never forget
the good times

never forget
the good times

A story of life in
British Columbia

merry Christmas Keith

joe garner

Joe Garner

Cinnabar Press
Nanaimo, British Columbia
1995

Available at most book outlets
or order direct from:
CINNABAR PRESS LTD.
P.O. Box 392
Nanaimo, B.C., Canada V9R 5L3

FIRST PRINTING - August 1995

Published by
CINNABAR PRESS LTD.
P.O. Box 392
Nanaimo, B.C., Canada V9R 5L3

Printed in Canada by
Friesen Printers
Altona, Manitoba.

Typeset by
Pat and Johan Gunderson
Langley, B.C.

FOR MY MOTHER

TABLE OF CONTENTS

FOREWORD

NAME ME ANYONE, Canadian or otherwise, who at age 68 would announce he was going to write a book. Amazed, his son asked, "Why?" The reply? "Because there's a story to tell," remembering he had begun life in a dirt-floor shed, the home of pioneer parents on Saltspring Island.

Joe Garner could tell of being a logger at age nine, doing more reading than arithmetic in a village school until Grade X, and slugging out a no-future life with tens of thousands of others during the Great Depression. He became a successful hardware merchant, supervised vital war construction work, ran as many as 20 logging camps, and was a driving force in community projects around Vancouver Island.

Retired, bored, he knew no more about writing than the deer and cougar which still roam around his big log home on Cinnabar Ridge south of Nanaimo. He had a kitchen table, a chair, foolscap paper and a pencil and he figured that was all he needed. Three years later, aided and abetted by friends with advice, he was the author of *Never Fly Over an Eagle's Nest* and in Nanaimo that was big stuff. It sold close to 100,000 copies in an age when 5,000 in sales was also big stuff. He was ignorant of publishing but he knew — he wasn't a free enterpriser for nothing — he could do better on his own after his first go-around with a minor local publisher. And he had more stories to tell about life, people, politicians, the outdoors and the fight and the plight of the little guy in the biggest game of all — the logging industry.

In a van loaded with boxes of trade paperbacks he entered the almost unknown market of self-publishing and sold store to store, door to door, across Canada, publicizing on television

7

and radio along the way. Audiences love his laconic style. Here was something new. The real article.

In the next 11 years he sweated out three more books, wearing out HB pencils by the gross. Nothing came easy. But they all were best sellers because they had the ring of truth, a rare commodity these days. Ask those hot shot publishers or successful bookstore owners about self publishing and selling and they'll sniff: "The system doesn't work that way." Mention Joe Garner's name and they'll say, "Oh, yeah, but that's Joe."

At 84, beset by diabetes and steel and plastic hips, he picked up his pencil again. In days long ago he could monkey-wrench an aging bulldozer back to life under the headlights of a pickup. But a word processor or even the typewriter were not for him. Ever onward despite suffering a stroke at Chapter Nine, he finished *Never Forget the Good Times*, chronicling his family life, his trials and triumphs, often feeling frustrated as he felt his mental machinery was not too well oiled. But as the daughter of one of his housekeepers said, "When Mr. Garner decides to do something, he just doesn't quit." Aided faithfully and patiently by his partner in Cinnabar Press, Joan Davis, he didn't.

Look again at the photograph on the cover. He's more gaunt now and he laughs: "I'm hearing the swish of the scythe." Is that the face of a quitter? No, that's the face of a man who's been there and while he knows this is his last book he says, "I'm in the sunset of my life, but sunsets are beautiful."

There is a phrase: "Seize the day!" This may be a Yuppie-type challenge and unfamiliar to Joe Garner, but by the Lord Harry, it fits him tight like a square nut on a steel bolt. No give. Just solid.

Barry Broadfoot
Nanaimo, B.C.
July, 1995

ACKNOWLEDGMENTS

F IRST, thanks go to my daughter Joanne for advice and guidance; Jim London for his help interviewing family members; Karen Girard for the initial transcribing of the various tapes; Barry Broadfoot for his research and support; and Jean Robinson for her help with the final reading.

My sincere appreciation to Bill Davis for his constructive criticism and advice, and for his time and knowledge so willingly given.

I also wish to extend my thanks to all those who contributed in ways both big and small to the completion of this book.

Then, a special thank you to Joan Davis for her patience and encouragement during the writing, and for tackling the arrangement and design of the final manuscript.

Descendents of Joseph Edwin Garner

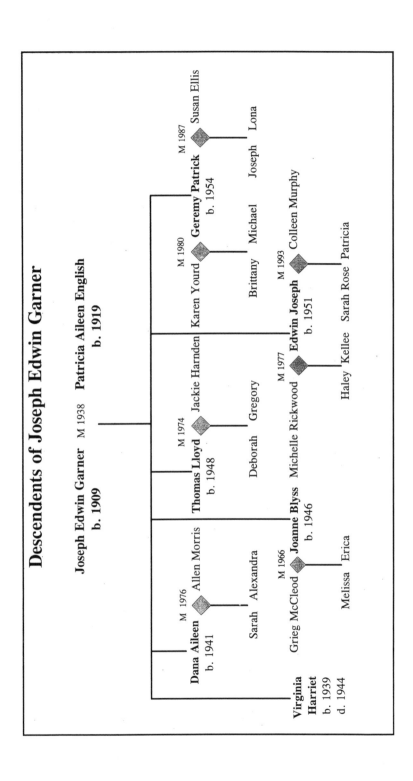

Joseph Edwin Garner
b. 1909   M 1938   **Patricia Aileen English**
b. 1919

Virginia Harriet
b. 1939
d. 1944

Dana Aileen
b. 1941   M 1976   Allen Morris

Sarah   Alexandra

Grieg McCleod   M 1966   **Joanne Blyss**
b. 1946

Melissa   Erica

Thomas Lloyd
b. 1948   M 1974   Jackie Harnden

Deborah   Gregory

Michelle Rickwood   M 1977   **Edwin Joseph**
b. 1951

Haley   Kellee   Sarah Rose   Patricia

Geremy Patrick
b. 1954   M 1980   Karen Yourd

Brittany   Michael

M 1987   Susan Ellis

Joseph   Lona

M 1993   Colleen Murphy

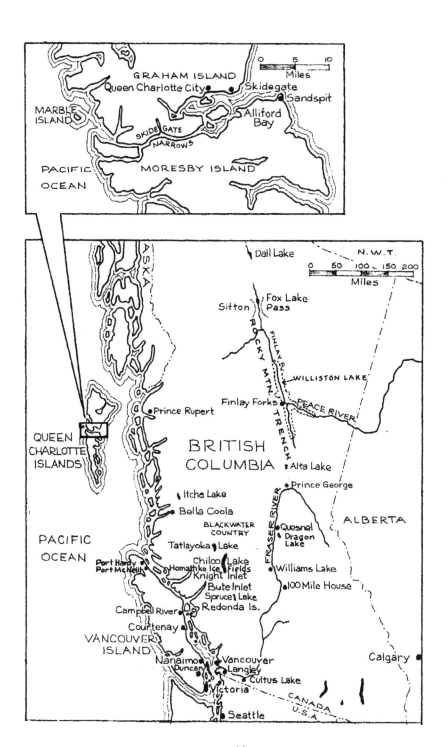

PART I

THE BEGINNING

EVERY STORY has to start somewhere: It was Sunday, October 18, 1992. Ed, my middle son, and I had planned an afternoon deer hunt in the back-country out behind Fourth Lake. Fletcher Challenge, one of British Columbia's logging giants, was closing its operations for the winter in that area some 20 miles southwest of Nanaimo. In that high and mountainous country it had already snowed the week before.

We had agreed to leave my home at one o'clock using my pickup, a 1988 Jimmy with low mileage and in excellent condition. Ed drove into the yard about ten minutes to one with his daughter Haley.

"Can't go hunting this afternoon," he said, apologetically. "We have promised to go and look at a horse Haley wants to buy." Girls and horses first, Grandads come second.

"Well, my 4 x 4 is all packed and ready, so I'll just head on out for a drive back up there and may be lucky enough to get a couple of grouse along the way. No problem. I'll be home in time for the World Series, with maybe a couple of grouse."

With their big brown Rotweiler dog bouncing around in the back they drove off in Ed's old truck, and I backed my GMC out of the carport and headed for the hills I'd hunted for 20 or more years. It could be a good day, despite my disappointment.

Most of the logging companies on Vancouver Island have locked gates where the publicly maintained road ends and their private logging roads begin. These gates are usually opened to let hikers, fishermen and hunters into the area when there is no logging going on. But you must stop and report, telling the gate man in what area you intend to travel, fish or hunt. He will tell you where there is heavy snow or washouts or obstructions. Because the government keeps records, on the way out everyone must stop and report what game they have encountered.

These gates normally open before daylight and close shortly after dark on the weekends. Only when there is an extreme fire hazard in summer do these gates remain closed.

At ten past two I went through the gate going into the Nanaimo Lakes area. The attendant asked my name, wrote it in his book along with my licence number and the make of the vehicle.

"This gate will be closed at six today," he advised. It would be dark by then anyway.

"I'll be back here long before that. The Blue Jays are playing their second game of the World Series and it's "play ball" at five. I hope to be watching it by then."

"Me, too," was his reply.

"Where do you think there might be some grouse?" I asked, holding up my cane. "Can't get around much in the brush anymore. If they're not by the road I won't be going tramping around."

"Some of our boys are having luck up on the west side of Fourth Lake, and the roads are still fairly good up there. So good luck."

"That's where I'll go then. Now if I'm not out by five I'll be in some kind of trouble," I said and drove off thinking about the baseball game.

The day before the Toronto Blue Jays had lost a cliffhanger to the Atlanta Braves three to one in their home town. If they could win today the series would be all tied up. I had played senior amateur and a bit of semi-professional baseball from age 15 to 40. No small wonder I wanted to watch this second game. Baseball is my favourite sport and always has been — not much ice for hockey where I grew up.

I drove up almost to the very top of the mountain, from where it's downhill to the open Pacific Ocean. I took the last logging road to the southwest. This old road was very rough for about half a mile to where a roaring creek crossed it. Here, there was a washout over six feet wide and six deep. This was the end of the line. No vehicle could cross this.

I put the truck in park and looked around. Having climbed almost from sea level, I knew I was well above 2,500 feet. I'd now been driving for an hour. Being 83, and bouncing over these rough roads it was necessary to get out and have a widdle. The door swung open on the sidehill, so the warning signal was screaming at me. I reached over and pulled the ignition key out. The silence was golden. I could have shut the door, but I didn't. It was foggy, grey, the silence deafening in

14

its own way and I was probably the only human for miles. This didn't bother me. I'd spent most of my life in the woods. Hell, I was even born in the woods in a tiny log cabin with a dirt floor. Isolation was as normal as breathing.

When I tried to start the engine again to head home, the ignition key would not go in far enough to turn. The steering wheel was locked, the gearshift mechanism was jammed and nothing I could do would make it shift. I tried desperately to get the strain off the gearshift, hoping this would help, but with no success. Both the steering wheel and the gearshift lever were locked solid. I've worked and owned trucks of every type, from a Model-T to logging monsters, and I knew them. Now I was in a very difficult situation — alone, old, partly crippled and miles from home. I was baffled and worried.

I had put a big jack in before leaving home — always be prepared in rough country — so I got it out and raised the front end until both wheels were clear of the ground. I spun the wheels and then tried to turn them in every possible direction hoping to free the gearshift.

No luck! "Damn it," I remember saying.

Without wheels, the rain beginning, and the afternoon waning, this view of the mountains and the lake below was little consolation to a man in desperate trouble.

This was getting serious, even dangerous. Dusk would be coming soon. I went to the glove compartment and got out the instruction book and spent half an hour reading it. The book did not help with the situation one bit, so I put it back and slammed the lid shut.

I went to the front end and lowered it back down. Then I took the jack to the rear and lifted those two wheels up, hoping beyond hope it might let some thingamajig go to free the gearshift and allow the key to go in. Again, no luck.

It was now coming up to four o'clock and the light was starting to fade. I let the back end down and put the jack away. I figured I'd probably bent the ignition key by now, so it wouldn't work anyway.

Looking back, I realize both operations were futile, even stupid and in my condition, dangerous. The problem was not the gearshift; it was that ignition key. It didn't fit anymore. But why? Why?

I had no hat or rain clothing with me. So much for being prepared for rough country! Still, the best thing was to try and walk out as far as the bottom of the steep part of the mountain, where the rough road I was on joined with the road going out to the west coast. I was betting my life that the gate man would either come as far as this junction looking for me, or would phone the Nanaimo Search and Rescue for help. These volunteers are efficient, dedicated woodsmen, experienced in searches and rescues. They could easily be there in an hour. There's always a phone at the gate, and this was the normal procedure when someone hasn't shown up by closing time.

On the front seat there was one medium sized banana. I am a diabetic and it was already over an hour past my all-important regular snack time. I cut off one third, then peeled and ate it. I carefully put the rest in my coat pocket. After putting the shotgun under the seat, I got my cane, closed the doors and set off. A misstep, a bad stumble and my plight would be perilous.

Both hips had been replaced with steel and plastic. My right knee was in such bad condition it was also ready to be replaced. I was to see the anaesthetist the next week before going in for the operation.

The logging road was covered with rocks and heavy gravel. From past and painful experience I knew a sudden slip or fall, or a turned ankle would be the end of any walking. I was being extra careful because I was wearing only a pair of old oxfords and light socks. Ed and I would have road-hunted, so boots weren't necessary.

There were huge puddles of freezing muddy water in various places. The water came up almost to my knees as I waded slowly through, gauging every step, using my cane as a feeler to try and avoid the rocks. My feet and legs soon became completely numb.

What in hell was happening to me — to die this way?

I did not dare to stop and rest a single minute going down that long three and a half miles in the rain which had started when I left the truck. I had estimated that if the gate keeper closed the gate at six he could get to the bottom of the hill I was on in 20 minutes.

When I reached the junction it was pitch black and I had to use one of my matches to see my wrist watch. It was 6:18 p.m. I had actually made it with just over two minutes to spare. But there was no vehicle to be seen and no headlights coming.

I had never felt so alone.

After waiting another ten long and desperate minutes I realized no one was coming. This could be the end of everything. The rain was now heavier, with big snow flakes mixed in. Between fatigue and the pain in my hips, I knew it was impossible to go any further.

A small fir tree that a bulldozer had pushed over hung alongside the road. Using my hunting knife I started cutting off some of the smaller branches to make a bed, a resting place I badly needed. Or was it to be my final resting place?

I also cut some bigger branches and piled them across the road. If someone did come looking for me they would have to stop to investigate this feeble barricade of brush.

By the time I'd finished I was so exhausted I just flopped down on top of the small branches with my feet and legs poking out towards the center of the road. I'm not quite sure whether I collapsed from exhaustion or whether I passed out in a diabetic coma. Everything was blurry. I think I had gone almost to the edge. Death from exhaustion and cold was a possibility, but I had to keep telling myself: Do not panic. Hold on!

In my confused mental state it seemed that brother Tom, who had now been dead for some 32 years, was there with me. Deep inside, a voice was saying, "Joe, you may not get out of this one alive. You could soon be with your brother, again."

Down the Nanaimo River Road — so busy in spring and summer with hikers, fishermen, families going on picnics during the weekends — there was no one. Further away, in warm houses, people were watching baseball, eating dinner, drinking, talking, laughing, and I waited — for what?

What goes through a man's mind? What thoughts? What triumphs? What regrets?

What memories?

Where the logging road forks — to the left, the one Joe stumbled down. On the right marked by Xs the spot where Joe, exhausted and weak, lay down to rest — six and a half kilometers from where he had started off and some 2,500 feet lower. This photo was taken nearly five months later, after the road had been cleared and graded.

TOM

TOM AND I sat down on a cedar log near the two stumps where we kept a record of our wages each day.

It was the fall of 1918 on Saltspring Island, largest of the Gulf Islands between the mainland and Vancouver Island, where in those days only a few pioneers lived. Now it is the island of choice for those who wish to retire or just get away from it all. It is now expensive, selective and getting crowded with people from many parts of the world.

Tom was eleven then and I was nine, two tough kids, keen and woods-wise. We were working for Captain Justice's small sawmill and hauling out logs with his team of horses. We kept the mill supplied with enough logs so they were able to cut about 2,000 board feet of special lumber orders every day. Tom and I were going to the Divide School, so we could only log in the evenings and on the weekends.

We had devised a system to keep track of our earnings. On our way home we each put a small rock on a stump for every dollar we had earned that day. We were each paid 25 cents an hour. If something happened that allowed only six hours of work we would put one rock in the tight little pile and place another a few inches away until the full dollar was earned. We were paid in cash twice a month. On pay days we placed the money on the stump and put the required number of rocks on each bill — one rock on a dollar bill, five rocks on a five dollar bill. Bills and rocks had to balance. Once, when it didn't add up, we walked back the half mile to tell our boss. When we explained how we kept track of our wages, he was so impressed he made up the difference without even looking at his books.

This day, long ago, it was shady and cool on that log and

we were tired. As we sat resting, Tom got to his feet and stood directly in front of me, quiet and intense.

"How would you like us to be partners for the rest of our lives?" he asked, with a big smile. He'd been doing some long-term thinking.

"Sure, I'd like that," I said, and I didn't have to do much thinking about it. A partnership seemed as natural as breathing. We were brothers, and as important, pals.

We usually walked to school with the three youngest Gilbert kids — Bert, Eileen and Phoebe. They lived half a mile down the hill from our rough shack and were our nearest neighbours. During the winter, fights often started when Bert hit one of us on the side of the head with a big wet snow ball. When this happened Tom and I doubled up on Bert who was almost two years older than Tom. We had a system. Bert never did catch on. Tom would tackle him with his fist, while I got directly behind him and lay face down in the snow. When Tom hit him hard enough, he would trip over me and go ass-over-teacup backwards. That was when we'd pile on him, and it would usually be the end of the fight. This was when I first learned how important it was to work together as a team.

As we walked the rest of the way home that day we talked about nothing but our future.

"I'd like to have a big logging camp and lots of good timber," Tom said. "That's all I would ever need."

"Well, I'd like to own an apartment block with a good hardware store under it," I declared.

We agreed we should work separately, but always be ready to help each other when necessary. Our pact was silent — no papers, no lawyer, no handshake even. Just brotherly trust.

Many years later, when both dreams had come true, the phone rang. It was Tom. He had just bought a new float-equipped Cessna 180 aircraft. We had had our ups and downs, but we each had prospered, cooperated and still were real pals.

"Let's go fishing today. I'd like you to see how well this new plane performs taking off from a high lake."

"When?" I asked.

"Get your fishing gear and meet me at the Aero Club in about 20 minutes," Tom said.

"Okay, but make it half an hour? What's the rush?"

Tom was waiting at the floating dock on Quamichan Lake, a few minutes drive from Duncan. I parked the station wagon, grabbed my tackle box and rod and put everything under the back seat of the new plane.

"Untie her and push off. She's ready to go," Tom said.

He started the motor which was already warmed up. My seat belt was barely fastened when he pushed in the throttle, and the 180 was up on the step and quickly airborne. This was some bird.

"Looks like she's got plenty of power," I remarked as he banked her to set his northeast course, mining country, wild, wild.

"We're headed for Spruce Lake, back of Bralorne, and almost due north of Anderson and Seton lakes," Tom explained. "This small alpine lake is more that 4,000 feet above sea level. She's full of trout," Tom said with enthusiasm. In all those years we'd never lost our passion for trout fishing, and now, a new lake!

"That should give us a good lunch and let us see how this baby performs at that altitude," I replied, pouring two cups of tea and tossing the thermos on the back seat.

We'd passed over Crofton and over the Gulf of Georgia, and soon were over Squamish following the Squamish River. We topped the Coast Range, and as Tom circled Spruce Lake I could see trout by the dozens making rings on the clear water as they rose to take the insects. He made his usual perfect landing, taxiing over near the inlet. I dropped a small anchor and we were fishing in a matter of minutes.

Tom, with spinning gear, landed a nice trout on his first cast. I put on a small mosquito fly, but made a mess of my first cast. A 14-inch rainbow grabbed the bait anyway. By the time I had netted the trout, Tom had put two more nice ones in his basket. After half an hour of this, he said to me, "There are some really big lakers in here. About ten years ago some cowboys cut a horse trail in and took out all the 15 and 20-pounders they wanted. Up on this isolated lake there's a thousand times better chance of seeing a bear than a ranger. I brought along this big spoon," he said, holding up a shiny Gibb Stuart. "We don't need any more little ones. So come over and watch." I put my gear away and climbed over onto his float. On the first couple of casts, nothing.

"Put some more weight on and cast out further," I suggested. On the next cast one of the biggest lake trout I had ever seen followed his flashing spoon to within five feet of the pontoon then turned and slid back down into the depths.

"Don't think I could handle one that big if it did get on," Tom said, hefting his small rod and light line.

"It's worth a try. Go ahead," I coaxed.

He made a few more casts with one or two of these beauties following his lure every time he reeled in. A new tactic was needed. Tom stopped reeling and left the big spoon dangling five feet under the surface. As he reached into his shirt pocket for a tin of Copenhagen with his left hand, his reel started to whirl in a hurry. His snoose tin dropped into the lake and drifted away. He tried to slow the monster down, but what can you do? His nylon line was only five-pound test. In jig time the reel was empty, the line parted and the big trout just kept on going. It jumped several times trying to shake the spoon. Tom reeled in what was left of his line. It had broken off half way along. Five pound test against a 20-pounder is a mismatch.

"Let's make a fire and cook up a few trout for lunch," I suggested, but Tom was still looking at the spot where that big lunker had made his last leap.

"Bet he would weigh at least 15 pounds," he said as we taxied for shore to tie the plane facing out into the lake. "More like 20 pounds," I suggested.

Tom cleaned the smaller trout while I started a fire from driftwood. We'd fry half a dozen. Three each would be just right. I rolled them in flour with salt and pepper, then laid them in the hot bacon fat in the old reliable cast iron frying pan. When brown and almost done I splashed them with a little wine vinegar and put in more bacon for that smoky flavour which makes all the difference. I can taste those trout today and remember the stillness of the lake, and the silence.

The tea was brewing as we ate our trout and bread. A can of Eagle Brand condensed milk whitened our tea. It also made an excellent desert when we spread it over the toasted brown buns Tom had brought. It beat dining at the Ritz.

We were sipping the last of our tea when Tom stood up and faced me as he had done when he was eleven, so long ago. With the same kind of smile and in the same soft voice he said, "You and I have been partners now for almost 30 years. I have all I will ever need. Two good logging camps and plenty of timber. You have your apartment block and the hardware store. We could divide everything and call it a day if you like. I got a hankering to live in Vancouver now, so I won't be able to do my fair share over in Duncan any more."

"I'd be glad to call it a day before we get any busier than we are now, and too old."

"You call Tom Gillespie, the accountant, and Dave Williams, our lawyer, and things can be settled next Tuesday. Let's say at 9:00 a.m. at your office. I'd like to clean this up neat and easy, no fuss, no bother. What say? Okay?"

We shook hands, washed up the dishes, stowed them away in a box and prepared for takeoff. Nothing more was said. We had agreed. What else was necessary?

Tom taxied as far up the lake as he could and turned into the wind. He tested the ignition, pulled on the carburetor heat for a few seconds to prevent icing, then pushed the throttle wide open and turned the carburetor heat off. Above the roar, he yelled, "Now we will see what this baby can do." The 180 came up on the step and was airborne half way down the lake.

"Wow! She sure has plenty of power even up at this altitude," I exclaimed, and he turned and smiled. He loved flying, the wilderness and life.

At the narrow outlet of the lake the motor coughed and almost stopped. In one quick motion Tom pulled on the carburetor heat again and eased the throttle back just a bit. We had lost about 100 feet and were almost brushing the tree tops. The motor coughed once more and my heart jumped. Then the motor went back to full power and we were climbing smoothly again into the clear, home free. Tom gave me a funny look, then pressed the lever that let the controls swing over to my side.

"Take her for a while. Good practice. I need a chew of snoose after that one," he said. "Remember I lost mine in the drink when that big one took off. I wonder how much it did weigh?"

I set a course for home as he began rummaging under his seat and came up with another tin of Copenhagen. After tapping the lid a couple of times — just out of habit — with two big fingers he wedged in a sizeable chew behind his bottom lip. He reached under the seat again and came up with an empty salmon tin. His spit can.

After a few minutes of silence Tom reached over and shook my arm, saying, "You know, Joe, if the motor hadn't cleared that carburetor ice back there, we were only about two seconds from crashing."

He looked away and then with that infectious smile, he said, "I don't suppose our lawyer and bookkeeper would ever have been needed as far as we were concerned." This time he was serious. It had been that close. Two bodies in a fire-blackened plane, if we were ever found. But it didn't deter me one bit from wanting to get my pilot's licence in the not too distant future.

Three days later we met in Duncan at our main office and divided about two million dollars worth of cash, land, buildings, heavy logging and construction equipment, several boats, two hunting and fishing lodges and three aircraft. Everything was priced at book value and we accepted values with a wave of a hand. That's the way true partners did it, a far cry from today.

Just before noon Tom asked our accountant, "What's left to settle now?"

"Just the hardware business with the building and the two new bulldozers," Gillespie said after some figuring.

"So what's the book value?"

"Bulldozers at just over $50,000 each and the hardware store at just under $200,000."

Tom's solution was simple and short.

"Joe has been doing most of the work around here for the last two years. If it's okay I'll take the bulldozers and Joe can keep the building, the business and all the stock, as is, where is."

He stuck out his big right hand, "Okay with you, partner?"

"More than fair, but if that's how you see it, that sure is okay. Lunch is on me, boys. What say we go. We're done here," I said.

Tom opened his club bag, and set four goblets on the desk. Then he reached in again and produced his trade mark. It was the familiar 26-ounce bottle of Crown Royal in a purple sack. Same old Tom. A handshake, a drink, a deal done. And the finest whiskey, always.

And that's how Tom and I ended our 30-year partnership, as easily and amicably as it had begun when we were kids and pledged allegiance to each other.

I WAS MISSING HIM terribly as I lay in the dark, wet, cold brush — the rain coming down and not even a star to let me know I was still in the real world.

Tom, my brother, partner, true friend.

GANGES

IN THE SUMMER OF 1924, when I was 15, we started to build the big house in Ganges on Saltspring, so the growing Garner family could be closer to the village's schools. Little did we know then that this house would become a heritage house and be turned into the Core Inn Youth Center, in a town grown large and busy with tourists and boaters all summer. Progress!

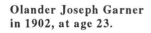

Dad had a better than average education, having attended a finishing school in South Carolina. He liked to read to us in the evenings. His favourites were *Brer Rabbit, Uncle Remus,* Jack London's *Burning Daylight,* Mark Twain and Shakespeare. And there was always the Bible. Dad would tell us what parts we should read, which naturally made us want to read the other parts.

Olander Joseph Garner in 1902, at age 23.

High fashion in 1902. At age 18, Joe's mother Lona Edwards one year before her marriage in Spartanburg, South Carolina.

Model T, vintage 1922, the first logging truck on Saltspring Island, driven by Tom Garner. This is the truck Margaret and Joe used to drive to and from Ganges to attend high school.

However, it was Mother who was determined her children would get a proper education, which meant attending school. When Margaret and I started high school, Dad was logging at the north end of Saltspring on the Cotsford's property. So Dad, being Dad, moved the family up there so Mother could cook for the crew. That left Margaret and me to batch in the big house at Ganges. We stayed there from Sunday evening until Friday after school when we went up to spend the weekend with the family. It was no holiday. We helped Dad with the logging.

We used our Model T truck with solid rubber tires on the rear wheels — a very rough ride over those rocky and narrow gravel roads. The front wheels had pneumatic tires that were 33 1/2 x 3 1/2 inches, smaller than today's motorcycle tires. If we had a flat it would take us an hour or more to work the jack and then do the patching. We'd put the tube and tire on the wheel, put the wheel back on the axle and tighten the nuts. Then we'd have to pump the tire up with a hand pump, taking turns when one of us was exhausted. And sometimes we ran low on gas. The gas was gravity fed, so when we were going up a hill the fuel couldn't reach the carburetor because the bottom part of the tank was too low. The only way we could keep going was to turn the truck around and back up the hill, then turn around again at the top and head for the closest gas supply. If the motor started spluttering and stalling we had to take the cover off the gas tank, which was under the front seat, and blow into it. Compare this to the monstrous off-highway logging-road trucks of today that are capable of carrying 120 tons or more. It was almost a toy.

Margaret was two years younger, but we were in the same grade. Margaret was going on fourteen and I was going on sixteen. I had been kept out of school by Dad for one full year so I could work as the donkey engine driver for our logging show. Margaret had skipped Grade I when she started at the Divide School, because the school trustees needed one more student to qualify for a government-paid teacher and she was it — a trick used everywhere in isolated villages on the coast and on the prairies.

We attended the "Jail House" school on Creamery Road for Grade IX. Before it was used for a classroom it had been the office of the constable. In the rear there were four jail cells. Some Grade VIII girls were fooling around one day and the teacher gave them the choice of spending a half hour either in the corner of the room — the punishment corner — or in a cell.

They chose to go to jail. Since that day it was called the "Jail House" school.

We took Grade X in "The Chicken House" school. Farmers had used this building to exhibit their chickens, ducks, geese and turkeys. It was downtown, and directly behind Mahon Hall.

We took Algebra, Geometry, Arithmetic, History, English, French, Latin, Geography and English Literature. We had no choices. Our teacher's name was Robertson and he taught all of these subjects to Grades VIII, IX and X. There were at times as many as 30 of us in that one big room.

Robertson was a great believer in the value of debate. It was a challenge but I loved it. Billy Mouat and I seemed to be the two who hung in there and usually ended up in the finals. It was great entertainment for the rest of the class and good training for us. Billy became school superintendent for the Cariboo District in central B.C., and later superintendent of the Abbotsford District in the Fraser Valley, where a high school was named in his honour.

Margaret was very skilled in languages, but I was better in the math subjects. Margaret still wonders how I was the one who ended up writing books.

Actually I didn't learn to read until I was in Grade III. I didn't have to. While the students in the higher grades read their readers out loud I found it easier to memorize them. Even when the teacher asked me to read from an old reader, I could recite the stories word for word. Everyone but the teacher and Mother knew I couldn't read. It was when I was asked to sound out the alphabet the teacher caught on. Then I had some heavy catching up to do.

While we were batching at Ganges, Margaret and I had a daily system and just one menu. We had five or six laying hens. On Sunday evening we'd cook up a big pot of potatoes. Then we'd have fried eggs and fried potatoes every day for the rest of the week. There were no other vegetables — a menu which would horrify any dietician, but we thrived. Potatoes alone kept the Irish alive for decades in the 1800s, before the famine. Neither of us missed one day of school due to sickness. The house was sparsely furnished, with a wood-burning cook stove, three beds, some dishes and an assortment of pots and pans. Margaret did the cooking. I'd chop the wood, split some kindling and fill the wood box for the following day. Having started logging at nine years of age and peeling telephone poles at eight, this was no big chore. The house was always nice and warm to come home to. After supper we'd wash the dishes, then do our homework together. We got on well and had a lot of fun. There was never a feeling of competition between us, just companionship.

Dad let us have a small charge account at Mouat's store. We got no spending money, but if we really needed something we could go to the store and charge it. Needless to say, ice cream and chocolate bars were not chargeable items!

I did the janitorial work at the school and also cut the wood for the heater. Dad got enough money from this to pay for both Margaret's and my tuition fees.

Sports were important to both of us. I played baseball, basketball and soccer and Margaret was captain of the girls' basketball team. She was tall enough to jump center and also to play on the Saltspring ladies team. We played against teams from the village of Fulford, Gabriola Island and Nanaimo. Everybody turned out for these events and it was exciting to cheer the home team on. We particularly wanted to put on a good showing against the private schools that most of the English remittance children attended. Subsidized by wealthy parents in England, some of those mavericks with their hoity-toity accents would even go so far as to treat us like second-class citizens. In truth they were second class. We were the Canadians, the pioneers, the workers.

There'd usually be a dance after the games. I was elected to keep enthusiasm high, to 'cheerlead' and help organize these events. There was plenty of homemade apple cider at these dances, drunk from jugs out back, so they were always well attended.

WE MADE IT through Grades IX and X, but before the end of our final year, the family was back at the big house in Ganges with us. Mother was expecting her tenth and last child, Dorothy. She was born at the end of May, 1926. Mother was told by her doctor she would never live through another pregnancy. She informed Tom and me she intended leaving Dad when her health returned.

As soon as school was out we started preparing for the move. Four weeks ahead of the planned departure, Tom and I were given $35 to go to Vancouver, buy a lot and build a house big enough for Mother and eight children. A $5 down payment got us a lot — and we got all the materials the same way — with money left over from the $35.The experience we'd had building the big house in Ganges proved invaluable, yet we forgot to put in the stairs up to the second floor. However, it was sufficiently advanced for us to move in on time so the younger children could start their fall term.

Pearl and Ollie were left behind with Dad. Pearl had just turned twelve and Ollie was only eight. At the time we really didn't think much about it, but Ollie was badly mistreated by our father and forced to work long hours. Ollie really had no childhood at all. If he didn't work as hard as Dad thought he could he got a whipping. Dad even picked up his paychecks from Mr. Lumovitch in advance. They were logging on the old Jameski farm, where former television personality Jack Webster now has his home.

Later, we all wondered why Ollie hadn't turned on Dad after the way he treated him. He was unusually big and strong and tough for his age. But in those days father was boss.

Pearl was abused by our father, too. When the neighbours became aware of what was going on, they took her under their wing. The husband was the Conservative Member of Parliament for the constituency. Pearl lived with them for a couple of years while she completed Grade XI under the expanded curriculum. We all felt she was the brightest of our family.

I was always considered Dad's favourite, although, when I was born and only weighed three pounds he wouldn't even pay for a birth certificate, or to have me circumcised. He didn't think I'd make it, so he didn't want to waste a dollar. I was the runt of the litter until I was in my early teens. I was 18 or 19 before I finally reached my full height of six feet. But what I lacked in size I made up for in toughness. Early on I realized if I flattered or praised Dad, things went smoothly. I only got one licking from him, the day I didn't get home from school in time to milk our three Jersey cows. There were some traits I saw in him that I was determined would never rub off on me.

Dad was jealous of Tom who was a very good athlete and had great natural talent and coordination. As a result Tom had some really bad times.

We had lots of companions in Ganges but we always had to meet them outside our home because they didn't like to be around Dad. However, when we moved to Vancouver our home on Second Avenue was always full of young people. Mother loved it and she would make all sorts of goodies for our late evening snacks.

Now that most of her worries had disappeared, Mother became noticeably happier and younger looking. A Mr. Formby, who lived two houses up the street, started visiting our house and he gave me a job as his helper. He taught me how to lay bricks and build a good fireplace the old English way.

After we got settled, a group of us, with our sleeping bags on our backs, would hike up Hollyburn Ridge after the Friday night dances to go skiing. We called ourselves the Spades Athletic Club. There could be as many as eight of us in our log cabin up the mountain.

Sometimes we went to Bowen Island on a Saturday night on the Union steam ship, which was always crowded. It was a two dollar trip and we danced in the community hall to a four piece orchestra playing all the favourite jazz songs. The ship returned to Vancouver around midnight. It was known as The Moonlight Cruise.

I continued to play baseball, and enjoyed playing for the Fairview Merchants against the great — and I use the word "great" sincerely — Japanese-Canadian Asahi baseball team.

Our home field was the Powell Street grounds just east of Main, between Powell and Cordova. Any ball hit onto Cordova Street was a ground rule two-base hit. Home plate was in the northwest corner of that block and right across the street was a Skid Road beer parlour frequented by many of the spectators. I played third base or shortstop. That was the corner where most of the inebriated spectators watched the game from the grandstand. Fans from everywhere were lined up four deep the full length of the Powell Street playing field. If you made an error they let you know about it in no uncertain terms. I hung in there for three seasons because the Fairview Merchants were a good bunch. They were a senior team with many good players. No community showed more enthusiasm than those Powell Street ball players.

The Asahi star player was Roy Namura who played shortstop. He could throw a ball like a bullet from either short or third. Those who hit the ball in his direction rarely reached first base safely. If there were visiting teams from the United States, Namura was usually asked to play for the Firemen or the B.C. Telephone teams, the semi-pro players.

The Japanese-Canadians played a daring and fast game. Sometimes a player stealing second would just keep running for third and occasionally made it. I've seen them with the lead, when they hadn't even hit a ball out of the infield. Because I batted left-handed, I always did well against them, with a batting average of .500 or over. Their pitchers didn't normally try to overpower you with fast balls, but they threw a lot of breaking stuff with good control.

31

In 1942, those same players of Japanese parents were evacuated from the Pacific Coast to other parts of the country after Japan sneak-attacked Pearl Harbour, the Hawaiian naval base.

When sister Pearl joined us in Vancouver in 1929, she and Margaret ran the Jiffy Coffee Shop in the 400-block of Richards between Pender and Hastings for a couple of years. Tom and I helped to get them started. They were now independent. Coffee was five cents, yet they were able to make money. It was an exciting time for them and both married while operating that little business during the Depression's darkest days.

At 14, sister Edie took a year off from school and worked in a garment factory at the corner of Main and Second, but the

Vancouver street photographer snapped Joe's sisters, Margaret on the left, and Pearl, near where they operated the Jiffy Coffee Shop on Richards Street.

Sister Edie at 16 years after graduating from high school in 1932, just before she started working for Nelson's in Vancouver as a seamstress.

next year Mother insisted she go back and take Grade IX. A studious young girl, she finished at the top of her class. Then she got a job working for Nelson's Laundry. There she operated an electrically powered sewing machine making sheets, towels and coveralls. Edie was 21 before she decided to marry.

Margaret and I usually went to the dances together until the night she met a six-foot four-inch Scandinavian who trapped in northern B.C. They met at the Commodore dance hall which boasted the only spring floor in Vancouver. Margaret went home escorted by her Scandinavian and I took Hazel home for the first time. I just had to go in and meet her mother, which was the beginning of a very warm friendship that lasted just over a year. She was one of Canada's top divers and was kept busy training for the Olympics.

Shortly after moving to Vancouver I took two years of industrial night school. I walked the eight blocks twice every week, and after the course I could figure out almost any construction problem with a carpenter's square. This was a turning point and enabled me to take jobs I would otherwise not have been qualified to handle.

One was the Ruskin Dam, where I fell out of a 50-foot tower, head first, towards the jagged rocks below. These rocks had been blasted out for the foundation of the dam on the Stave River, a quarter of a mile from where the Stave River crosses the highway and flows into the Fraser River just west of Mission. I could plainly see the first of three sets of guy lines as I dropped from the tower. By some miracle I grabbed hold of the highest one, and, as it sagged as low as it would, I let go to drop and catch the next lower wire. The last of the three guy wires was almost 20 feet above the rocks. When it stretched down as far as it would, I let go and landed on my feet near the river among those jagged boulders. All this grabbing and dropping seemed to be done in slow motion. My subconscious had awakened.

I clearly remembered meeting two men running with a stretcher. I stopped them and asked where they were going and one said, "We saw someone tumble out of the tower and we're going down to pick up what's left of him."

"I'm the one that took the tumble," I told them, and opened both hands to show where the skin was torn away from the palms. They looked at me in disbelief.

"Please walk with me up to the first-aid shack and wait a while to see how I feel after I'm bandaged. If things are okay I'll be back to work in half an hour."

And I was. That was the spring of 1929, and I had just turned 20. The month before I had been made night-shift foreman, overseeing the concrete pouring for the main dam. I was responsible for gathering the 5 x 12 inch cylinders full of the concrete that was being poured at various locations. These samples were labelled and placed in a test room for 30 days prior to the engineers testing each and every one of them so they had proof that the concrete was up to or better than the specifications called for. These samples were collected at least three times each 12-hour shift. Government specifications demanded this testing be done.

I knew I had to get back to finish the shift if I possibly could. We were working 12 hours, seven days a week. My take home pay was $400 a month plus board. This was an absolute fortune in those days.

TOM HAD MOVED to Vancouver Island where he met and married Marie Sandigard. They were living with his in-laws in Westholme between Duncan and Chemainus. In 1930 he asked me if I would go over and help build him a house. So I packed my belongings into my pride and joy, my Oakland Roadster, with its straight-8 motor that could travel at speeds well in excess of 100 miles an hour.

Tom and I continued to give money to Mother to help support the family. Later, she and the three youngest children, Al, Lloyd and Dorothy, would join us in Westholme.

CROFTON

WHEN I'D FINISHED TOM'S HOUSE I went to a tax sale and bought us three lots in Crofton for $35. We paid $15 for one corner lot and $10 each for the two inside lots, but we had to wait one long year before we could take possession and start building.

We each took an inside lot and kept the corner lot as an investment. A couple of years later we sold it for just under $100. Now, 60 years later, it is still vacant and priced at $60,000.

I decided to build a house to live in on my lot so I would be able to walk to the booming grounds where I now worked. I salvaged enough lumber and bricks from the defunct old smelter down by the beach to put in the foundations, lay the floor, and build a fireplace and chimney. No permits or building inspections were necessary. You just registered your house plan at the municipal office for one dollar and started building. The houses in Crofton were on septic tanks. To get water, you dug a well about 20 feet deep and lowered a galvanized bucket on a rope into it.

Every single thing that went into building my house was bartered for. Shingle bolts were exchanged for shingles, logs for lumber, and firewood for windows and doors. Tom and Marie's homemade dandelion wine was exchanged gallon for gallon, by the deck hands on the freighters in the Crofton Harbour, for linseed oil and white lead. These two ingredients mixed with a little turpentine made an excellent exterior paint.

Those were the ways of the "Dirty Thirties".

While I was working on the roof, my new girlfriend, Claire, came and helped me put on the shingles. After the last nail was driven, Claire declared, "Now I can move in."

"Let's go get a couple of beers and head to Nanaimo for your blankets."

This was the first time I had actually lived with a girl. It was to be a bitter-sweet experience. During our second year Claire informed me she was pregnant. She wanted an abortion, but I was dead against any such idea. There was no more discussion about it and I thought all was well, until late one night Claire left in a hurry for the bathroom. Unknown to me she had used the bark of the *Cascara* tree, a frequently-used method of aborting in those days.

She came back out saying, "It's all over now, Joe."

In her hands she carried a small roasting pan with the whole mess in it and asked me to bury it. I could tell it would have been a boy. I walked to the lower back corner of the lot and dug a hole. In the dark I buried what was left of my dreams. I placed some heavy rocks over the grave so it would not be disturbed.

Next morning Claire quietly packed her things and after breakfast we loaded her belongings into the rumble seat of the car. In silence, I drove her to her sister's place in Nanaimo.

During the Depression the collection of *Cascara* bark provided a living for many otherwise unemployed people on the Island. *Cascara* trees for half a mile on either side of a road would be stripped of their bark in spring. The bark was rolled up, dried and sold to China and Japan for its medicinal value. To induce an abortion a small roll of bark was inserted for one or two nights.

JIMMY MAXWELL, who also worked at the booming grounds, moved in and stayed until he got married.

A year later Ollie, after enduring a 20-minute beating from Dad, decided he'd had enough. He packed his belongings in a suitcase and wrapped his three guns in two Hudson's Bay blankets. He left a note on the table under a dirty porridge bowl. It read: "Dad, your cow is at the Price's place. The chickens I fed and let out. I am leaving you forever. Your son, Oliver."

He walked the eight miles to the Vesuvius wharf, transferred everything to a dugout canoe he had fashioned the previous winter and paddled the four miles across to Crofton. He arrived on my doorstep just in time for a late supper. He was 16 but looked 21. Ollie had never been inside a beer parlour, so we went for a beer at the Crofton Hotel to celebrate our reunion and his newly found freedom. It was a wonderful day for us both. He batched with me for just over two years until he married.

Since Claire had left, Cuzzo Takarabbi, a Canadian-born Japanese girl, came in after school to do the housework and have supper ready. Cuzzo, who lived down the street, was happy to get her small weekly wage. Her father was the caretaker at the summer home of the well-known Vancouver dentist "Painless Parker". It was on the ocean and about a quarter of a mile south of my house. Years earlier, in 1919 when I was ten, I went to Vancouver with Dad when he was going over to have a troublesome wisdom tooth pulled, free of charge, by this same dentist. To gain publicity when he first started using a form of freezing, Dr. Parker would seat his patients, four at a time, on a wooden platform outside his office at the northeast corner of Hastings and Columbia. As many as 150 people would gather to watch him perform this feat. While he was pulling teeth the traffic would be detoured to Powell Street for up to two hours. Writing this, I realize how much times have changed!

WHILE LONGSHORING I formed a friendship with "Shorty" Berkey that would last to this very day. He was called "Shorty" not because he was short, but because his brother Ken, two years older and two inches taller, hung that handle on his "little" brother. Shorty and I worked together all up and down the Island, but mostly at Chemainus. It was tough to get into the longshoremen's union at that time, but Shorty and I had no problem. The Longshoremen needed a good pitcher and a good third baseman and we filled the bill. In Chemainus I would again play against Namura and many of the Asahi ball players.

We worked hard, played hard, and celebrated even the smaller successes. After winning a major ball game in Duncan we all went for a few beers at the Tzouhalem Hotel. Before heading home we went to the Chinese restaurant for some chow mein.

Leaving the restaurant, our coach George Syrotuk stuck an old metal teapot inside his shirt saying he needed it to mix a few on the way home. When we pulled into Chemainus and turned left at the Green Lantern Hotel on to River Road, there, at the other side of the railway track we saw chief constable Sam Service. He turned on his car lights and waved us to the side of the road. As he walked over I rolled

Chemainus longshoreman's baseball team from left to right, back row: Bob Cadwallader, Bill Jackson, Joe Horton, Shorty Berkey, Danny Wyllie, George Syrotuk, Corp Robinson, Tom Garner and Bill Horton (assistant manager); front row: Jimmy Syme (manager and coach), Joe Garner, Haley Jackson, Bill Syme (bat boy), Fred Sommerville, Jackie Gill and Pete Hawryluk. (1938)

my window down anticipating trouble.

"Good evening, sir. What can we do for you?" I asked.

"You boys are lucky tonight," Sam growled. "All I want is that teapot you fellows borrowed from the Chinese restaurant in Duncan."

I handed it to him and he just turned on his heel and headed back to his vehicle without another word. Service was a baseball fan and we were all still in our uniforms.

THINKING OF RIVER ROAD brings back vivid memories of both boxing and learning to dance the Charleston. It was the autumn of 1927 and Tom and I had come over to Vancouver Island for a few months to run a tie mill for H.R. McMillan at the top of the first hill on River Road.

We went to the local dances and the frantic Charleston was the in-thing. If you were good at it the girls wanted to dance with you. So most evenings Tom and I would practice the intricate steps on our way down the level dirt road to the rough shack we called home.

We had thrown this one-room shack up on our first weekend. The Green Lantern Hotel was charging us an exorbitant two dollars a day. Tom cut the lumber and I hammered the nails. We'd bought two small secondhand windows from Hong Hing for a dollar twenty-five and a big mirror for fifty cents. A low-sloped roof kept the rain out and a rough wooden floor kept us up off the ground. I nailed two bunk beds to the wall on the low side of the shack and a sink and the mirror on the high side. There was one small stove, a table and two chairs, one trunk, some shelves, and nails underneath to hang our clothes on. Crude, yes, but fine for two young bucks.

Red Howard was my falling partner. He was the light heavy weight boxing champion of B.C. and I was his sparring partner. Each day, usually before work, we'd jog for three miles and then put in a full eight hours falling fir trees with hand tools. I returned to Vancouver as fit as a fiddle.

H.R. MacMillan had asked Tom and me to come and work for him at a fixed wage. I told him, "No. A man's got to have more to think about than just pulling in a wage." This was my first contact with H.R., the B.C. timber giant of this century. Back then, he had numerous small tie mills working on contract around southern Vancouver Island.

BUT TO GET BACK to Constable Sam Service. Once, when he was patrolling the old Chemainus highway he was following

Mural of Hong Hing in front of his store in Chemainus.

behind Hong Hing, the owner of the secondhand store on Oak Street down near the government wharf.

Hong turned right onto Mill Street without giving a signal. Service followed him and pulled him over.

"Hong, you did not signal when you turned off the highway, and you should know that's illegal."

Hong got out of his truck, spat on the road right in front of Service, and said, "Mista Sam, whatcha malla you. Gotdamn, everybody know where Hong go."

Service just shook his head and without another word they

Mural of Hong Hing's Model T truck.

both drove off in different directions.

Sam Service combined being a good policeman with a soft heart. He was an innately humane person, like his brother Robert, the famous Canadian poet who wrote his first poem sitting under the big maple tree just below the bridge at the head of Cowichan Bay. Later, when Robert Service went to the Klondike he wrote many more wonderful poems and those poems are still loved today.

Hong ran a gambling joint at the back of his store and sometimes sold beer and whiskey to his friends — the mill workers, the longshoremen, the fishermen, and anyone who could ask for it in Chinese. Small in stature, he would not hesitate to pick up a cleaver and clear his premises of anyone who was being unduly noisy.

One of the famous Chemainus murals depicts Hong standing outside his store. The mural is painted on a building at the corner of Oak and Esplanade, half a block from where his store and home used to be.

One day, four fellows who lived at Mrs. English's boarding house a block away decided to play a trick on Hong. They found two blocks of wood just the right size in a woodshed by the side of his store. While one of them went into the store to buy cigarettes, two went around to the back end of Hong's truck and lifted one side while the fourth put a block just inside the wheel under the axle. The hard rubber-tired wheel was now just a half inch off the ground. They quickly put the second block under the other side and headed into the store. They told Hong where there was an old wood stove for sale for only $5.

"I go get um," he said as he ushered them out the door and locked it. They headed for the corner to watch.

Hong cranked the motor and got it started, then climbed into the driver's seat. But when he put the truck in gear it wouldn't move. He got out to see what was wrong and didn't notice the blocks partly hidden behind the wheels.

One of the boys hollered, "Give her more gas Hong. Maybe she go."

"Hong, your wheels go around, but your truck don't move. Maybe we can help," one said.

As he stepped down the boys on the far side took out the block. When Hong walked around to look at that side the two boys on the other side whipped out the second block.

"Try um again, Hong, and we'll give you a push."

In Hong climbed, thoroughly confused. The wheels skidded as he pulled down hard on the gas lever. The truck leapt forward, and Hong was on his way with a wide grin and a wave of his hand. That $5 stove he would sell for $10 and declare he had made a one percent profit. Percentages baffled him, but money didn't.

Hong Hing was the name over his store, but his real name was Fong Yen Lew. After half a century as a shopkeeper, secondhand dealer, bootlegger, gambling house operator and general junk collector, he returned to China, presumably to die. Instead, he married a woman some 40 years younger than himself and before he died she presented him with an heir.

AS WELL AS longshoring together, Shorty Berkey and I took

on many construction jobs. During these tough times, there might only be one ship to load in a month, or you could be busy every day for two weeks. Everywhere, thousands of men were unemployed, but we found lots of jobs, building chimneys and fireplaces, putting on roofs and even building houses. We had begun a working relationship which would continue until 1949, but our friendship continues today. He's one of the last of my special handful of friends who is still alive.

My next job was looking after the construction of the export booming grounds for Lake Logging. The International Woodworkers of America (IWA) were getting organized. We had only just finished driving the three big dolphins and putting up the gangway when we were called out on strike by the Log Export Branch organized in Crofton by Joe Morris, later to become a national and international labour leader. We were asked to put pickets up on the wharf to prevent the longshoremen from loading the ships. But the court classified it as an illegal strike and the police from both Chemainus and Duncan escorted the longshoremen to work.

As a result of this I was blackballed by the Lake Logging Company from all the logging camps in the district. I had to go out on my own. Tom asked me if I would look after his log dump and booming problems.

I was fortunate. The ban was my good luck. I really never looked back. When I had all Tom's problems sorted out, much to my surprise, I was asked to oversee and build a second booming ground just south of the government wharf for the Crofton Export Company. I was not eligible to join the union because I was now classified as management.

Though the Great Depression was wrecking most of Canada and the U.S. these were busy times for Crofton. There could be as many as 19 ships in the harbour waiting to load logs. This was in the mid-thirties when to hope seemed hopeless. But for me they were some of the good times I remember so well.

PART II

The War Years

ON THE MOUNTAIN, when I regained consciousness and some semblance of rational thinking, the rain was still pelting down. My clothes were soaked. I was shivering violently. I felt around and found my cane among the branches I had cut for a bed, a tangle of boughs by any other description. Rolling over onto my stomach I struggled to raise myself up to a standing position. I was swaying like a drunkard. I knew that I had to get moving very soon or collapse, perhaps forever. My situation was now desperate.

I felt in my jacket pocket, fished out what was left of the banana, cut it in half and ate the larger piece. Diabetics need snacks at least every four hours — some snack! However, this seemed to clear my mind and steady my legs. I was soon able to take a few steps, heading downhill towards an old shack I had seen on the way in at the next fork in the road. I just kept walking slowly, feeling my way along with the cane. It was so dark, that the only way I could follow the road was by looking up toward the sky and following the slightly lighter gap between the trees.

On this second stage of my walk in hell, I lived again my entire life, the good things and the bad. I thought of my early married life in the coastal village of Chemainus, not too many miles to the east from where I was now struggling. I thought of the frame around my neck.

MEMORIES OF CHEMAINUS

CHEMAINUS IS WHERE I met and married Pat English. I was building a house on Chemainus Road. Pat walked by every day on her way to and from school swinging the little red lard pail she carried her lunch in. She was 12 then, and I was 22, but she would stop and talk. She often stayed until I was ready to quit for the day, then I would drop her off at the end of her road on my drive home to Crofton.

She was 13 when her father died at their farm on Crozier Road, now part of the Chemainus Golf Course. Near their farm I later built a house for Len Williams and a shingle mill and house for Gil Clarke. I cut enough shingles from old cedar buried in the swamp back of the property for the roofs of both buildings.

After her husband's death, Pat's mother sold the farm and opened a boarding house next to the old telephone office on Maple Street.

Pat had lots of girl friends. Her best girl friend was Virginia Humbird whose Dad was one of the owners of the Chemainus sawmill. The Humbirds were friendly with the Weyerhauser family who owned a huge sawmill in Everett, Washington. Virginia and Pat had started school the same day. We named our first daughter after her.

When Pat turned 17 and I was 27, we met again in Chemainus on the badminton court. Tom and I had come to Chemainus having just won a major tournament in Duncan. Pat thought we were both good-looking guys in our white flannels, but she didn't think much of me. I was too damn conceited, she told her girl friends.

As luck would have it, Pat and I were booked to play

Patricia English, at age 16.

together. The teams were posted on the board, but she refused to play with me. However, I wasn't going to give up that easily, so I went over to where she was sitting.

"I hear you don't want to play badminton with me," I said. "Did it ever occur to you that maybe I could teach you a thing or two about the game? It could be to your advantage." She picked up her racquet and walked onto the court with me.

At the time I was going with a girl who worked at the telephone office. Jo Murray was my age and my usual partner in the mixed doubles. After dropping her off for her night shift, I would sometimes walk over to see Pat at the boarding house next door. Within a few months Jo moved to Port Alberni to

47

marry her high school boy friend.

I still lived in Crofton but I was building two houses in Chemainus so I would often visit Pat and stay for supper. Afterwards we would go out together. We knew each other this second time around for less than a year when we became engaged.

I asked Mrs. English if I could build a small, three-room cottage just up behind her boarding house. I told her when we moved on we'd give it to her. After all, it was on her land.

We were married on February 26, 1938. Pat's brother Terry gave her away and also acted as best man. Ruth Radcliffe was the bridesmaid. Afterwards, the four of us went to Nanaimo to have our pictures taken. Pat and I then took the C.P.R. steamship to Vancouver where my sister Margaret had a nice reception waiting for us.

Next day we drove south as far as Everett. As a wedding present, Pat's friend Virginia and her father arranged for us to spend a few days at one of the Weyhauser's guest cabins.

The day we returned to Chemainus, I bought pork chops for supper and to my surprise, Pat threw a crying tantrum, saying, "I don't know how to cook these things!"

It hadn't taken long to find out that she hated cooking. Pat had three older brothers and three older sisters, and I think she'd been spoiled by them. It so happened that barely three weeks after our wedding I was in hospital having my appendix out. You can bet Pat got a lot of teasing from the boys at the boarding house about that.

We played badminton and often went to the community socials. We'd go to Nanaimo almost every weekend because Pat was crazy about dancing. She especially loved to jive and jitter-bug.

I well remember her fiery temper during those early days of our marriage. I loved to tease, and she loved to throw anything at me she could get her hands on. That first year she broke most of our china. I remember a bottle of ketchup barely missing my head, and smashing into the wall I had just finished painting, in fact the paint wasn't even dry yet.

"You can look at that mess for a while," I said, and walked out.

We stayed in this little three-roomed house for almost a year, then bought the land to the north of what is now Garner Road, and subdivided it into 48 lots. There were three roads in the subdivision, and lots sold for $150 each. We had a good deal going — $5 down, $5 a month, at five percent interest.

Wedding picture of Joe Garner and Pat English, taken at Nanaimo just before leaving on the C.P.R. ferry for their honeymoon. (February 26, 1938)

Easy bookkeeping. We had a grand opening and all the lots were sold within a week.

I first built a house for ourselves at the corner of Garner and Cook Streets. There was a big stump right where we wanted to put the house. We tried to push it out with our bulldozer. No luck. I phoned brother Ollie: "Could you blast this stump out?" That was like waving a red flag in front of a bull.

Joe and Pat's first home built in 1939 in their subdivision in Chemainus, as it was in 1994.

"You get enough powder, Joe, and I'll move that big baby for you," Ollie promised.

"One box of twenty percent enough?"

"Plenty."

Next day I gave him the box of powder and some blasting caps then went deer hunting. He'd asked me to just go away and leave him alone. That afternoon he blasted that huge stump right up over the top of the power lines and it landed square in the middle of the railroad tracks, roots up.

Ollie set out a couple of big red buckets filled with rocks on each side of the stump about 100 yards apart. He knew there was a work train somewhere nearby so he phoned the railroad station master. He then went home, got his gun and headed up the mountain to see if he could find me, or shoot a deer if one

50

got in his way. Ollie was nowhere to be found for the next couple of days, and by then the work train had loaded the stump on a flat car and hauled it away.

Up the hill from us on the corner of Garner and Victoria Roads we built a house for Mother. She wanted to get into a house of her own with her three youngest children. Brother Lloyd packed all the bricks for the fireplace and the double chimney I was building, even though he was only 12 years old. Al started shingling the outside walls, but when he left in September, 1939, to join the army, the walls were less than half finished, so Lloyd completed that job also.

I remember coming home one Saturday night having had a couple of beers on the way. Pat was mad because I was late and I got mad at her.

"Okay, I'm going right back where I came from," I told her. She pulled down a big picture of herself hanging on the wall, and yelled, "That's what you think," and brought it down full force on my head. The picture, glass and all, popped right out and I was left with the frame hanging round my neck.

I decided enough was enough, and said, "Patsy, that wasn't very nice." Then with the frame still draped around me, I walked straight out the door.

WAR

VIRGINIA, our first-born, arrived on August 10, 1939, in the old Chemainus Hospital. Pat had unexpectedly gone into labour. Her brother, who lived next door, rushed her to the hospital, where they took her directly into the delivery room. She was asking for me and one of the nurses sent a messenger up the hill to the baseball field half a mile away. I walked into the case room dressed in my uniform and the nurse quickly slipped a white gown on me.

"And put your shoes back at the door," she ordered.

Within minutes Pat and I were the proud parents of a red headed, noisy, ten-pound baby girl. Little did we know then, that within a month war would be declared and our comfortable and secure lives would be changed completely.

I was a contractor and was actually working on the upgrading of this little hospital. It involved making screens for all the windows and outside doors, as well as building a dark room for the development of X-rays.

Mother packed her belongings and moved back to Vancouver shortly after the war started, and Pat and I moved up the road to her place because it was a bit bigger. Lloyd stayed with us until he graduated from the Ladysmith high school a year later.

On May 2nd, 1941, in the same hospital, our second daughter, Dana, was born.

Within a month we were forced to close our contracting business in the Cowichan area, not because we were so patriotic, but because most of our crew had already joined the army and building materials were available only for war purposes. After closing down the various jobs I phoned Hugh Martin of

Marwell Construction in Vancouver and explained my position.

"I'm ready to go on war construction till it's over," I declared. "What have you got on Vancouver Island that needs a good carpenter foreman or a superintendent?"

"Glad you called Joe. I've been phoning every man I know that might be able to handle the sea plane base at Patricia Bay. How would that suit?"

"What would you want me to do there?" I asked, eagerly.

"A huge sea plane hanger with a wharf and repair shops. You can report to Glen Harris, our assistant superintendent at the Pat Bay airport tomorrow morning. Be ready to take over. It's for both heavy and light aircraft. The base is to be a training area for our sea-going pilots. What time can you be there in the morning?" Hugh asked.

"How would eight-thirty be? That should give Glen sufficient time to get his day organized," I replied.

"Okay. Joe, I'll get him on the phone and let him know you are coming down. How about your construction crew? Can you bring them with you? We need some good men. We are having real problems."

"I can get about a dozen men who could be there within a few days," I assured him.

"I'll advise Glen right away," he said and hung up.

Pat had been listening to the phone call.

"Are we going to have to move to Victoria or Saanich?" she asked anxiously. Understandably, she didn't want to leave our comfortable home. Virginia was now two and loved to sit in her high chair and feed herself. Dana was barely a month old and we were enjoying our life just the way it was.

"Well, I certainly won't be able to get enough gas coupons to drive there every day, so we had better get ready to move," I declared. "This rationing is making travel tough. And it could get tougher."

"Let's put some chairs and other furniture and stuff in the pickup and go down there today. See what we can find," she suggested. We drove around Saanich, in and around Sidney and the airport. Absolutely nothing. Air Force and construction crews occupied every livable house. We were advised to try Victoria, so we bought the morning newspaper and started searching. Everywhere we phoned or went was taken. It seemed hopeless. We finally stopped in Beacon Hill Park to think over our problem.

As we were putting our lunch things back into the pickup,

Pat said, "I know someone living down on Moss Street in an apartment. Why don't we go and ask them if they know of something?"

Her friends were home when we got there. While we were chatting outside a carpenter walked by carrying a door. It was getting heavy so he stopped for a rest close by. We got chatting.

"Where are you going with that?" I asked.

"This door is for the last apartment in the block," he told me.

"Are you the contractor for the building?"

"Sure am," he replied. "This is the last one I'm going to even try and build until this war is over. Can't get men or material anymore."

"I'll go along with you and help you put the door in place and have a look," I said, hoping against hope.

It was a modern little three-roomed deal with stove, fridge and plenty of kitchen cupboards. Not big, but nice.

"Is it rented?"

"Not yet, but it will be before dark," he assured me.

"We are looking for something about this size. How much is the rent?"

"Seventy-five a month," he said.

"I'll take it," I told him, holding out a $100 bill. He took it with a smile, took the keys out of the lock and handed them over to me. We signed the papers and that was that. He agreed to let us do the inside painting and take it off the rent.

The luck of the Garners!

"You'll have to wait until tomorrow morning to move in," he said. "But it's okay if you leave your chesterfield and other things you have with you here."

"What are you planning to do now that this block is finished?" I asked.

"Look for a job."

"Come and work for me next week at the Pat Bay Airport." He did, and we shared our vehicles for travelling to and from work for the next few months.

We took our furniture into the apartment, then drove back home to Chemainus where we loaded the rest of the stuff we needed.

Early next morning Pat drove me to the airport and picked me up at quitting time. By then she had everything set up and we had our supper in the apartment after the little ones were in bed.

The next week we sold our first home in Chemainus, with

54

some of our furniture, to Mr. and Mrs. Fred Deacon. Shortly after we sold Mother's house to Mr. and Mrs. Boyd, with the rest of the furniture we couldn't bring with us.

Things were working out just fine.

A few months later during the autumn of 1941, the big seaplane hanger was completed, ready to house and service the fleet of amphibious bomber aircraft stationed there. Both Hugh Martin and Doug Welch, the owners of Marwell Construction, came over for the grand opening. Glen Harris and myself made sure all the construction details were properly explained and understood.

The airport officers had a bar in the hangar with plenty of sandwiches and other goodies. It was a welcome treat because only service people were allowed to buy more than one 26-ounce bottle of liquor per month. If you remember, we were on rations!

AFTER THE PARTY Hugh and Doug called Glen and me aside. We were both congratulated for a job well done and we drank a toast to its completion almost a month ahead of schedule. Hugh informed us, "Our company has just been awarded the contract to construct the Vulcan Airport south of Calgary. It's a multi-million dollar job. We will develop and handle this project entirely, just us. Doug and I want you fellows to get things underway. Glen can take on the superintendent's job. Joe, you'll be his assistant. Okay?"

"How soon?" Glen asked.

"No real hurry," Welch said, grinning happily. "If you both could be in Vulcan tomorrow it certainly wouldn't be a bit too soon. All your expenses will be paid and your salaries will be almost double what you're getting now. This is a rush job. Everything is rush-rush these days. This war!"

We nodded our agreement. Hugh poured us each a Scotch and soda, then raised his glass: "To the future of the Vulcan Airport."

"A Beaver aircraft will be here at the new docks by seven-thirty tomorrow to take you both to Vancouver," Doug told us. "Glen, you and Joe be there with your baggage. I will have your airline tickets and some cash to get you on your way.

"We'll go to our office to collect the blueprints and discuss plans for getting material and equipment on the job site as soon as possible. In Calgary there'll be a couple of U-Drives waiting to take you to Vulcan. Two of our office staff are already there and have a temporary office set up in one of the hotels downtown. Their phones are hooked up and they're expecting you tomorrow in the late afternoon.

"Take a couple of days to look things over, then give me a call," Doug said to Glen.

That's how quickly things can happen when there's a war on!

Leaving our little apartment at six next morning we drove out to Pat Bay. Dana was tucked in her basket on the front seat and Virginia was asleep with her head on Pat's lap. She woke up long enough to say "Bye, Dad."

"You'll have the car, and I'll phone you as soon as I find a place for us to live," I said to Pat. With a quick kiss she was gone.

The Beaver had just landed in the bay and was taxiing up to the wharf when Glen arrived. We wheeled our gear down to the plane in a cart and stowed the four heavy suitcases on the back seat. In less than half an hour we were docking in Vancouver. Doug Welch was waiting.

"You have reservations on a noon plane to Calgary, so we don't have a minute to waste," Doug explained as he sped north on Granville Street. He passed signs reading 30 miles per hour with his speedometer needle steady on 60.

The staff had most of the blueprints already packed in wooden crates. We spent an hour going over the general plan. He gave us his ideas and told us what had been done so far. They had already been able to rent or buy several houses in Vulcan for key personnel, so Glen had a place to move into right away.

We made it to the airport just in time. They were starting to remove the boarding steps as we arrived.

In Calgary we piled our gear into the waiting U-Drives and arrived at Vulcan by way of High River about five that afternoon, hot, tired and dusty.

Little did I realize that afternoon when we arrived in Vulcan that I was participating in one of the greatest achievements in the history of war — the British Commonwealth Air Training Plan. Across Canada residents of cities, towns and villages realized something important was happening. They saw land being bought or expropriated and concrete being poured for runways and dozens of buildings both large and small being erected. Even in Canada wartime secrecy was tight, but something was obviously going on.

During the First World War thousands of airmen and ground crew had been trained in Canada under the auspices of the Royal Flying Corps, later to be named the Royal Air Force. So, in 1937, when it appeared that war with Hitler's Germany was inevitable, although futile efforts were still being made to contain that madman, the government of Great Britain decided that a similar scheme was absolutely vital. Germany had air superiority and its bombers and fighters could pound training bases in England and France endlessly, while shooting training planes out of the sky like a professional gunner breaking clay pigeons at a trap shoot.

The bases had to be in Canada, the nearest member of the British Commonwealth and the only one with the land and the workers. Another important element was a large group of expert flyers known as bush pilots.

After much negotiation and much nitpicking by Canada's fussy little prime minister Mackenzie King, the deal between the R.C.A.F. and the R.A.F. was eventually signed. The Allied pilots and support crews would be trained in Canada. When the war ended against Japan in August of 1945, Prime Minister Winston Churchill would remark that the British Commonwealth Air Training Plan was "one of the major factors, and possibly the decisive factor of the war."

In 1941 my job with Marwell Construction was to help build the air base at Vulcan, on land known as the Galbraith Farm.

We were the major contractor. Money was no problem. Ask for it and it was there, just as it was for the other bases being constructed across Canada. Materials in short supply? Just order them and they would arrive. The government would find the materials and skilled men. This vast task of building 230 training bases, both large and small, had a triple-A priority.

Even though men were desperately needed for the fighting forces, the government made sure that every type of tradesman was available and the orders went out to all contractors: "Full speed ahead." The results were magnificent.

But strangely, during the war and for many years after this historic accomplishment, Canada never got the full recognition it deserved. In recent years several books have been written on this achievement. I can hardly do it justice, except by quoting a portion of *Behind the Glory*, a first class account of the British Commonwealth Air Training Plan (BCATP) by Toronto writer Ted Barris, published in 1992 by Macmillan of Canada:

> In its five and a half year span — from December,
> 1939, to September, 1945 — the BCATP would

expend $2-billion, a vast sum then, in the training of air crew from nearly every nation of the free world. It would ultimately deliver air superiority to the Allied war effort. The product of its training — nearly a quarter of a million air and ground crew — would spearhead the major land and sea operation to win back Europe, North Africa and much of the Pacific. It would supply R.A.F. Bomber Command with the trained airmen for a third of a million sorties.

It would produce some of Canada's 160 fighter aces who accounted for more than a thousand victories in the Second World War. It would help sustain the flow of bomber and fighter aircraft to the European theatre of war by supplying trained pilots and navigators to Ferry Command. And it would ensure the success of military operations on all fronts with the qualified airmen of Transport Command and Coastal Command. And it happened almost entirely in Canada.

There it is, in black and white. What Canada did. Unfortunately, because the Second World War or any war is barely taught in Canadian schools as history, two generations of Canadians have grown up in ignorance of this great achievement and sacrifice.

But all this was to come. As far as we were concerned we had a job to do. We had the plans, the workers, the materials and we were told to build a base which would be used to train pilots as instructors and then, those instructors would train young men from around the Commonwealth and the world to be pilots.

Often under miserable conditions, we worked day and night, literally creating a small town with mess halls, living quarters, H-huts for the trainees, a 38-bed hospital, sewer and water systems, headquarters, garages, warehouses, recreation halls, and, of course, a "digger" or jail. The bases that were strung along the foothills of the Rockies were important because the weather and terrain there were excellent for flight training.

Future pilots were moving into their quarters even as the painters were moving out and the double-decker iron bunks were being set up. Pilots were training four months after we broke the first ground. It was high pressure and top priority from day one, with as many as 700 tradesmen on the job.

When the base was completed there were often up to 4,800 Air Force personnel on it. During those years it sent out thousands of young men, some no older than 19, to fly the deadly skies over Europe.

And today? The town of Vulcan is prosperous with its fields of canola and wheat and its beef cattle. There are still a few of that town of 1,000 who remember the influx of the "fly boys" as they called them. Many a garage, basement and attic was converted into living quarters for the wives and children of the personnel of Number 9 Service Flight Training School.

"Saturday nights could only be described as a madhouse," said Harris Matlock, a retired Vulcan farmer who was born there. He took his training and instructed in Vulcan, and when the war was over he went back to farming.

What remains of this base? The runways are there, used by local flyers who have their own planes, including Matlock. The seven hangars are used for various businesses, including two for farm and cattle auctions. The rest of this huge assemblage was hauled away, pulled apart and sold or burned. Matlock even knows where some very expensive equipment was buried by bulldozer because it could no longer serve any useful purpose.

It was much the same story all across Canada. Some bases were maintained by the R.C.A.F. Some were sold to flying clubs after most of the buildings were taken away. The rest? Just disappeared off the face of the earth. Many a returned veteran's first home was built with lumber salvaged from the buildings.

The Flying Finches, the Cornells, the Harvards, the twin-engined Ansons and the small Piper Cubs used in training practically all went to the scrap heap. Only a few of these planes went to private owners, and a very few went to museums. Once the war was over they were expendable. Good for scrap, and scrap they became.

This is a wonderful story, one that every Canadian should know and be proud of. But the training of pilots, flight engineers, air gunners and navigators, and the indispensable ground crews is pretty dull stuff when compared to tales of flying bombers through heavy flak over German cities, or dog-fighting with German aces.

I was proud to have taken part in this grand plan, even though at the time it was just another rush wartime job.

The task was incredible, and it was done by Canada, a nation of less than twelve million in 1939. I, like others who remember those days grieve for the 3,000 young men and their instructors from every Allied country who died in training accidents in Canada, and the many thousands more who were killed flying bombers and fighters over Europe in defence of freedom.

But that day back in 1941, we moved into the two hotel rooms that had been reserved for us. After a quick shower and a meal we hit the sack for some much needed sleep.

At six next morning, Glen was hammering a breakfast call on my door. He had already arranged for the general manager and the purchasing agent to come with us. The purchasing agent would be responsible for the acquisition of all the building materials. The general manager was to locate and hire the heavy equipment to start shaping the runways and do the excavating for the buildings.

We drove off for our first look at the site, 10 miles southwest of town. The first thing was to locate ground for an office and half a dozen storage sheds. By noon these were staked out and the material ordered. Within a week the office building was ready, with lights, phones and heat. A week later the storage buildings were rough but usable, all temporary and on the northwest side of the main airport.

About 40 engineers and surveyors were laying out the runways, hangars and other buildings. We were told this was to be one of the largest training centers for the British Commonwealth Air Training Scheme.

There are two humorous memories of those dark days. Shorty, who had come with me from the Pat Bay job, and I were driving to High River when a truck ahead of us hit a coyote and kept on going. We pulled over to check. The animal was dead.

"Joe, what do you think a coyote hide is worth?" Shorty asked.

"You tell me and we'll both know."

"Well, let's find out," he said, taking out his hunting knife and skinning the coyote. He sold it in High River for twenty-five bucks.

When a wartime construction site was close to a town there were always some local girls — and some from afar —who lived "like there was no tomorrow," nor did they hesitate to "do their patriotic duty." Both wartime expressions! I can still see a couple who used to show up at Vulcan, strutting about in those imitation leopard skin coats that were popular in the early forties.

One night the two "Leopard Skin Girls" hooked up with Shorty and me. One drink led to another and I ended up in the back seat of our car, parked beside a building. We needed

Shorty Berkey (carpenter foreman) left, and Joe (assistant superintendent) on airport construction job at Vulcan, Alberta, in 1941.

privacy, so I strung a rope along the windows and hung the lady's clothes on the line. When Shorty returned to the car he slapped his hand on the roof and shouted, "What's going on in there, Joe! You trying to get a closer look at the leopard's spots?"

Shorty was a good sport and a fun guy to be with. But when this job was completed he joined the Air Force as a mechanic and we weren't to get together again until just after the end of the war.

It was generally believed there was imminent danger of a Japanese invasion on the British Columbian coast so there were blackouts and panic everywhere. I was sure Pat would be nervous. I learned later she was living near an apartment where there were lots of Air Force and Navy people and she was having a ball. She had no trouble getting a baby-sitter. As soon as I was able to get a partly furnished house for us I phoned Pat.

"I'll be on an Air Force plane to Pat Bay first thing tomorrow morning," I told her.

In Victoria, after helping her pack I bought her and the children train tickets for Calgary. The plane was waiting to take me back to Vulcan that evening.

The dust storms in summer and the severe cold during the winter months made for some very miserable living conditions and the alkali water tasted horrible. By the time the second autumn set in, the job was practically completed, and Pat and I packed our belongings and moved back to the coast. We rented a house in Vancouver off east Broadway.

Vulcan had gone so well, and I wondered what the next big challenge might be. I was soon to find out.

Pat with daughters Virginia (3) and Dana (1), taken in Vancouver during the autumn of 1942.

STORMY WATERS

WITHIN TWO DAYS of getting home from Vulcan that fall of 1942 Doug Welch talked me into building a radar station on Marble Island, the most westerly piece of land in Canada. There was a fear the Japanese might invade the Queen Charlotte Islands and use them as a springboard to attack the mainland. For a year, the R.C.A.F. had been attempting to get the job under way but they lacked the know-how. It was not their thing.

"Radar is the only means of detecting an invasion in time to do something about it," Doug said. At the time, radar was new and unsophisticated.

Plans prepared by the R.C.A.F. were produced along with some engineering reports. Everyone believed a station could never be built on this isolated, rainy and wind-hammered rock. I pointed out to Welch, with some concern, that the engineer's closing comment was written on some water-stained brown paper, which stated: "Camp and tents blown off the island in a storm."

"You will have a free hand to do the job as you see fit, Joe. Men can be called from any industry, in or out of the armed forces. The commanding officer at Alliford Bay, the seaplane base on the Queen Charlottes, has guaranteed all possible protection and assistance."

I thought, I'll need it, and more. I had a tough one!

"Well, Joe, what do you say?" Doug asked.

"Sounds like this could be a bit of a challenge. When do we start?"

"What about this afternoon?

"I'll have a crew ready in a week and we'll want air

transportation to Queen Charlotte City." I informed him.

"We have an accountant who is also a timekeeper and he is familiar with the procedures of progress draws and the book work required by the Treasury Department. He'd be a good man to have along," Doug said.

"Have him packed and ready to leave by tomorrow noon."

I spent the rest of the afternoon calling a crew, brothers Tom, Oliver and Lloyd. I asked Fred Robson, my brother-in-law, if he could handle the job of master mechanic.

"Hell, yes! I fix everything from alarm clocks to 1000-horsepower diesel engines, and keep them going."

"You'll do," I said. "Be ready to leave in a week for at least four months, so make a list of the equipment you'll need and pack everything — except a girl."

Fred laughed. "I'll be there. You can count on it."

With these men to supervise, I knew it would be a first class crew.

The accountant and I landed at Alliford Bay just before dark the next day. Harry Winnie, the commanding officer, welcomed us with enthusiasm. We were going to give this project another try. We talked with his engineers until well past midnight, then slept in the officers' barracks for a few hours.

Dawn was barely breaking when we put our sleepy-eyed accountant on the dock at Queen Charlotte City with instructions to establish an office and charter a boat. Harry Winnie and I headed out to look over Marble Island from the air. The little island was no more than a half mile long and 200 yards wide and looked much like a huge ship. We checked some sheltered inlets on Graham Island, a mile to the east, which could possibly be used for storage. It was a quiet day for the west coast, yet any attempt to land near the island was out of the question.

It would be impossible to get a scow near enough to unload without having it smashed to bits. Landing people and food from a supply boat would be a perilous manoeuvre. A power boat would be useless. We would need a strong boat that could be manhandled high up onto the beach, a river-boat, with seating for two sets of oars and four passengers, or equivalent cargo. Just how the heavy equipment might be put ashore was much more of a problem than either of us had anticipated.

Flying low through the passage that separates the two main islands of the Queen Charlottes, we could clearly see the shallow channel and its jagged reefs. Further east two big

A-frames were yarding huge spruce logs into the water. The size of these logs gave me an idea.

"Harry, do you know the boss of that outfit we're looking at down there?"

"Sure do."

"Where can he be contacted?"

"He should be in the cookhouse about now," Harry guessed, looking at his wristwatch.

"Let's land and have a chat with him."

Winnie banked the flying boat and made a perfect landing. The man we wanted to see was there to help us tie up. Jim Carstairs, "Bull of the Woods" in logger's lingo, invited us to stay for lunch.

We explained what we were going to try to do. Jim's opening remark was direct.

"On the west coast of these islands, it is rough and dangerous at any time of the year. Right now I wouldn't want to chance it in a battleship."

"I need a raft using a dozen of these big spruce logs, lashed with double headsticks and heavy cable. It should be forty feet wide and eighty long, with logs not less than three feet in diameter at the small ends. Can you do it?" I asked. Jim looked at each of us in turn.

"I think your project will be impossible to complete. If we build you this raft, it will be twice as strong as anything we've ever built and it just might hang together long enough to put your machines and supplies off on that surfbound piece of real estate. I'll have my men double-lash everything. It can be ready one week from today," Jim said.

I considered this briefly. "Jim, let's make it ten days from today, and instead of double lashings, make it quadruple."

"Who's going to tow it out to the island?" Jim asked.

"Jack Hann has a big seiner called the Bertha G, and knows this passage about as well as anyone around here," Harry suggested.

Jack was contacted that evening. His comments were also to the point: "You fellows must be more than a little crazy to try to build on that damned island. Only thing it's good for is eagles and seals. The winds will probably blow the buildings into the ocean even if you do manage to get them up."

Next morning shortly after daybreak, I was airborne for Vancouver to finalize the loading on scows of all the equipment and prefabricated cedar buildings. Ten days later, the Bertha G towed all this through the narrows and we transferred everything to the log raft in a cove, where the Skidegate Channel meets the Pacific Ocean.

The cargo consisted of dishes, 20 beds with bedding, two diesel lighting plants, five prefab buildings, plywood, two dozen barrels of gas, diesel fuel, one big oil burning cook stove, one complete water system, three 10,000 gallon fuel storage tanks, food for thirty men for four months, first aid supplies, two machine guns and thousands of rounds of ammunition including three cases of tracer bullets, a Murdie logging donkey, one TD14 International bulldozer and my brother Tom's portable sawmill. There was one complete four-bed hospital unit, including drugs and supplies. All this had to be loaded in such a way that the items loaded last would be off first, to be used in that order. Just to feed and shelter thirty men out on that island was going to be a major undertaking.

There was a big cave on the island where the men slept and cooked for the first 10 days. We managed to land more than half the equipment and buildings. If a bad storm had come up during that period, the seas would have washed our entire camp out into the ocean.

Crew of portable sawmill on Marble Island at the start of construction of a radar station in 1942.
From left, Tom Garner, Fred Robson, John Vonkerman, Ollie Garner, Earl Devlin, Jack Bursey and a Prairie boy.

We got the cookhouse and one bunkhouse roofed before the first storm hit. All hands were busy moving stoves, beds and groceries under cover, when suddenly everyone stopped.

"What the hell is that noise?" Fred Robson shouted.

"It's a storm. All hands hurry and get things tied down or into the bunkhouse," I ordered. I could see the storm off in the distance, black clouds swirling towards us driven by 80 to 100-mile an hour winds. The line squall struck the island with a sound like thunder. Within minutes, our gauge was registering wind speeds over 105 miles an hour. The noise became so great that any voice communication was impossible. The seas roared up the rocky beach like tidal waves. Rocks as big as a man's fist were being blown through the air. From a cave, I watched our bags of cement and piles of bricks disintegrate. The wind was so strong, it blew most of the wet 3 x 10 floor joists right out of the tight lumber piles and carried them as much as a hundred yards out over the foaming waves before they dropped.

The worst of the storm lasted about an hour. Over half the lumber was gone and nails and other hardware soaked in sea water had already begun to rust. Fortunately, we had carried most of the plumbing and electrical supplies into the buildings the previous day. We had lost almost all our groceries. Sacks of flour and vegetables, and cases of canned goods had been swept off our storage ledge.

Next morning when our supply boat came out, we hoisted our prearranged signal, a red flag, to show the Gale brothers we considered it too dangerous to attempt unloading. They would try again the next morning and if a green flag was up, they would stand by until the big skiff was launched.

In our crew were six men from Alberta. They were a rugged group of individuals, but this storm had scared the hell out of them. They announced next morning they would rather leave now than stay to starve or drown at some later date. It was two days before we could get these men out to the packer. The Quallace was a 45-foot west coast fishing boat owned and operated by Jim and Frank Gale.

Fred Robson and I took the terrified men out, two at a time. The waves were such that one minute the big skiff was 10 feet above the decks of the packer and the next minute we could see the propeller and keel. It was imperative to keep the boats close without allowing any actual contact. This was done with poles and ropes handled by men whose very lives depended on every move. The prairie boys needed no coaxing to leap from the skiff onto the packer. Their bags and suitcases were tossed to them from a safer distance.

It was now my turn to leap across. Not my idea of fun either. I had a grocery list sufficient to feed an army for a year. Coffee, tea, sugar, and meat had all been rationed by the government and were available only with coupons. This was indeed a problem from our standpoint. The storm had taken four months rations away in a matter of minutes.

The Gale brothers gave notice: they would not carry on unless a second boat was chartered to stand by in case of trouble. They suggested I try to charter the Burnaby M, a 50-foot seiner owned by the Haida Indians of Skidegate Village.

When we arrived at Queen Charlotte City, Frank Gale and I headed for the Skidegate Reserve. I was introduced to Ed Collison, their chief, and his half-brother Jim McKay, the skipper of the Burnaby M. Their big boat was up on the beach being caulked and copper-painted. Because we paid good wages we had no trouble hiring a dozen men. The big boat was launched at high tide that evening and we arranged to leave at daylight the next morning.

Gales' store provided the groceries. We purchased almost everything they had in stock. But when Frank Gale Sr. learned we had no ration coupons, he refused to let the goods go.

"I can't replace those rationed things without coupons," he stated.

I got on the phone to Harry Winnie and explained our predicament.

"Hang tough! I'll be over in our crash boat."

Twenty minutes later there was a great roar down by the dock and Harry stepped ashore. He had with him the two purchasing officers from the base. Papers were produced and signed, stating that we had received the groceries as emergency rations for the west coast radio detachments. "If there's a court-martial because of this, I'll come out and get you so we can face the Ration Board together," were Harry's parting words. A month later in Vancouver we did. After explaining what had happened we were assured that in future a phone call would give us all the ration coupons we needed.

In minutes the crash boat was out of sight in its own spray. With its two big straight-8 Rolls Royce engines, it was capable of doing well over 40 knots.

Our arrival back at Marble Island with the two packers, replacements for the crew, plus enough good food to see us through, shot morale from very low to high. I was able to inform them that a scow was already on its way from Vancouver with cement, nails, bricks and lumber.

We were astounded at the way the young Indians handled the big skiff and hauled the supplies and men ashore. Few words were spoken — they worked as one. Each seemed to know exactly what was needed, and they anticipated each other's every move.

Sharks up to 12 feet long sometimes followed the skiff in towards shore. We never knew if these were man-eaters and no one was in a hurry to jump in and find out.

When the Haidas had stowed their gear in the bunkhouse, Lloyd, Fred and I went in to introduce ourselves. They were fine young men, with an average height of over six feet. Many had attended colleges, and had studied music and the arts.

George Brown told me he was Captain of the Rangers, the local defence force on the Queen Charlotte Islands. All the men were members with combat training, and each had brought his own rifle with 500 rounds of ammunition, hand grenades and emergency food rations.

Fred Williams told us, "I am the leader of our orchestra. We're known as 'The Harmony Boys'." He asked if it would be okay if they practiced. They had brought along some of their instruments — a set of drums, saxophone, trumpet, violin, a couple of guitars and one banjo.

The last man introduced was six-feet three inches tall and weighed over 200 pounds.

"This is Phil Watson ," said George. "I suggest you make him your labour boss." Shaking hands with Phil was like putting your hand in a vice.

"You are now the official boss of the Marble Island Haidas and you will be paid accordingly," I said, rubbing my right hand to get the circulation going again. It was easy to sense the respect everyone had for him.

The Harmony Boys were already tuning up their instruments as Fred and I headed for the office. It was now early December and cold. As a full moon came rising out of the ocean the strains of "White Christmas" drifted out over the little camp. The combination froze us in our tracks. Fred broke the spell, "That's some good crew you hired today, Joe. Might get this bloody job done with men like that around."

I had bought four bottles of Scotch at Alliford Bay the previous week and we took them up to the bunkhouse. It was a great evening with everyone getting acquainted. The music and Scotch had done a great deal to bolster the sagging spirits of everyone in camp, especially the Air Force boys who manned the wireless and lookouts 24 hours every day. Phil was the one who called the party to a halt. At eleven o'clock he blinked the newly installed electric lights three times.

"Okay gang! Party's over! We've got a war on and plenty of work to do tomorrow." Everyone tied into his job with vigour and enthusiasm next morning. In only a week, we had the main cookhouse completed and a gravity water system operating. The diesel generators were now in operation so we had hot water and a stove with an oven for the first time since landing. We had to get a second cook to help with the extra work for this larger crew. Bread and pastry could now be baked.

Then another storm struck. The big log raft with a full load of supplies was partially unloaded when heavy seas started to pound the island and push the raft up on the rocks. Our big raft was left high and dry.

Three days later we got a cable out to the Burnaby M and with the boat pulling and the bulldozer pushing, we were able to move the damaged raft a few feet. Then she stuck again and the cable broke. When the loose end tangled in the propeller it looked as though the Burnaby was headed for a watery grave among the jagged rocks.

Again, the crew did the impossible. Fred Russ cut the cable with a fire axe and hammer, then launched their dory. He and the deck hand cleared the cable from around the propeller shaft using pike poles and a long gaff hook just in time to allow the skipper to apply power and pull out to safety. Next day, at low tide, Ollie and his helper drilled a hole in a rock and put in a big eye-bolt anchor and fastened a block to it. They rigged the mainline from the donkey through the block and back to the raft.

"I don't think the donkey will have enough power to move that raft one inch," Ollie declared emphatically.

"What do you suggest then?" I asked.

"Hell, we got lots of dynamite in the shed. Why don't we blast her loose? Sure as hell no good to anyone where she is," Ollie remarked as he spat on the headstick.

He and his crew carried a dozen boxes of dynamite to a big crevice under the high side of the raft. They piled boulders on the boxes to keep them from floating, then ran a fuse through a piece of water pipe. After coating the pipe with grease, the cap end was put in one of the full boxes of dynamite and tied securely. Shortly before high tide Ollie stretched the main line from the donkey singing tight. Everybody, except the donkey puncher and Ollie, was cleared from the area.

At exactly three minutes before the tide was at its fullest, Ollie lit the fuse, then took over the donkey driving. The dynamite was now under several feet of water. There was a deafening boom that actually shook the island. A huge spray went up and the raft seemed to heave 10 feet into the air. The donkey roared, and through the smoke and spray we could see the big raft lunge towards the open ocean. Everyone let out a great cheer.

The boatmen again took the cable out to the Burnaby M and this time she hauled the raft free and back to the inlet for the final load.

"All she needed was a bit of a jolt to get her going," was Ollie's remark and we both laughed.

We had built a railroad from the beach up to the radar building. The little rail car was first pulled up a steep incline by a single-drum gas winch. There were about 200 feet of level track from the top to the radar building. This level portion was operated by manpower. A team of experts came to install the special tubes and wiring. There was a recess left in the main concrete foundation about fifteen inches deep and a foot square.

"What in hell is that square hole for?" I asked.

"That's to be filled with high-test dynamite and wired to a secret circuit. If the Japs land, the orders are to throw the switch and blow the building to smithereens."

A destroyer was used to bring the radar equipment from the war supply depot in Vancouver to Alliford Bay, where the cargo was then transferred to a small scow. On each corner of the scow, a machine gun was mounted and manned during the trip out through Skidegate Channel. Two bombers escorted us all the way. Harry Winnie had explained that two Japanese submarines had been sighted in the area and he suspected they might try either to destroy the equipment or steal it.

The Bertha G, with Jack Hann at the helm, was asked to tow the scow through that narrow and treacherous Skidegate passage and on to Marble. He asked me to be on his boat to help coordinate this risky manoeuvre. As we approached the narrowest turn in the passage, he handed me a razor-sharp fire axe. It was a tense Hann who gave the instructions.

"Now listen carefully, Joe. Our lives may depend on what I have to say. The tide is travelling out towards the ocean at over ten miles an hour. The front end of the scow will strike the rock shoulder as we go through the turn ahead. It should bounce clear and follow, but if it hangs up and swings on us, you will have to instantly cut the towline. If I swing my left hand down, you chop. If you miss, we will be jammed against the jagged reef. At the speed we will be travelling this could sink both scow and boat. I'll have to use full power to keep the boat under control," he told me.

I took my position where the two-inch hemp rope passed over the stern. After taking a couple of practice swings with the axe to make sure there would be no mistakes, I glued my eyes on Jack and waited.

We flew past the rocky shores as we travelled with the riptide, swirling and boiling like rapids in a river. It seemed only seconds until we were into the turn. The corner of the scow struck the rocks with a crash. I watched Jack's left hand as the towline came up so tight water actually squirted out of it where it passed over the hardwood rail. The scow groaned and bounced, then cleared the rock shoulder to follow like a trained seal. I wiped the cold sweat off my face and walked to the wheelhouse where Jack stood with a tight-lipped grin.

"Was about to give the signal when she broke free," he said.

"Wouldn't want many like that!" was my hoarse response.

Before we hit the big ocean swells the four machine guns were taken from the scow and mounted on the two Air Force boats that were following. The gunners needed no coaxing to leave the scow and get aboard their boats.

Brother Ollie and I left the Bertha G to ride the scow and handle the line changes and signals when we neared Marble Island. Plenty of advance preparation had gone into this key manoeuvre. We planned to beach the scow on the east side of the island during high water. The Burnaby was to have the cable strawline stretched out from the donkey on shore, and held tight so it couldn't snag on the boulders on the ocean floor.

As prearranged, the scow passed as close to the Burnaby as conditions would allow and Jim McKay threw me a light line which was tied to the end of the strawline. This was pulled over and shackled to a bridle at the back end of the scow. The boat then cleared the strawline from its tow bits and the donkey was signalled to go ahead and the cable tightened. This caused the scow to swing around and head towards the narrow entrance to the cleared beaching area. The Bertha G had been instructed to hold the scow in position by pulling on the towline as needed. Thanks to the skill and good judgement of Jack Hann, the scow and cargo were manipulated to within feet of the prepared landing spot. When the lines were secure and tight, the Bertha

G was cut free. With a wave of his hand, Jack turned his boat and headed for quieter waters.

Both Air Force boats circled the island until well after dark, but no Japanese subs were to be seen.

By dawn next morning, the big glass tubes in their crates were safely off the scow and on their way up the railway to the radar building. This was quite a trick — the crates had to be kept upright at all times, as we were told the tubes would explode if tipped more than ten degrees in any direction. All hands had worked through the night to again accomplish the seemingly impossible. None of our crew was allowed inside the building once this top secret equipment was put in place.

At high tide the next afternoon the Burnaby M pulled the scow off the beach to find the bottom had been smashed. When it hit the big ocean swells the towline broke and the battered little scow drifted on out towards the open ocean. We all felt a bit sad to see it go, after it had so nobly done its perilous job.

The completion of the radar station was now assured. An end to the hazards and isolation seemed only weeks away.

When the job was nearing completion, the air vice-marshall and his aide flew up from Pat Bay. An Air Force boat met them at Alliford Bay and brought them out to Marble Island and we went out in our river boat to pick them up. As we reached the shore a wave caught the boat and turned it sideways, spilling us onto the rocky beach. What a welcome! We struggled to our feet, undamaged but uncomfortable, and headed for the cookhouse and some hot coffee.

We dried out a bit, then inspected the radar station. Back down on the beach I checked the surging seas and asked a simple question, "When do you want to head back out to your boat."

"When you think its safe enough we'll go," the air vice-marshall replied.

After 10 minutes of carefully watching the seas with my Haida boatmen, there seemed to be a bit of a lull. Maybe I just sensed it. I don't know.

"Let's go," I yelled.

We ran down to the boat and the waiting Haidas shoved us off. In minutes we reached the fish packer. The two officers were helped aboard by the Haida deck hands. The air vice-marshall's last words as the boat pulled away were, "Keep doing what you're doing and don't let anyone interfere." This suited me fine.

We'd had rough times. But little did we know the worst was yet to come. On the opposite side of the island a big sea was running with waves 15 feet high. Our supply boat, the Burnaby M, was standing by to be unloaded. Charlie Williams and Don Moody were on boat duty that day. Don had neglected to remove his gum-boots and he and Charlie were rushing the job. The big skiff fouled the tow line and instantly flipped over, spilling the boatmen into the heavy surf.

The alarm went out and all hands came on the run. Their boss Big Phil Watson never hesitated. Throwing off his heavy clothes and boots, he dove into the foaming surf to pull Charlie up and tie him to the boat.

Don had disappeared. George Brown threw Phil a rope and miraculously he caught the end and dove. Again miraculously, he found Don and looped the rope around the drowning man's waist. Unconscious, he was hauled onto the rocks and revived.

I headed out to help Phil who was still holding onto to the drifting boat. I was running along the top of a reef some 15 feet above the normal breakers. The swells were breaking at least 40 feet away, so there was no thought of danger coming from that direction. If you don't know what is meant when a West Coaster warns, "Look out for the three big ones!" I'll tell you what can happen.

The first wave came over the top of the reef in a solid wall 10 feet high and knocked me into a pothole of foaming water. I was sucked down so deep that all light disappeared. The second wave shot me up from the depths and I was able to gulp one breath of air. The third wave came over the reef like a small Niagara Falls and I was driven back down into the darkness again.

It seemed forever before I saw daylight. Pulling off my heavy gloves, I clawed frantically for the surface. Fortunately I neither blacked out nor panicked. When I made it out onto the rocks and lay with my head down it seemed as though quarts of water ran out of my nose and mouth. Unable to stand, I crawled off the rocks towards shore and safer ground. Some 20 minutes later I staggered up the beach and surprised brother Ollie, who thought I had joined my ancestors.

Within days a letter was sent to our lieutenant governor explaining the courage and bravery of Phil in saving the lives of the two boatmen. We received a reply saying that he was to receive the British Empire Medal and there were instructions as to where and how it should be presented. A two-day holiday was proclaimed. One day was spent travelling to attend the ceremony and the other was spent recuperating and returning to the island.

The big Skidegate hall was decorated for the occasion. A

large crowd was in attendance. Phil, Chief Ed Collison, Harry
Winnie, Jim McKay, the senior officer of the R.C.M.P. and
myself were all up on the stage. Two young Haida Princesses
served us tea and drinks.

Following the welcome by Chief Collison, I was introduced and asked to present the medal to Phil. I spoke of the
near-tragedy and the courage displayed by our hero, his quick-
ness, his skill, with his own life at stake.

That evening Phil and I decided to become blood brothers.
Chief Collison agreed to solemnize this ancient rite, in the way
of the Haidas for many centuries — cutting our wrists and
mixing our blood. I was given the name which, translated,
means "Stormy Waters." Some Haidas believe it is spelled
"GUIWA". Others say it cannot be spelled, only spoken. It
does not matter. It was a proud moment of my life.

In the sixties a huge tidal wave hit the coast and wiped out
everything except the miniature railroad now moss covered and
rotting, and the radar building, its roof sagging looking much
like an old swayback horse. I know because I went there in a
hired helicopter from Alliford Bay. It was as though we had
never been there.

Men were desperately needed during the war, but I was
considered more valuable as a construction boss, building hangars, radar stations and airports. The Air Force offered me a
flight lieutenant's ranking but when I talked to Harry Winnie,
commanding officer at Alliford Bay, he said, "Stay where you
are. You can do ten times as much good for the war effort doing
what you're doing than if you got pinned down as an officer
with all the red tape that goes with it."

The same applied to many thousands of young men, as any
nation dedicated to an all-out war effort needed an enormous
and experienced back-up force. The war had to be won, but the
smooth running of the nation was a very important factor too.

When "Johnny came marching home again," as the First
World War song went, I had no trouble looking each and every
one in the eyes and thinking, I did my share. I was in the front
lines too.

But nobody ever asked me, "Why weren't you in the service?"

They knew what had to be done at home as well as over-
seas, and we all had done our bit.

VIRGINIA

BY THE LATE SPRING of 1943 the Marble Island Radar Station was completed and taken over by the R.C.A.F. I phoned Doug Welch for instructions.

"Just get down here as fast as you can," he said. "I have a good job waiting for you right here near the city."

"See you tomorrow, Doug."

Harry Winnie, the commanding officer at the Alliford Bay seaplane base was flying their big amphibian to headquarters in the morning and I was welcome to come along. We arrived in Vancouver and said our good-byes. Marble Island had been a remarkable and gratifying experience for both of us.

Doug's good job was the building of a Radio Rhombic Station near Mission in the Fraser Valley, an hour's drive from home. It was to be constructed of brick and concrete and would be the last rhombic relay station on the west coast of Canada.

"The foundations and building cannot be one thirty-second of an inch out of line," Doug emphasized. "Another thing that's even more important is that every piece of reinforcing steel in the entire building has to be electrically welded together, otherwise it could possibly throw the rhombic beams off course. It's a long, long way to Australia from here.

"Our surveyor will be there to stake out the exact location for each corner of the building," Doug said, as he handed me several rolls of blueprints and two thick books of specifications.

"Be here at seven tomorrow morning and I'll introduce you to the engineer and the construction men who are already out there," he said, adding that a dozen of the men had worked on the Vulcan job.

Doug and I went over the plans for several hours and he

left with these parting words: "We will order and supply you with all the material you require, except for the concrete. That will all come from Evans, Coleman and Evans in Vancouver as you need it. You can order that directly from here."

When we had the footings ready to pour and were prefabricating the forms for the first phase of the concrete walls, I phoned Evans, Coleman and Evans and ordered 68 cubic yards of ready mix for that Friday morning. This gave them almost a full week to get things ready.

Three hours later their shipper called. There could be no concrete for at least two more weeks. When I phoned Doug he said, well, we would just have to wait. To hell with this nonsense, I thought.

"Do you want this job to go ahead or not? We can't possibly operate unless we get our concrete when it's needed."

"I don't know what else we can do. They're the only ready mix outfit big enough around here to handle this job. Got any other ideas?" Doug asked.

"Bellingham is closer to us than Vancouver by almost 20 miles, and I'm sure they have trucks and ready-mix. I can drive across the border and be back here by noon. Okay if I give it a try? Winter is coming and we don't want to be pouring concrete if there's a sudden cold snap."

"Sure, give it a try and call me any time. Good luck."

I was back by noon. Everything was arranged. Good old American know-how. Bellingham could have 20 cubic yards at our job site by 8:00 a.m. Friday, with the next two trucks by 9:30 and the complete order filled by noon. Their price was a dollar a cubic yard less than Evans, Coleman and Evans' price with a guarantee the quality would be as good as, if not better than, the specifications called for. I had advised the customs officer just south of Abbotsford what we were planning to do.

"Go ahead," he said. "There is no duty on concrete as long as it has been paid for before it crosses the border."

I phoned Doug, and told him, "Bellingham will supply the sixty-eight cubic yards at $25 a yard, and have the concrete on the job and ready to pour this Friday morning. Guaranteed. All you have to do is wire $1,700 to their bank. And we'll be saving $68 plus a very expensive job delay."

I gave him the name of the firm, their bank and the account number and the phone numbers.

"You sure everything will go ahead?"

"Certain of it!"

He called me back within the hour, saying "The money is

now in their bank account and the rest is up to you."

"Okay," I said. "And thanks."

We didn't hear another word from Doug until one o'clock that Friday, when he drove up in his big black Buick station wagon. Hugh Martin, his partner, was with him. Our crew were just finishing their lunch and standing around the yard. Doug and Hugh, without a word, walked over and looked down into the nearest foundation trench. They both started laughing, then went to their Buick and took out four dozen cold beer and put them on the Dewalt saw table.

"Finish the beer, boys," Doug announced. "Then take the rest of the day off with pay." There were a dozen men in the concrete gang and they drank every last ounce of the four dozen in less than half an hour. They said thanks and were gone.

To this day I've wondered how Hugh got hold of four dozen beer so fast, as it was strictly rationed and also in short supply. But that was the way things were done in wartime construction. Rules were bent.

I suppose some of them went to the beer parlour in Abbotsford to brag and relax. They had made that pour in record time and they deserved the break. From then on we had a crew that worked their hearts out for us.

Doug and Hugh stayed to enquire how I felt the job was progressing. "First class," I said. They asked what materials were needed most urgently.

"More concrete and bricks seem to be the only thing we could have trouble with."

They both laughed.

"No problem," Hugh said. "Within an hour after your first trucks came through customs this morning we phoned Evans, Coleman and Evans and told them what we had done. That shook them up. They assured us they would promptly fill every order you phone in."

Doug shook my hand saying, "You're to be congratulated. We never would have given such a wild idea a second thought."

"Keep up the good work," Hugh added, "and you'll be looking at a big bonus when this job is completed."

I was already getting $450 a month plus living expenses. During those war years of frozen wages, if a worker made over $5,000 a year the government took 100 percent of the excess for war purposes, so a higher salary was of no benefit. But a bonus wasn't taxed. The weather cooperated and by the middle of January the job was complete. I was given a month off with full pay — a belated but welcome Christmas holiday.

Virginia at left, and Dana, Christmas 1943.

WE WERE NOW living in a four-room house away out in South Vancouver at 1911 East 54th Avenue. We had moved in the previous weekend and it had snowed. A family two houses away came and helped us unload and put the furniture in its proper place. Their son Harry, about 12 years old, worked like a little Trojan. He carried in my shotgun. He watched and asked questions when I wrapped it in an old blanket and put it away up on the high shelf in the master bedroom closet. I wrapped the rifle the same way and put it beside the shotgun. He asked about the caliber of each gun and I told him the rifle was a 32-special and the shotgun was a 12-gauge.

"Golly, all we have at our house is one old .22," he said.

"Maybe I'll take you hunting one day when this war is over."

"Oh, I'd like that," he said, enthusiastically. Harry and his dad hung around helping and it was well after dark by the time all the beds were set up and the dishes, pots and pans put away. Harry's mother came over. It was supper time. Pat came out of our kitchen looking very tired, with Virginia and Dana tagging along. The mothers got talking and she invited us over to their house for supper.

"I have a roast chicken ready to come out of the oven so it won't be much trouble at all," she said, very neighbourly.

We hadn't stopped to eat since breakfast. There was precious little left of that chicken but a big bowl of bones. We sat and chatted for a bit and then left to get our children tucked into bed. They were already asleep before Pat got their door closed.

Harry would take four-year-old Virginia for a ride on the handle bars of his bicycle almost every afternoon when he came home from school. They would speed around several blocks. Virginia loved these rides and she waited for Harry almost every day. This was the beginning of a tragic friendship, and of memories which have never left me.

Two weeks into my month off Doug called me: "We need you on a job in the old part of town. It's an old brick apartment building just one block west of Burrard Street and two blocks south of Georgia. It's tricky and the foreman just quit. Would like you to take over."

"Sure, I'll do it, but I would like to have four of my old hands come with me."

"No problem," Doug said. "Come in and look the job over and meet the crew this afternoon?"

"Be at your office by one."

The building was at least 40 years old and none of the doors would close properly. On the fifth floor I attached a chalk line to the top of the floor at two opposite outside walls and stretched it tight. The distance from the line to the floor in the center was almost two inches. Doug looked at me in disbelief. He had a crooked building. I laughed.

"The builder must have conveniently forgotten a wet or green 2 x 12 shrinks over an inch as it dries, whereas brick walls stay where they are," I explained.

On the ground floor I measured the same way. The center of the floor was just over one inch lower than at the outside walls.

"You will have to scare us up half a dozen big hydraulic jacks. We'll need two five-horse Dewalt saws so we can rip long wedge shaped strips of dry two-inch lumber and nail them right on top of the present flooring. We can put a plywood floor over all this, then build new partitions to make a more modern and useful design. We'll have to use Gyproc lath, because all five apartments will have to be replastered. There is not too much wrong with the old ceilings but they will have to be completely stripped and replaced. If we try to patch them the job will cost twice as much and take twice as long to do."

The government was anticipating a shortage of housing for returning war veterans. These suites were part of a massive remodelling and building program which kept the economy booming for several years after the war. I knew this was another government priority job when he said, "I will have your material and equipment on the job this afternoon."

I outlined the plan to the crew. The materials arrived and we were able to get started the next morning. It must have been a nasty job, tearing out all that old plaster and piling it on a truck, but that part of it was almost finished when I took over. The old wiring and plumbing had been stripped out and was being replaced with new material to pass current city inspections.

We had many hands helping and in four weeks the floors were levelled, new partitions erected and everything was ready to be plastered. Earlier I had asked Doug to get us a good plastering contractor. We were almost finished when he came to the job and told me he had searched all of Vancouver, New Westminster and the small towns up the Fraser Valley as far as Chilliwack.

"All the plastering contractors are busy and it will be at least a month before we can get one."

"I'll try getting a crew for next week," I told Doug. "Delays like this cost money."

Our neighbour, who was building a duplex to cash in on the housing crunch, had told me his plasterers should be finished that day. That evening I asked him if he knew where they might be found.

"Sure can, I just left them in the beer parlour at the Marpole Hotel. I'll take you over and introduce you."

We found the contractor with his crew all sitting at one big table. After 15 minutes of negotiating and drinking he said, "Let's go and have a look at the job."

"Sure, no time like the present." He threw a five dollar bill on the table and told his crew he'd be back within the hour. In those days that was 50 beers.

At the apartment block on the second floor, which had just been completed that afternoon and was swept clean, he took out a steel tape and asked me to hold one end so he could measure the yardage.

"All four floors exactly the same as this one?"

"Exactly," I said.

Scribbling in his note book he quoted a price per square yard.

"We'll finish this thing in less than two weeks."

I phoned Doug for his okay, knowing it would be an enthusiastic yes. "Tell him to start tomorrow. I'll be over with a formal contract before noon. Thanks again, Joe," Doug said as he hung up.

On the short drive back to the hotel we discussed the quickest and best way to get his equipment and material on the job. He introduced me to his crew and I shook hands with each of them and then threw down another five dollar bill. Another 50 beers, but they were short ones, small one gulp glasses, so they'd be on the job in the morning.

"Have one on me, boys. I'll see you all tomorrow morning."

THAT NIGHT I felt a desperate need to get home. Approaching our driveway just before 10 o'clock I could see two police cars parked in front of the house with their lights flashing. I put my car in the garage and went into the house through the side door. Two policemen were standing in the hallway.

"Is there something wrong here?" I asked anxiously.

"We have just returned from escorting your daughter Virginia to St. Vincent's Hospital. She and the babysitter managed to get both your guns off the top shelf in your bedroom closet.

The boy somehow got a shell into the rifle barrel, pointed it at your daughter and pulled the trigger," the sergeant explained. "Why, we don't know."

His words hit me like multiple blows.

"She was apparently holding your shotgun in both her arms. The rifle bullet struck the shotgun just a bit behind the triggers, carrying chunks of hardwood and steel into her arms and chest. She was already unconscious when we got here. The boy had run home to his parents and they phoned us. We called an ambulance and escorted it to the emergency ward. Get over there right away if you want to see your daughter alive. Her condition is critical."

Police are trained to be efficient, and through experience, are usually non-committal, but his voice could not conceal his grave concern.

"Your younger daughter is with the babysitter's parents, the people who called us," he added. "They'll take care of her. Now get over there, fast."

The officer said he would take both guns and all the ammunition back to Cordova Street, their headquarters.

"Take everything," I said. "I never want to see the guns again. The ammunition is locked in a cupboard out in the garage. I'll bring it to your station before noon tomorrow," I promised.

Then, with its siren on, one car escorted me to St. Vincent's Hospital. I was in such shock I remember very little of the drive.

The head nurse met us at the front door and led me directly to Virginia. She had assisted the doctors as they tried to remove the pieces of lead, wood and steel from Virginia's body. A tray with a small pile of fragments was by the bed.

"Your daughter did not show even the slightest sign of consciousness during the hour the two doctors worked on her. There was absolutely no possibility she could have lived through this. There was nothing more they could have done for her. I'm very sorry."

Virginia looked so peaceful as I looked down at the small still body of my dear child. She looked quite normal, just a little girl sleeping. My mind could not accept that she would never wake up. I just could not believe it. I could not believe that she would never smile at me again. I could not tear my eyes away. I remember noticing they had washed her face. It looked so clean. I gently touched her cheek with the back of my hand. It felt cool.

The nurse took my arm, saying, softly, "You might as well go home, Mr. Garner. Do drive slowly and carefully," she warned.

I could not speak. I was in a state of shock far different from anything I had ever known. As I write this, those same feelings come back.

I cannot remember the drive home. As I opened the car door I could hear the phone ringing. Running into the kitchen I lifted the receiver off the hook. I heard, "Is that you, Mr. Garner?"

"Yes, it is."

"This is the nurse at the hospital." she said. "Virginia has somehow regained consciousness and is calling for you. Please drive carefully, but get here as quickly as you can."

"Okay," I said, not even realizing the impossible had happened. My little girl was calling for me.

Ten minutes later I was back at Virginia's bedside. She had been propped up with pillows, almost to a sitting position. The nurses stood by, silently.

"Hi Dad. We were playing cowboys and Indians when he shot me. I've been out there in another place and it's so nice and warm. It's very bright and sunny. There is music and we can hear birds singing. But I wanted to come back and say good-bye to you."

"Don't go yet," I said. "Wait and see your mother. She should be here soon."

"Mom is not coming, she's away downtown," she said quietly. "I can see her."

Then in a small clear voice she said to me, as if she was the adult and I the child, "I don't want to be here any more. It's so nice out there. I'm going back now. Good-bye Dad."

Then she slowly closed her eyes and was gone from me for ever. I was devastated. I knew I would never again look into her blue eyes and see her smile at me. I knew I would never get over the feeling of utter desolation and helplessness. I had never felt so alone in my whole life. There was a void there that could never ever be filled.

I got back home again shortly after midnight. Just then Pat arrived and, as gently as I could, I told her what had happened. She broke down, sobbing. I lit a fire in the fireplace, and tried to comfort her. We just sat and talked until daybreak, about our children and our lives.

"Let's go up to the hospital, I have to see Virginia," Pat said.

A nurse took Pat to where Virginia lay. I waited. Pat stayed for only a short while, then came out and stood beside me. We said nothing. What else was there to say?

A day I will never forget — March 2nd, 1944.

We later talked about the funeral. It would be at the Forest Lawn Cemetery. It was a nice place. My mother had already arranged to be buried there and she was very fond of Virginia.

After the funeral we all went out to my sister Ethel's place for tea. It was a very sad occasion. She was so young — a whole life ahead. When Pat and I went home, brother Tom and his wife came with us. They were both very fond

Virginia's grave.

of Pat and Virginia. I lit a fire and they stayed for the rest of the evening.

"It won't be good to stay in this house," Marie said. "Come back to Vancouver Island and live with us for a while."

"There's plenty of building and logging to keep us both busy. Remember, we're still partners," Tom added. Tom, always faithful, always kind.

Pat and I looked at each other, then got up and walked into the girls' bedroom and sat down on Virginia's bed. Pat had made it up early that morning and put a pretty pink bedspread on it. We just sat there holding hands. Pat started to cry and I did too. When we had calmed ourselves and gone back into the living room we both spoke each other's thoughts: "We can't live here anymore."

Marie took Pat into our bedroom. Tom and I talked about the accident. How could it have happened?

I told him that I had been at the police station the day after the accident and discovered a dent near the end of the magazine. Very slight, but enough to jam a shell and prevent it from being injected into the barrel. Tom was the last person to use the rifle, on a hunting trip to the Cariboo years before. Had the magazine, which was directly below the barrel, hit against a rock at that time? This was the only explanation we could come up with. The gun had been considered empty ever since.

I knew the children could not get near the shells in the garage because the box was padlocked and the key was hidden. While pulling the gun off the shelf the boy must have dropped it and the shell was jarred loose.

It was an accident waiting to happen. Never point a gun at anyone, at any time is a rule not to be taken lightly.

When Marie and Pat rejoined us, they had fresh makeup on and their hair neatly combed.

"I'm going to quit my job tomorrow," I told them. "It's almost finished anyway. Just the plastering and that's being done right now. Pat, you start packing as soon as you feel up to it. I'll pick up some boxes first thing tomorrow morning and get back here by ten. We'll pick Dana up at Mother's and try and catch the noon boat to Nanaimo. If not, the later one. I'll make all the necessary phone calls from Duncan."

Tom nodded to me and Marie began helping Pat wrap some of the dishes, ready to put into boxes.

Tom and Marie caught the late boat to Victoria that night. It was the old C.P.R.'s Princess Marguerite that left Vancouver Harbour at midnight for Victoria.

Pat and I couldn't sleep. We sat and talked and kept the fire going until another dawn.

When I told Doug Welch I'd be leaving for the Island he asked if there was anything he could do to help. There wasn't.

He phoned Hugh Martin at his office. When he put the phone down he turned to me. "Go put Emil in charge of the job, Joe. Then come back here for your severance pay and bonus cheque. We're both terribly sorry for you and Pat and little Virginia ."

Hugh was there to say good-bye when I got back. We parted good friends. It was a sad way to leave Vancouver, but our lives lay ahead of us and they had to be lived.

PART III

OLD DUNCAN

ON THE MOUNTAIN the pouring rain had now turned to big flakes of snow, making walking even more difficult. The snow was not only wet but exceedingly slippery. The rubber tip on my cane had worn off an hour before, so I no longer had any confidence in it as a safe support. Extreme care would be needed as the thing I feared most now was a hard fall on the rough gravel. If that happened I was certain I could never make it back up on my feet again. Brother Tom was no longer with me as I shuffled along the rough gravel road.

But something told me to stop. "Joe, you've got to think," I told myself. "How do I get out of this?"

Until now, I had never really considered myself stupid. But after standing there and silently taking stock of my predicament I wasn't at all sure. I wasn't likely to be picked up until daylight, if at all. Who would be coming up? My son Ed would get out Search and Rescue, but what if he didn't check on me for a couple of days? My assistant might think I'd gone to Victoria and had forgotten to phone her. I wondered if I would see again the beautiful, soft beige carpet that had been laid in my log cabin two days earlier. It was foolish, thinking about a carpet. My mind wasn't working.

I remembered my life in Duncan not too many miles south from where I was now struggling.

100 HOUSES

THAT SPRING of 1944 when we moved back to Vancouver Island and went to live at Old Angus with Tom, I became a workaholic — losing myself in hard labour, trying to get over Virginia's cruel and untimely death.

Two of my foremen from the Vancouver job moved in with us since there was no other place in the Duncan area for them to live. Like her mother, Pat now had her own boarding house.

On top of that, Tom and Marie separated and he was leading a very active social life. This helped increase the hectic life at Old Angus. There were numerous poker games and pool and billiard parties on his full-sized table.

Within a few weeks of getting back to the island I bought my first piece of heavy construction equipment, a half yard Insley power shovel with backhoe and shovel attachments. Tom owned a new TD14 bulldozer, one of the most popular-sized cats for logging in those days. We agreed to pool these two pieces of equipment and form Garner Bros. Ltd. We issued equal shares. Almost immediately we contracted to clear the site for a high school in the village of Lake Cowichan, a growing community some 20 miles west of Duncan where Lake Cowichan empties into the Cowichan River.

When the job was done Colonel Boyd called us into his office, gave us a cheque in full payment for the clearing, and asked, "How would you two fellows like to build our new high school on a cost plus ten percent basis, with progress draws paid at the end of each month?"

"You're the builder, Joe," Tom said.

"Sure sounds great to me."

"Go for it then," the colonel said, and the Garners were on

their way. Hard work is a healer and we both had problems.

Next morning we began excavating for the foundations, septic tanks and sewage, plus a new water system for the village. That Insley shovel turned out to be a job getter.

While we were building the school we applied for and were granted the only lowbed trucking service license between Victoria and Nanaimo. When the equipment wasn't on construction jobs we always had timber to haul, so the truck was kept busy and earning money. A good friend, Bill Heaney, had the only lowbed licence in Victoria, and there was more than enough work for both of us.

Tom rightly decided we needed a garage and office. We bought the BA gas station with its two-bay repair shop so we had somewhere to service our equipment. Behind the shop we put up three small temporary offices and moved into one of them. Hardly more than four walls with a roof, but at least we had a headquarters with decent lighting. When it got really cold we just plugged in a couple more electric heaters.

Our lawyers, Dave Williams and Jack Davie, who had just been called to the bar, moved into the other two small offices. It was a convenient arrangement for both of us.

We now formed Garner Builders' Supplies Ltd. and bought the lot and building directly to the south of the old Chinese Hand Laundry in downtown Duncan. It would be our permanent office and we would soon open a small hardware store. Always conscious of economy, and money, we decided to go two stories high to accommodate three apartments on the second floor. I built them so each opened out onto a common patio about eighteen feet square. Yes, this was the beginning of making my childhood dreams come true. We were moving at a terrific pace, yet Virginia was always in my thoughts.

The Whittaker family from England, who had owned the old Cowichan Merchants store in Duncan, had recently sold out to David Spencer, the big Vancouver retailer. The T. Eaton Company one year later bought the David Spencer store lock, stock and barrel. John Lawrence, a friend of the Eaton family, was brought over from Vancouver to manage it.

Garner Bros. was asked to do the necessary alterations, both inside and out — shelving, counters, new floors, closing in all the windows with brick, then stucco and painting the outside. This was another cost plus 10 percent job, so a good profit was assured.

In a main floor office of the Eaton building was a huge fireproof steel walk-in vault that weighed at least a ton. When

I asked Lawrence what to do with it, he said, "Get rid of it. It's yours if you can use it."

We needed the lowbed and a small bulldozer to move the vault and we put it in our new building even before the concrete was poured. It was a God's gift to our lawyers who moved into their new premises near the back door even before they were finished. They had now become Williams, Harvey and Davie and were very busy.

THERE WAS AN enormous demand for housing right after the war and our three apartments were occupied the day they were completed. Tom Gillespie, our bookkeeper and accountant, moved in with his wife and Joe and Lea Gergel moved into the second apartment. Joe had come to work for us as a cost accountant and he was a good baseball player. Edith Rudd, who moved into the bachelor apartment, worked for us for almost 30 years.

Mrs. Gillespie was a choreographer who also had direct-ing experience in opera. She and Gillespie, a top athlete, had come from England after he had graduated from St. Andrew's College in Scotland. There he met and became friendly with the Prince of Wales, who in 1938 abdicated the throne of England to marry Mrs. Simpson, the American divorcee. This precipitated a political crisis in Britain while a shocked British Empire looked on. Edward, reputed to be one of the finest bird shots in the British Isles, brought Gillespie to Alberta so he could look after his ranch near Calgary. They travelled to-gether when the prince was in Canada, and he was with him on his famous Royal Tour marked by scandal involving lovely society girls, which the press never reported. Brother Tom met Gillespie while he was on a shooting trip to Alberta and told him if he ever needed a job he would like him to come out to Vancouver Island and work for us. That's how Gillespie ended up in the little town of Duncan which for better or for worse was sometimes referred to as more English than England.

And Tom loved entertaining. He decided to hold his first garden party shortly after we had finished remodelling Old Angus, a major job at considerable expense, but the money was rolling in. Who could better arrange this occasion than the Gillespies?

It was to be a formal affair with all the trimmings. A large tent was erected in the main garden near the house. On the day, Mrs. Gillespie wore a stunning long white gown. Gillespie was also attired in white except for a blue silk handkerchief tucked into his left sleeve, his usual "duds" for posh social events. This had been expected of him when he travelled with the prince. In truth, the Gillespies weren't at all what I had expected any of our apartment dwellers to look like. Yet, despite their backgrounds they fitted in well and were accepted by both the remittance people and the pioneers of the district.

The war turned in favour of the Allies following D-Day in June of 1944 and it was a foregone conclusion that the troops would be returning home within a year. Some would be bringing war brides with families and all of them would need a place to live. Accommodation was already in very short supply. When Germany and then Japan surrendered unconditionally in 1945, all this became reality.

Quick off the mark, Tom and I formed Cowichan Construction Ltd. with Alex Richardson as a third partner. We were contracted to build 20 Central Mortgage and Housing units just north of the old Cowichan Creamery building on Garden Street in Duncan.

My old pal Shorty Berkey returned to Vancouver Island after V-E Day. He took the C.P.R. ferry to Nanaimo and came down to Duncan and went up to the Elks Club for a beer. He walked over and sat down at our table.

"How's business?" were his first words after we greeted each other.

"Busy, very busy," I replied. "Got more work than I can handle, and I need you on the job tomorrow morning. You came along at just the right time."

"Joe, I was really thinking about taking a bit of a holiday. I haven't even hung this uniform in the closet yet," Shorty replied, but he had a smile on his face. Three days later Shorty was supervising our Central Mortgage and Housing Corporation project. We worked like hell and got them done in record time. Our reputation as builders was now made.

When the project was finished Alex Richardson took over the company and changed the name to Richardson Construction Ltd. A few years later, Alex was killed learning to fly at the Cassidy Airport south of Nanaimo when his plane stalled and plunged into trees near the runway.

Jobs were coming thick and fast. Shorty and I started rebuilding the hotel at Cowichan Bay which had burned the previous winter. Reg Higby, the owner, asked us to take on the job. We put in a new concrete foundation and added a second floor. But within a few years it burned to the ground again. In the late seventies, a concrete-block condominium, three stories tall, was built on this same foundation. The Cowichan Bay Arms, overlooking the water, is reputed to be the only fire-proof concrete apartment block in Cowichan Bay.

We were also remodelling Domingo Ordano's boat works just down the street from the hotel. It was here, with a dull skill saw and some knotty hemlock lumber I neatly sliced off the ends of my two middle fingers on the left hand. I put the cut-off finger tips in a clean white handkerchief, and, feeling faint, I staggered out to the car and drove to the emergency ward of the Duncan Hospital. Ordano had phoned ahead, so a doctor was waiting when I arrived after a wobbly drive over the old lower road. I handed Dr. McCaffery the hankie with its precious contents and asked him if he could sew them back on. After taking a good look he said, "It's too late for that, Joe, but come along with me anyway."

He froze the hand, then removed some bone chips and stitched up the stumps of my fingers. They kept me there overnight. Next morning, I asked the doctor if I could return to work if only to supervise the jobs.

"You can if you are very, very careful. he said. "But come back and see me in a couple of days."

It was late summer. Baseball fever was high. There was one game left in the playoffs and it was to be played the evening I went to have the bandages changed. I was still at the hospital when brother Tom and George Syrotuk came by in their base-ball uniforms. Would I like to come and sit in the dugout with the team? They just happened to have my cap, the top part of my baseball uniform and my spiked shoes with them. Just a coincidence, of course.

"Okay," I said, and went along.

In the ninth inning we were at bat, one run behind the City Service team with two out and runners on both second and third base. The classic double situation. George was coaching. He looked over at me. I'd changed into my uniform. He must have considered deeply the wisdom of putting a crippled pinch hitter in, but this was winner take all. A fly ball or a weak grounder and we were gone.

"Will you hit, Joe, we need two runs."

"Sure," I said and went to the plate. My hand didn't feel too bad when I got hold of the bat. I batted left-handed and usually tried to drive the ball through somewhere between first and second base. But, because of the sore hand and poor grip, I swung a bit late and the Texas Leaguer sailed out over the third baseman's head. Both runners scored standing up and I wound up on second base. The double we needed. Game over. It was the end of the 1945 baseball season. Those sawn-off fingers had won the playoffs. Every cloud must have a silver lining.

When I went to Cowichan Bay next day with my hand still in bandages, Laurence Myers was cutting lumber for the hotel job on the big Dewalt saw. "How's the job going?" I asked. He turned to look at me and, while he was asking about my fingers, he somehow pulled the saw forward. It suddenly caught the board he was holding with his left hand and sliced his four fingers clean off just behind the first joint. I instantly felt sick to my stomach. First me, now him. But he was far worse. Joe Gergel ran for the first aid kit and put a tourniquet on to stop the bleeding. We got Laurence into my car and took off to the Duncan hospital. Again!

Was it someone's idea of a practical joke, that somehow two of Laurence's fingers ended up in a can of red paint? When our painter stirred the paint the following day and saw the fingers he passed out. A bucket of cold water in his face brought him around, but it was almost a week before he felt able to look into a paint bucket.

The Cowichan Bay projects progressed without any more mishaps, and by the next spring we were ready to take on other jobs. The country was booming.

OUR BUSINESS was growing at such a rate we needed to get some extra space and the dilapidated old laundry building next to us looked like a good bet.

Gillespie went to see the Chinese owners one morning. They wouldn't even talk to him about selling. A couple of days later brother Tom and I were having a beer at the Elks Club when Lem Traer, the woods boss for the Hillcrest Lumber Company, sat down at our table. We told him about the problem we'd run into trying to buy the old Chinese laundry.

"I don't know why there should be any great trouble getting that old building. Just go over to your bank and get $10,000. Try to get five $1,000 bills and fifty $100s. Then go by the liquor store and pick up a bottle of Johnny Walker Black Label. I'll wait here and then we'll both walk over and make the deal," Lem said.

The bank only had three $1,000 bills so the manager Barney Cox went down the street to the Royal Bank and borrowed the extra $2,000. This held things up some, but I was back at the Elks Club with the money within the hour.

"Give me the money and let's go," Lem said as he put the five $1,000 bills in his wallet and stuffed the rest in his coat pockets. I carried the Scotch. On the way I told Lem he could keep any money left over from the $10,000 if he successfully closed the deal.

The Chinese owners showed us into the kitchen and made a big fuss over Lem, who was then employing over 50 Chinese at Hillcrest, building logging roads in the hills back of Mesachie Lake. Some of these men had also worked for Lem during the past 15 years building logging railroads at Sahtlam.

Lem and I sat on one side of the table. A small bottle of cheap whiskey and four glasses were set down. The two Chinese who owned the building sat across from us. Lem pointed at the label on the bottle and, in pidgin English, said, "Me no likey!" then handed the bottle back. Lem then took the Johnny Walker — the favourite drink of most Orientals — out of the paper bag, uncorked it and poured a good-sized drink for each of us.

"You hip likey?" Lem asked, holding up the bottle.

"Maybe I likey buy your building," he said looking at the two men. One had run the laundry for several years. The other was responsible for hiring the Chinese crews Lem needed for road maintenance. They both addressed Lem as "The Bossee Man."

Lem introduced me as his advisor regarding the condition and value of the building. "Could we look around?" Lem asked. We carried our glasses as we explored the various rooms. One of the doors had been bolted shut.

"I like look see inside," Lem said, as he tried the door.

"No! No! Nothing inside, just dark."

Lem insisted, and the door was opened. Three squawking Rhode Island Reds flew past us down the hallway, to disappear through a hole in the floor.

"Him lay eggs," the laundry man explained rather proudly.

"Him not velly good," Lem said laughing and held up his empty glass. So back to the table, to sit in the same chairs.

The glasses were refilled. Lem took three $1,000 bills out of his billfold and laid them neatly side by side on the table. Beside them he laid out ten $100 bills. Pointing to the money he asked, "You likey sellum?"

The Chinese looked at each other and shook their heads.

"By and by, you likey," Lem suggested, smiling, as he placed another twenty $100 bills in two neat piles alongside the others.

"You likey?" Lem asked.

"No likey," they answered in unison.

He took out one more $1,000 bill and put it on top of the other three, then put ten more of the smaller bills beside them.

"Him $8,000," Lem said, pointing to the piles of money on the table.

"Now you likey sell?" he asked yet again.

"No likey sell," was their reply.

"Bye and bye you likey," Lem said, and he began talking to the one responsible for hiring the road crews each year. He explained how he might need about 25 additional men because they were going to use more heavy trucks and less logging railways in the future. This created much interest. The boss man asked a lot of questions about this new type of road building and the tools that would be needed.

When their glasses were almost empty, Lem poured another drink, then asked again, "You likey sell?"

Same answer, but there seemed to be a bit more interest now. Lem then placed another ten $100 bills alongside the rest.

"Him $9,000," he stated, pointing again to the spread of money. "Now you likey sellum?"

"No likey," they said again.

Lem stood up and motioned me to do the same. Then he said, "Too bad," gathering up the bills and stuffing them into the paper bag. I slid the bottle of Scotch across the table, saying, "You keepum."

When only a few of the bills were left on the table, one Chinese held up his hand, palm outward, and said, "We likey sell."

"We likey sell," said his partner.

Without further delay I handed Lem a paper our lawyers had prepared earlier. It just said they had been paid in full for the property as is, where is. The amount of the sale was written in and the sheet of paper was signed. We had the old buildings we wanted and Lem was $1,000 richer.

In a week the old building was torn down and the concrete foundations poured for the bigger hardware store, with three more apartments above, to tie onto what we already had. When our crew was ripping up the last section of the old wooden floor they found the three hens hiding out between the floor joists. One had died, but the other two seemed fine. I told the foreman to put the two live hens in a box and take them over to the laundry man who had already set up his business only a block away on the opposite side of the street.

The building remains today almost the same as when we

My childhood dream, the hardware store in Duncan.

built it nearly fifty years ago, when it certainly did a lot to
improve the look of that end of town.

In his retirement Frank Davie, our lawyer Jack Davie's
father, and a former Speaker of the B.C. Legislature, had been
one of the first tenants to move into the new apartments above
the hardware store. When he was getting older and spending
more time in his bed I would drop by. On one of my last visits
before he died he had two boxes packed and sitting on the
dresser by his bed. He pointed to them, saying, "Joe, I would
like you to take these to remember me by." They were pictures
of his early days in government. Years later, I would gather the
pictures together again and give them to his son. Jack and his
daughter Patsy were living on Maple Bay Road at that time and
raising a few Hereford cattle.

LAKE COWICHAN was then a booming sawmill and logging
district with three very large lumber mills (Lake Logging,
Hillcrest Lumber and the Youbou sawmill owned by Western
Plywood) and several smaller ones. They had to have more
workers to keep up with the postwar orders pouring in. These
mills were all working double shift.

In the thirties, Hillcrest Lumber had moved from Sahtlam,

just west of Duncan, to Mesachie Lake. This deep little lake was tied into the big lake by a narrow channel. Hillcrest had the money, the timber and the mill, but like the other mills it did not have sufficient suitable housing for their workers. Carlton Stone, the owner, got the bright idea of contacting the federal agency Central Mortgage and Housing Corporation with a proposition. C.M.H.C. were contracting the building of houses in blocks, and he offered them, free and no strings attached, sufficient land for a 100 house project near the village of Lake Cowichan.

The land was little more than an old logging slash — big stumps everywhere and some huge boulders. One long deep gully ran almost diagonally across the northwest portion of the proposed development. But it was strategically located, adjacent to the new high school, close to the town center and with a view of the majestic mountains on three sides.

The C.M.H.C. manager for Vancouver Island came to me in 1946 and asked if we would be interested in building these houses on a cost plus 10 percent basis. In every way a sound deal for all concerned.

"Let's go up and look at the building site," I suggested. "We better know what we're talking about."

He had a blueprint of the general layout. The plan was to scale, showing every contour and even the shrubs and lawns planned for each house. It was a magnificent job of surveying and draftsmanship.

"What do you want us to do?"

"Absolutely everything," he replied. "Clearing and grading the site, sewers, water, blacktopped streets, concrete sidewalks, shrubs, lawns, painting the houses."

He stuck out his hand and asked with a smile, "Will you take on the project?"

"Yes," I said, and that was all there was to it. The perfect way to do business.

"This will all have to be confirmed in writing," he advised. "But you can start the clearing and the burning of the rubbish as soon as you can get at it."

"We'll move the equipment in tomorrow," I assured him. This was the fall of 1946. Perry Ross was our top equipment supervisor and did an excellent job of preparing the site. Tom and I believed in rewarding our top hands, so that Christmas, Garner Bros. gave a large parcel of land to Perry as a bonus. Years later the North Cowichan Municipal Hall and work shops were built on that land and Perry became the municipality's public works superintendent for the Cowichan District.

We were blessed with good weather that year and the project was well underway with the arrival of spring.

Joe Gergel was our office manager, purchasing agent and time keeper. Tom Watson was our bookkeeper and Tom Gillespie would go up twice each month to supervise and help with the payroll. Accommodation was so scarce we had to build living quarters for our bookkeeper, a four-room house finished in a week on a water-proofed concrete slab at the corner of Auchinachie Road and the old Island Highway. The house still stands as good as the day we moved Watson and his wife in.

Shorty Berkey was general superintendent, and Jack Griffiths and crew did the plumbing and water supply. George Hamilton did the electrical and Claude Green did the painting, both inside and out.

Crews were organized to act as an assembly line. They moved from one house to the next, where they repeated the same phase on each building. This speeded construction considerably and eliminated any errors that might otherwise have occurred.

The floor sanding and finishing, the last job to be done, was contracted out to my old friend George Syrotuk, who also managed our baseball team, "The Concos" — short for Construction Company and sponsored by Tom and me. We brought in players of known ability from as far away as Alberta and Trail and gave them jobs. There was great enthusiasm for the sport in Duncan and intense competition between teams.

I well remember the day George finished the floors in the first house. He came out the front door, humped over, dragging his equipment. Lifting his head to look at Shorty and me approaching, he groaned, "Only ninety-nine more to go, fellows," as he slumped against the railing, feigning exhaustion.

"Good God, George," I laughed. "You're all humped over like a dog trying to screw a football," and Shorty laughed too. Always clowning around, George was a pleasure to have on any job.

The first house put up was the nerve center for the project. The area immediately south of this was used for prefabricating all the buildings, as well as for covered storage space for the cement and other building materials that needed to be kept out of the rain. This whole area is now a children's playground. Complete prefabrication was also an innovation, saving much time and labour.

The first house also included office space for Stevens, the

This 100-house project at Lake Cowichan was constructed on an 'assembly line' basis in 1947. Stevens the engineer for Central Mortgage & Housing Corporation looks on.

Construction crew and office staff of Garner Bros. Ltd. on 100-house project, August 1947.

engineer for C.M.H.C. who did an excellent job of the general layout. Stevens Crescent was named in his honour after he collapsed and died while walking up the hill to inspect the dirt removal and grading program that was to create 12 more lots planned for that area. The dirt was used to fill in part of the gully to create building lots for eight additional houses on the north side of Stone Avenue and west of what is now Ravine Park. Stevens could be seen several times a day climbing the steep little hill to see how this important job was progressing. The whole area had to be prepared perfectly to contain the 100-house subdivision. We actually had to slice down the higher area more than 20 feet before starting to build.

Stevens' replacement was another qualified engineer who was very fond of fishing. Luckily for him, there was little engineering work left to be done, so he spent the best part of his time on the lake or down the river where there were some beautiful rainbow trout.

Most of our workers lived in Duncan, so we had two small buses, called crummies, that travelled back and forth every working day of the week. We had no labour problems, except for one carpenters' strike which lasted two hours. Shorty phoned and I rushed up from Duncan. At the picket line I asked who was in charge and one of the men stepped forward.

"I am," he said. He was our best foreman.

"What is it you fellows want?" I asked.

"We want our pay raised from 90 cents to a dollar an hour," he said with real determination.

"Is that what all this fuss is about?" I asked.

"It's exactly what it's all about," he replied.

"Well, you've got your raise and there will be no dockage of pay provided you're all back on the job within the hour," I told them.

That was just the beginning of soaring increases. Within six months the carpenters asked for, and were given, another 25 cent increase. Today if you want to hire a qualified carpenter it can cost you twenty times that if he is in a union and the contract is ironclad.

It was a big job for us but we managed to do it for almost 15 percent less than the originally estimated cost. This was a saving to C.M.H.C. of some $60,000. It took us just under two years to complete the 100 houses. There were two basic plans. The single storey sold for $3,800 and the storey and a half with two extra bedrooms upstairs went for $4,200. These same houses today are selling for $90,000 and over, even though they are now close to 50 years old. Many owners have improved them, adding bedrooms, another bathroom and patios.

As the 100 houses were approaching completion we undertook the building of 50 houses out at Honeymoon Bay for Lake Logging and another 40 or more at Youbou to look after the extra crews needed for the night shifts at both mills. This reflected the increasing demand for lumber.

AS THE HOUSES SOLD, there were dozens of additional children who needed schooling. Even while we were working on the houses, we were asked to build another large school close to the high school we had finished earlier. Everything on the school went along smoothly until we ran out of nails. We hadn't been able to get an order number to purchase nails or other hardware for anything other than the postwar housing. Everything came to a halt. If we couldn't get nails right away the school would not be completed for the beginning of the fall term. We needed at least 500 pounds of assorted nails.

I contacted Colonel Boyd who was superintendent of the school district as well as the Justice of the Peace at Lake Cowichan. I told him there were sufficient nails in our store if he wanted to go and see Joe Gergel and make some sort of an arrangement with him. Gergel explained that he couldn't let them go unless they were covered by a government purchase order number.

"Is that so!" the colonel exclaimed as he turned and headed out the door. He went directly to the new police station and, using military savvy, explained what he needed to Sergeant Les Jeeves.

"As magistrate, I want two of your men to go over and seize these nails from the Garner store and put them in the back of my car."

Colonel Boyd signed a slip saying he was responsible for taking the nails from us. Joe Gergel helped load them. Little did he know he would have to wait almost four years before those nails were replaced. But the new school was finished on time and the children started their fall term on schedule.

As men became available we started work on the only business block in Lake Cowichan. It included a much needed bank for the area and a nice cafe, as well as stores and a real estate and insurance office. To say I was a busy man would be putting it mildly.

CAPTAIN PRESSEY had bought the old Lloyd house in Westholme. It had a steeple and church services had been held there in earlier days. Could we remove the steeple and lower the roof?

While working on this job I was offered a keg of three and a half inch nails for $100. The regular price would have been $5, if you could get them. I knew they had been pilfered from some other job, so I refused to accept them. We had to salvage some of the old square cut nails, but they did the job. This old house has recently been renovated yet again, restoring it to its original design complete with a new steeple.

We had a crew of up to twelve men continually renovating houses in and around Duncan. Two I remember clearly were the Chaney's. I met Lon Chaney Jr. while we were working on his father's house at the end of Garnett Road on the southwest side of Cowichan Bay. The dad had been a big Hollywood star, and Lon himself had played in a number of movies.

Lon was a big fun-loving man, who loved to do impromptu little acts that always left my children laughing. He bought an older house on the water on Balsam Drive near brother Al, just

Home of Lon Chaney Sr., a famous actor in Hollywood's silent film era, where he lived at the end of Garnett Road on Cowichan Bay near Duncan.

off Garnett Road not far from his father. He asked me if we would do the renovations for him. Over the next few years he returned to his Cowichan Bay summer home regularly. He usually arrived when the big spring salmon were about ready to go up the Cowichan River to spawn. Lon loved to be outdoors and was an excellent fishing partner. He visited our house often, and over the years we had some wonderful trips to the Cariboo for trout.

I ALSO had several men working weekends helping me build a house for ourselves on Grieve Road. Both Pat and I were anxious to be on our own again.

Furthermore, Tom, reflecting his impetuous nature, announced at supper one evening that he was going to get married again.

"I'm going to South Carolina for a month. I intend to bring back a bride."

Surprised, Pat said, "No, Tom. You can't find one in a month. That won't work out."

"You'll see. You'll see."

In less than a month Tom was back with his Southern Belle. Unfortunately Pat was right. It didn't work out. It wasn't long before we realized Helen was a confirmed alcoholic. Their marriage was to fall apart five or six years later.

This was a stressful time for Pat and me. We were looking forward to moving into more tranquil surroundings on Grieve Road. Since Virginia's death, our relationship had become very strained. We'd never really talked about the tragedy, never cleared the air. Pat was blaming me for having a loaded gun in the house. I felt she should never have left the girls alone with such a young boy that night.

ON OUR OWN AGAIN

OUR LOT ON GRIEVE ROAD was part of a four-lot package which Tom gave to Garner Bros. Ltd. We later sold two of them to our foreman, Shorty Berkey, and his brother Ken for $250 each. The remaining lot, next to ours, was later sold to Tom McEwan, a reporter for the Cowichan Leader. We built a lovely house for him and his wife Margaret.

We had been living on Grieve Road just under a year and were getting nicely settled in, when, on June 23, 1946 at 10:14 a.m., we were shaken by the worst earthquake ever experienced on Vancouver Island. This quake did extensive damage along many parts of the coast as far north as Alaska. It was also felt south along the Washington and Oregon coasts.

It was a Sunday and I'd arrived home just minutes earlier after an hour's work at the office. Instead of pulling on the hand brake, I left the pickup in gear and went in for breakfast. Pat was looking out the window and asked me why my truck was moving back and forth in the driveway. Just then the house shook and the dishes began rattling in the cupboards.

In the time it took us to get Dana out of her chair most of the dishes were smashed on the floor. Outside, the ground was moving like waves in the ocean.

We had built our house on the southeast corner of the Old Angus property, directly under one of the main power lines. The lines and towers were swaying violently. We just hung on to each other watching and waiting.

The house inside was a shambles. Broken dishes mixed in with the pots and pans off the stove. The dining room wall clock that once chimed every hour had been shaken off its nail, broken beyond repair.

Damage in Duncan was practically negligible. A few bricks popped out of chimneys. Yet, 10 miles to the west where Cottonwood Creek empties into Cowichan Lake near the Youbou Sawmill there had been a lovely sandy beach which was now under some 15 feet of water. The slide caused by the quake sent out a wave big enough to damage many of the floating houses and boats moored along the shores. Most of the log booms were broken up and the wind and turbulence scattered logs for miles.

Photo by the Geological Survey of Canada shows deep crevices on Island Highway south of Courtenay.

South of Courtenay a crack opened up and split the blacktop for several miles. That part of the highway was closed or bypassed for a month for repairs.

BUSINESS just kept booming during those postwar years. It was a great time to be in the building business, and Tom and I had our fingers in many pies. I was logging in the Duncan area and Tom was already logging in a substantial way along the mainland coast. It seemed as though we were starting a new endeavour almost every week. Having my own plane to more easily keep an eye on everything, especially the logging, seemed to be an excellent idea. I could see it was certainly working well for Tom.

I met many Indo-Canadians in the logging and sawmill business. Mayo Singh built a huge fortune from a small sawmill he operated at Paldi in the 1930s. Paldi village between Duncan and Lake Cowichan was then a thriving East Indian community, with its own public school, large general store and post office. It eventually even had its own airport, which Tom and I located and helped build in the late forties for Mayo's son, Rajindi, a competent pilot with an instrument rating. We brought in our bulldozers and cleared the land, and rough graded the runway. Rajindi then brought in his own graders and finished shaping the runway.

The Mayo family was prominent in furnishing the new King's Daughter's Hospital. Other lumber companies in the Cowichan District also chipped in to help furnish this new building. These companies, after all, brought in their injured loggers, many seriously, from their camps and sawmills. Logging was a very dangerous business, and still can be. But the Mayo family did more than their share.

There were several sons in the second generation of the Mayo family and old Mr. Mayo would have liked them to retain most of the East Indian traditions. However, the sons had been born and raised in the Cowichan Valley and had acquired "new world" values. When he arranged a marriage for his oldest son, Rajindi, he found unexpected resistance. As it turned out, Rajindi had already decided to marry his white high school sweetheart. He did, and Joan and Rajindi went on to have a fine family of six, five boys and one girl.

Paldi, almost a ghost town now, is being considered for both residential and business development, as it is near booming Duncan and not far off the new Lake Cowichan highway.

A LANKY YOUNG Indo-Canadian trucker who lived nearby on Grieve Road walked over one evening to talk to me about making money. I guess he figured if I could, then so could he. Rajindi Mayo had told this young fellow that as long as he kept his trucks in good condition and rolling he would keep them busy.

"The first thing you do," I told him with emphasis, "is to get rid of that piece of junk you're driving. Go out and buy yourself the best and most up-to-date heavy duty highway truck you can find. Borrow all you need from the bank. You'll also be establishing your credit that way."

That was all this young man needed to hear. He borrowed to the hilt and within a month had three new Kenworths on the road. His name was Herb Doman, and he is now one of the most successful businessmen in British Columbia. Owner of pulp and paper mills, saw mills, controller of hundreds of millions of dollars and stock and very possibly Canada's number one Indo-Canadian success story — an employer of thousands.

YEARS LATER another young trucker, Howie Davis, asked me for some advice. It hadn't changed: "Get rid of that piece of junk you're driving and buy yourself six brand new Kenworths. I'll finance you."

An independent young man, he decided to do it on his own. He bought one shiny new Kenworth, the best he could find, and, before he could properly afford it, another one. H.A. Davis is now the proud owner of over a 100 trucks, some new, some not so new. Another success story I feel I played a small part in.

PAT AND I now found more time for each other. Dana began to talk excitedly about starting school and Pat told me she was pregnant again. Our daughter, Joanne, was born on September 27, 1946, at King's Daughter's Hospital in Duncan. This beautiful baby did a great deal to brighten our lives.

One afternoon, months later, Pat started hemorrhaghing. Our doctor came to the house and immediately rushed her to the hospital. I was working out of town. By the time I got to the hospital Pat was really in bad shape. They could not stop the bleeding. Her brother Terry, who was one of the few people who had her blood type, had donated all he could. I met him as I was going in.

"You'd better hurry. I'm going to get Mother," he said, as he hurried away.

Dr. McCaffery directed a nurse to take me to Pat's room. There they hooked us up vein to vein. Since I was a regular blood donor they already knew our blood types were compatible.

I watched her drift in and out of consciousness, sometimes speaking aloud about the beautiful place she had visited, but not always making sense. It brought back terrible memories of another time, when Virginia had spoken of that beautiful world beyond.

Pat told me later what was happening during the long hours she hovered close to death.

"I'd float away," she said. "I could hear screams and

didn't know they were mine. Then, suddenly I was in this beautiful place. The birds were singing and I seemed to be swaying gently on the branches of trees. It was a quiet, peaceful world out there, and I wanted to stay.

"I could hear the voice of Dr. McCaffery. 'No, Pat. You've got to stay here and take care of your two little girls.' They kept coaxing me back, but that beautiful, peaceful place was so inviting."

I recall seeing the nurse, Mrs. Eileen Forest, slapping her sharply on the cheek several times to bring her back. In the end, although she balanced on the edge through most of the night, by morning she was back with us once again, gaining strength. Her life had been spared but she was still very weak.

Dr. McCaffery explained, "This miscarriage has taken a lot out of her, Joe, and due to complications, she may not be able to have any more children. In any case, I strongly recommend that she never get pregnant again."

I didn't think much about the implication right away. I was too concerned about her health then to think of what the future held.

Later I began to think about not having a son. But when I talked with Pat about what Dr. McCaffery had said, she just smiled and said, "We'll see what happens."

Eighteen months later, in August of 1948, Pat was back in King's Daughter's Hospital again, delivering our first son. We named him Tom after my older brother.

TWO YEARS LATER, in the autumn of 1950, I decided to build a larger house for our growing family on one of three lots we owned on Alington Road. We had barely finished pouring the concrete when Herb Dickey, a local agent, dropped by and talked insurance. I mentioned that I was thinking of building another house on the adjoining lot to the north.

"Well, I'm having to move out of downtown Duncan by the end of next month, Joe. I would like to buy or rent it if you can have it finished by then."

He went to his car and showed me a plan. It was out of a builders' magazine — a very livable, four-room bungalow. I looked it over and made a few minor changes to improve things and save him money.

"It could easily be ready by then," I assured him, and as I write this I chuckle, thinking how long it takes to build a house today even with new materials and better equipment.

"How would a cost plus ten percent deal suit you?" he asked.

"Okay with me," I replied.

We shook hands. A few days later it became obvious I would have to raise some more money for this construction. Herb Dickie already had the insurance on our Grieve Road house. When I phoned him and told him we wanted to put a mortgage on it he said, "Why don't you phone Bob Whittome. That's more in his line of business than mine."

When I talked to Whittome, another businessman who had seen Duncan grow and prosper, he agreed to meet me at Grieve Road at four o'clock that afternoon. He thoroughly inspected the foundations and the upper rooms, the roof and chimneys.

"How much money do you need, Joe?"

"At least five thousand," was my reply. I explained I already had our house sold for $10,000 if a decent mortgage could be arranged.

"Forty-five hundred at six and a half is the best I can do," he offered, and added, "You will have to cancel your present insurance with Dickie's and insure with us before we advance you any money." He waited, watching my reaction to this unethical — to me — offer.

I looked him straight in the eye and politely said, "Bob, this is a dead end street. You can use our yard for a turn around. I hope we can meet again some day with the tables turned." I went into the house and phoned our bank. We had our mortgage money at six percent the following morning.

When I told Dickie he just laughed and said, "Sounds like Bob."

A year later, we were nicely settled into our new house overlooking Somenos Lake. Herb Dickie and his wife were living next door and they had already planted a really nice flower garden. One evening I walked over and asked Herb to renew our insurance policy and add another $5,000 to cover new furniture.

"I'll do it tomorrow. I was just going over to see you. Just listen to this," he said with a big grin. "Bob Whittome has asked me to sell his acreage and home on Maple Bay Road. He has just bought a property southwest of Duncan, on the ridge overlooking the town. He's anxious to move. Do you want his old place for $10,500 cash? It's a real bargain. If you want to get even, just make me an offer."

"Why not? Give it a try. I'll give you a certified cheque for $8,000 tomorrow morning for everything, as is, where is. But don't let him know who's making the offer. If he accepts okay, but if he doesn't I'll leave the cheque with you until someone else buys it. If nobody does he might come around if he's in that much of a hurry."

"Okay," Herb said. "I'll be glad to deal for you," and we both laughed. This could be fun.

Four months and no action. The frustrated seller was really anxious to know who was behind the offer. Herb made like a clam. Then, one evening he came over, all smiles. I knew what was up.

"He bit?" I asked.

"He swallowed it! The Whittome place is all yours as of noon today. When Bob looked at your cheque he just said, 'I thought so.' Here are the signed papers. Now you're even."

Herb laughed as he witnessed my signature on the contract.

A done deal and an insult paid back in full.

FREE IN THE SKY

A GROUP OF young Duncan businessmen wanted to learn to fly on floats, and get nearby Quamichan Lake licenced as a float plane training center. But some of the people living near the lake and along Maple Bay Road tried to prevent us.

Many were remittance men, receiving money from their families in Britain on the understanding that they stayed in the "colonies". They were somewhat eccentric and certainly resistant to change of any sort. They circulated a petition and sent it off to the Department of Transport in Ottawa. There were just over 50 names on it. This petition stated that aircraft would create too much noise and takeoffs and landings would scare away nesting geese and other waterfowl.

In the end we hired a local lawyer, Frank Davie, and sent him to Ottawa to argue our case. He said he had won a similar case 30 years earlier. The old petition demanded that all motor vehicles be banned from using Maple Bay Road because they were considered too noisy and dangerous to the horse and buggy people travelling to and from Duncan.

When Davie showed this defeated petition of long ago to "the powers that be" in Ottawa, pointing out that most of the same names were on both petitions, we were granted approval for a licence to use the lake for our flying school.

We immediately began building the necessary facilities for our Duncan Aero Club: clearing and grading of Indian Road down to the lake, a floating tie-up for planes and a small clubhouse and office. We all pitched in, each giving what we were able to in building materials, time or money.

Quamichan Lake in 1993 showing how wrong the protesters were in 1952 when they claimed the swans, ducks and geese would be frightened away by the float planes.

HELEN HARRISON joined the Duncan Aero Club in the fall of 1947, and she and her young son moved into our new clubhouse. Helen was one of the most qualified instructors for float flying in the world. She had logged over 10,000 hours and was the first instructor who had multi-engine and instrument endorsements. She was one of the pilots that ferried the four-engine planes from Alaska to Russia across the Bering Sea during the war. An unsung breed, women pilots were not un-usual, but she was exceptional.

We had the use of a Cessna 140 on floats as our first training plane — CF EKP. It had an 80-horsepower Continental motor and was owned by brother Tom. The club rented it from him. For a while this little float plane was used to check out pilots from all over British Columbia.

Helen trained the first eight men who signed up under the Department of Transport's approved course for Private Pilot Flying Training. We took our ground school lessons in the new clubhouse under her supervision. There were Lindsay Loutet,

Martin Braten, Jack Lawless, Ted Robson, George Hamilton, my brother Lloyd and myself, all of Duncan, and Andy Olson from Cowichan Lake. This slight woman in her late thirties was matching wits daily with these hefty loggers twice her size, but she was undaunted and was in complete control at all times. Loutet, Braten, Lawless and Lloyd Garner were the first group to complete their flying training with her.

A year later, in the fall of 1948 she moved to Vancouver where she continued float training and charter flights to all parts of the province. By now the club had the use of a second plane, a Stinson — CF FFW — also owned by Tom.

Before leaving, she checked out Hall Mackenzie, a former R.C.A.F. wartime pilot. Using the Stinson, from September to mid-November, Mackenzie logged many hours of flying time on charter flights servicing the logging camps of the Gulf Islands and the southern parts of B.C. He also checked out many wheel pilots for qualification to fly on floats. This Stinson was the same aircraft Tom lost to a Nanaimo logger in a poker game at his home in Duncan later that November. Shortly after, some of our club members went to Nanaimo and made a deal to buy FFW back for the Aero Club.

IN NOVEMBER of 1948, Doug Williston took over the pilot training and moved into the clubhouse with his new wife. Doug asked if he could use FFW to fly over to Vancouver for their first Christmas together.

On December 22, the weather turned bitterly cold and the lake froze over. That morning I got a call. "We'd like you to bring us over a load of dry wood for our stove when you can," Doug said. "It's getting mighty cold in this shack."

We were building a house nearby so I filled the pickup with short 2 x 4 scrap ends and arrived at the clubhouse just before noon. His wife was shivering in bed with her winter coat on. We built a roaring fire in the stove then went down to check the planes. The floats of the Cessna and the Stinson were frozen tight in half an inch of clear ice. It wasn't thick enough to hold a man's weight but it sure held the floats solid against the dock.

"We should take the planes up on the ramp until this ice melts," I suggested. We cut away enough of the ice with an axe to let us manoeuver the Cessna up out of the water and onto the dolly. I hooked the pickup to the dolly with a stout rope and pulled it up the concrete ramp and parked it out of the way.

"We'd better chop the ice from around FFW also and nose

One of the Duncan Aero Club's training planes at Quamichan Lake.

it up on the dolly." We used the pickup again to pull the Stinson part way up the concrete ramp.

Rubbing his hands together, Doug said, "Come on in and warm up with a cup of hot coffee."

As we sat at the kitchen table chatting, Doug asked, "Do you think we might put the Stinson back in the water tomorrow and take it over to Vancouver?"

"If it turns warmer, okay, but if it doesn't warm up considerably it certainly won't be safe to try a takeoff," I warned him.

"Can you come over about noon tomorrow and take another look?"

"Sure, and we can then better decide what to do. If the plane is best left where it is, you can get the 2.30 ferry from Nanaimo."

Next morning it had warmed up slightly. Doug phoned me, "Come and help me get the Stinson back in the lake. I've promised my parents I'd be coming over for Christmas and be in Vancouver before dark."

"Be there in 15 minutes," I told him, but I was wondering why they just didn't take the warm and comfortable ferry. His wife was outside in her heavy winter coat with their luggage. She was wearing a heavy pair of woolen gloves and socks and looked ready for the Arctic. Doug was warming up the motor.

"We've decided to give it a try," he yelled from the cock-pit.

"That ice is thick enough to knock holes in the pontoons." I yelled back, emphatically. "You're risking your lives. I can drive you to Nanaimo in plenty of time to catch that ferry."

"Well, I'm the instructor here and we're going to give it a try," he said with more than a little determination. I was beginning to worry. This was crazy.

"I'm pretty sure those floats are not sturdy enough to get you off the lake," I argued.

"It's my neck, not yours, so let's put her back in the water. There's no time to loose."

"Okay," I reluctantly agreed. He shut off the motor so we could turn FFW around and push her back into the water facing out. His wife climbed into the passenger seat and fastened her safety belt, and we stowed their suitcases on the back seat. He climbed back behind the controls and started the motor up. I gave the plane, still on the dolly, a good shove out into the lake. As he opened the throttle I could hear the ice breaking under the floats.

As the Stinson moved slowly and noisily away I wished them luck, and thought, "It's your neck and your decision." I could hear big chunks of ice hitting the floats as the plane taxied further out.

This had to be a lesson in float flying I would never forget. Jack Lawless, a club director, had arrived and he and I watched the plane taxi half way down the lake and begin to sink. Immediately Jack ran to the clubhouse and called the phone operator in Duncan asking her to contact Search and Rescue, the fire department and the members of the Aero Club. He knew this was going to be a bad one.

We watched helplessly as the Willistons scrambled out on to the ice which was not strong enough to hold their weight. They had to stay with the plane which was slowly turning upside down, the engine going under first. They climbed along the struts and stood on the bottom of the floats which were now keel up. Some mess, some Christmas, some stupidity and some trouble coming up.

Lindsay Loutet who was recently licenced to handle EKP arrived first. Jack had boiled a kettle of water in the clubhouse so we thawed out the ropes and untied the knots holding the Cessna in place and launched her. He taxied slowly through the broken ice alone to try and rescue the freezing Willistons. He used good judgment and kept the Cessna going slowly so it gently pushed the broken chunks down under the water and saved the pontoons from being punctured. The upside-down Stinson was so far out we couldn't see whether all was going well or not. But there was now a good chance this daring manoeuver might work.

By now brother Tom, George Syrotuk and several other club members had arrived. They put our big rowboat in the water and we started out to help. Lindsay had already made it halfway back to shore when we reached him. Mrs. Williston was in the passenger's seat and Doug was outside on the float, blue with the cold. Lindsay stopped the engine so we could get Doug out from under the wings where he was hanging on for dear life. When we had him safely in the boat we gave him a paddle and a pair of mitts. "Hypothermia" was not a word then, but we all knew what could happen.

"Start paddling back to the wharf as fast as you can before you freeze to death," I yelled at him. I grabbed the spare oar and stood in the front end to push the bigger pieces of ice out of the way. It took us half an hour to get back to the wharf with the Cessna following close behind. A brisk north wind was blowing and it was getting darker. Their clothes were frozen stiff. They stripped and climbed into bed while we got a fire going again. "Well," I told them, "this is one helluva a mess." My understatement of the year.

Next morning the ice was two inches thick. Tom and George Syrotuk took out a couple of empty 45-gallon gas barrels and fastened them to the floats of the Stinson hoping to prevent her from sinking any deeper and losing the whole thing. To put it mildly, the Willistons didn't have a Christmas dinner in Vancouver, and we had a plane to rescue from under the ice.

Right after Christmas, Tom organized several of his loggers and some of our club members and set up a huge tripod on 4 x 8 sheets of 3/4 inch plywood. They borrowed two five-ton BB winches that had to be operated by hand. Horace Nault, a qualified aero engineer, who had spent 10 years in the north country, came over from Vancouver to supervise the raising. Under his supervision, we slowly lifted the plane up out of the water and placed it right side up on the ice. This meant getting all the water and ice out of the plane as it was raised, and that was no easy task. There was a gaping hole in the right hand float and several smaller holes in the left one. The gang spent the rest of the day making a sleigh out of the material we had used to make the tripod and manoeuvered FFW onto it.

Ingenuity — the mark of a coastal logger.

CF-FFW, the training plane being kept afloat with two 45-gallon gas barrels. George Syrotuk contemplating problem.

That night it turned colder and snowed. The temperature plunged to just about the lowest temperature recorded in more than 20 years. Next morning eight of us walked out on the ice again and, with strong ropes and plenty of determination and muscle, we slid the damaged plane over the snow-covered ice for almost a mile back to the ramp. There it was put on the dolly and parked where it had been two days earlier when this mad adventure began.

When the cold spell let up, Tom phoned Horace Nault again to come over and do the necessary repairs. These were expensive, but the Stinson was back in flying condition by the end of February. Not as good as new, but she had a complete overhaul and a new certificate of airworthiness from the Department of Transport.

Williston got impatient, quit and started flying out of Vancouver. You could hear the sighs of relief!

ALLEN BEACH gladly took his place, and I started my flying training with him on the Cessna near the end of the year. Along with me were Robson and Hamilton and Olson, the last of the eight original club members. It cost us $300 each, but we would get $100 back from the federal government when we got

Tom Garner's amphibious plane, a Cessna 195, is no longer being manufactured. Horace Nault standing to Tom's left before takeoff.

our licence. Poor eyesight caused Ted and George to drop out about halfway through. Ted was short-sighted and didn't like doing spins. George was colour-blind and he actually couldn't tell the difference between red and green.

I trained with Beach until April when Fred Snell took over. Fred was excellent. Some of my training with him was done on a rented Luscombe — FGN. When he left in June,1951, he went with Okanagan Helicopters and soon became their chief pilot.

HELEN HARRISON came over to Duncan occasionally, and one day at the club she said, "Joe, I'm going to do you a nice favour for those you've done for me. I'll stay a few days and check you out. It won't be a snap and you'd better be on your toes."

Do I remember my first flight with her in the Luscombe? She read my log book, then we walked down to the floating dock. She carefully checked all the controls, including that all-important check to see that there was no water in the floats.

"You get in the pilot's seat. I want you to take off down to the north end of the lake and climb to 3,000 feet." I did, an easy climb. Without another word Helen reached over and pulled the throttle back to the idle position.

"Now hold the nose up to the normal flying position until

119

she stalls. Then kick the left rudder hard and we'll go straight down in a tight spin," she said.

Believe me! This all happened in a hurry. I remember it looked like the fields were coming up toward us in a terrible rush. I looked at Helen. She sat there, calm as could be, a smile on her face. The hard ground seemed to be getting mighty close.

"Now push the stick forward and gently put some pressure on your right rudder. That's right," she said. "Now when she stops spinning, ease the stick back and gently push the throttle in to normal cruise. That's perfect." she said. "Now pull her nose up to a gradual climbing position," she ordered. I did. Lesson Number One.

Helen gave me a pat on the back, saying. "That was almost perfect, Joe. How do you feel?"

"Okay," I said. I was a bit shaken up but I wouldn't admit it, not to Helen.

"Climb to 3,000 again and we'll do another spin, this time to the right." But this time I knew exactly what to expect. Helen never said a word and when we reached 3,000 feet again she just reached over and pulled the throttle back, then sat there quietly and watched as I did the manoeuver completely on my own.

"How do you feel," she asked again.

"Okay." And this time I did. I knew what I was doing.

"Now climb back to about 2,000 feet, then shut the motor off and do a dead stick landing," she ordered. I had been practising this type of landing for the past two weeks so I made it almost on the exact spot where she told me to touch down.

After tying up to the float we walked up to the clubhouse where she was bunking down while visiting Duncan. She mixed herself a cold rum and Coke and handed me a cold beer.

"Here's to 1909, Joe," she said as we touched glasses. "Checking your log book, I noticed that we were born the same year. Well, you are about ready for your licence. You certainly got the hang of it fast. All that's left is your cross-country. Can you be here tomorrow morning about 8.30? I want you to fly up-island to Comox, tie up at the wharf and leave your card with the wharfinger with the precise time of your landing on it. Then take off and land at the seaplane dock on the Fraser River at the Vancouver Airport. You had better fuel up. Then phone the control tower for takeoff clearance and fly back here.

"You might like to just stay here tonight and leave on your cross-country a bit earlier," she suggested.

"Sounds good to me," I told her. So I did.

Next day I flew the triangular circuit in under three hours. When I got back Helen insisted on pouring us a hefty rum and Coke to celebrate. Then she wrote out a permit so I could fly on floats anywhere I liked. I was not permitted to take passengers up until Carter Guest, the federal government's head man for aviation in the province, came over and gave us our final tests. This was done on June 19 of 1950.

That night we held a party for the graduating pilots, Andy Olson and me. My official licence to take up passengers was presented to me at the clubhouse. Carter Guest stayed on for a while, then said his goodbyes and took off for Vancouver. Helen handed me another large glass of rum and Coke. She stood up on a chair and loudly announced, "Here's to Joe. He has just received his private pilot's licence number P1799."

My wife, who didn't like flying too much, drank to that anyway. The evening went along smoothly, with some of the older couples leaving.

The clubhouse only had two main rooms. One was a kitchen-living room with a wood stove, a chesterfield and a table with half a dozen chairs around. There was a sink with wall-to-wall cupboards. A large window looked out over the lake to the north. The bedroom was a bit smaller with an en-suite bathroom and a clothes closet. It also had a window overlooking the planes.

Helen put her arm around my waist, whispering, "Come help me get some booze from under the bed," and gave me a good tug towards the open bedroom door. As we went through the door she pushed it shut with her toe. She went towards the bed and pulled me over beside her. Helen wanted to do some smooching and I was happy to accommodate. A couple of minutes later the door burst open and there was Pat. Helen stood up and Pat charged and butted her square in the stomach with her head, knocking her backwards onto the bed. Pat grabbed a handful of Helen's long red hair and pulled some out by the roots. She walked back into the kitchen, placed Helen's hair neatly in the middle of the table and carefully smoothed it out. She pointed towards the hair, and in a loud voice said, "That will teach her."

Pat then stomped out the door, got into her car and drove off. I didn't think she would want my company just then, so I didn't follow.

Helen began doing more charter work around Duncan and checked out many wheel pilots wishing to get their float en-

Inauguration of Helen Harrison into the Canadian Aviation Hall of Fame in 1984. Standing: left to right, Lloyd Garner, Edie Garner, Al and Barbara Garner, Margaret and Fred Robson. Seated: Helen Harrison, Joe Garner and Ruby King.

Helen Harrison and Joe at her inauguration.

dorsements. However, 1952 saw the last of the aero club's training school. Fred Snell and Helen had both left for Vancouver where there was more demand for their services and there didn't seem to be any more people around Duncan who wanted to learn to fly.

Helen continued to move around quite a lot, and I've been told that any time she moved away from a town she left at least one irate wife behind her.

When she retired in 1969 she had logged 14,000 hours as pilot-in-command of 75 different types of aircraft without injury to passenger or crew. She was in her seventies when she finally quit flying, but she was still instructing part-time when she was inducted into The Aviation Hall of Fame in Edmonton in 1984.

Helen Marcelle (Harrison) Bristol passed away in April 1995 at the age of 85 shortly before this book went to press.

MOTHER'S TRIP

ON A SUNNY MORNING the following April on my way to the air base, I stopped at Mother's home on Maple Bay Road and invited her to come along for a ride.

"You'll be able to see Duncan, all the streets and roads. We'll fly over this house and then we can go up over Chemainus so you can look down at the house you were living in when war was declared."

"How long will all this take us?" Mother asked.

"An hour at the most."

Thinking it over she gave me a big smile and asked, "Will it be cold up there?"

"About like it is down here."

She grabbed a blue sweater coat and said, "Ready to go when you are, Joe."

Mother would be 66 years old in a couple of months. She had a quick mind and rarely hesitated once she made a decision.

When I started checking for the flight, Mother watched every move I made and asked me why it was necessary to do all those different things, like pumping a gallon of water from the right hand float and checking the oil dipstick.

"You wouldn't want us to be forced down if we're up a couple of thousand feet, would you?"

I opened the right hand door and helped her up into the passenger's seat and showed her how to fasten her safety belt.

I untied the plane and pushed it around facing into the wind. Inside I cranked up the motor, and taxied out. I did the final check while the motor warmed up further — every precaution taken — then I reached over and tightened Mother's seat belt another notch and opened the throttle. Because of the steady wind we were up on the step and airborne in less than 30 seconds. Mother looked relieved and happy as we climbed smoothly. I circled back and pointed out Old Angus, the house where Tom had lived.

"Are you nervous or scared?" I asked.

She shook her head, but did not say a word for the next few minutes. She just kept looking at the scenery as it passed by below.

Smiling happily, she said, "I know you well enough to feel sure we wouldn't be up here unless you believed it was perfectly safe. You know, son, I've seen more of Duncan in the last few minutes than I ever knew existed. Let's go on up to Chemainus and and you can take me over the house you boys built for me. I'm sure I'll spot it. If you remember, Joe, that is where our family was living when Slim Hayes and your brother Al joined the army. To my dying day I'll never forget watching Al get ready to go, all soldier-like and determined-looking in his uniform. And me, his Mom, realizing I might never see him again."

"You must have been very happy when he came home after the war was over."

"I sure was, even though he did have that limp because of some shrapnel in his back."

I made three complete circles so she could have a closeup view of the house where she had spent time caring for her three youngest children, Al, Lloyd and Dorothy, while they were still in their teens. I pointed out the little house that Pat and I moved to shortly after we were married.

"Let's fly on up and have a look at the Ladysmith High School," Mother suggested. "That's where Lloyd put his hip out of joint. You should remember that," she said smiling.

"I sure do. I was the one who drove him to the hospital and when he was home again I made him a shoe using a short piece of 2 x 4 for the sole so he could walk without being lop-sided. I remember his right leg was almost two inches shorter than his left one."

After climbing, we headed towards Ladysmith, a few miles to the north. Three minutes later we were over the new high school, making more circles. I could see Mother was not enjoying all this circling, so we started back towards home. Nearing Chemainus again we passed the western shore of Saltspring Island where Mother and Dad settled when they left Victoria in the summer of 1905. She was comfortable again and interested in the magnificent ocean and island views below.

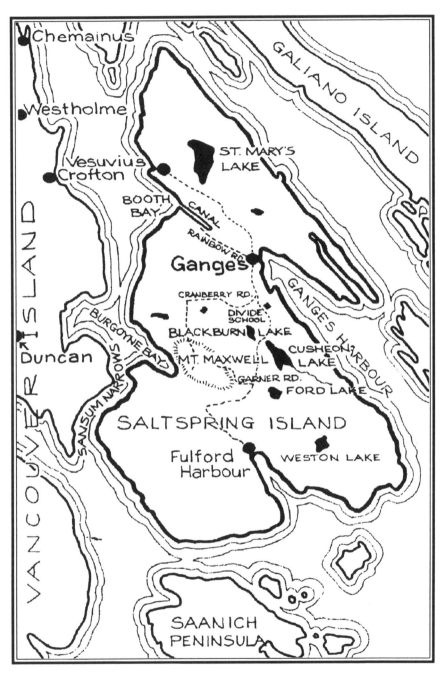

Saltspring Island.

"It wouldn't take us much longer to see all our old houses," I suggested. "Enjoy seeing them again?"

She patted my shoulder and answered, "Son, I would just love to see it all again."

I swung the nose east over Saltspring to take us directly over the old Beddis home and the beach at the outlet of the creek that drains Cusheon Lake. There Mother and Dad, with Ethel their first born, had landed many years ago. From over Ganges Harbour, dotted with islands of varying shapes and sizes, she could see The Trading Company store and Mouat's Store, and close by our big house where Ollie, Al, Lloyd and Dorothy were born.

It brought back memories of my first brush with aviation, shortly after the First World War in the summer of 1919. I was 10. We had seen pamphlets describing an exhibition of "barnstorming", as it was called in those primitive days of flight. Ernie Eaves and a stunt pilot named Brown, two pilots who had flown during the war, would show us islanders what it was all about. Tom and I had a great curiosity about airplanes. We decided we would save up our money and go see the show.

It was a dollar a minute to fly over the harbour, over beautiful St. Mary's Lake and around Vesuvius Bay. The "aerodrome", as such, was the hay field behind the Croftons' summer resort overlooking the harbour. This was the only field around large enough to allow safe take-offs and landings. The pilots had carefully roped it off. They took turns taking passengers on these sight-seeing trips throughout the day. We were able to pay for all this with money we had earned cutting firewood for the Saltspring Island Creamery and the Lady Minto Hospital. I asked Mother if she remembered that day.

"I most certainly do. I spent most of it keeping my young ones clear of the plane."

Arthur Drake, whom Mother had known well, was the manager and butter maker for the creamery. I was working for him the day his wife committed suicide. I well remember hearing the shot and seeing him rush out of the building and up the hill to his home where he found his wife lying dead on the floor. The shotgun was still smoking by her side. He just covered her up, phoned the undertaker and then came down and told me what had happened. We later learned she had been suffering greatly from cancer for quite some time. I recall they even closed the public school until after her funeral.

We flew over what we had known as "The Point". There was not one house there in 1926, the year Mother left Dad to go and live in Vancouver. Wild flowers bloomed there all spring and summer. Twenty-five years later we still looked down on a sea of blue and yellow bloom, with a house here and one there, but the end of this paradise was near. Now, in 1995, the shoreline has side by side houses costing vast sums — inconceivable for a pioneer to understand — with blacktop roads and concrete sidewalks everywhere. I'm glad Mother didn't have to look down on that. In the seventies Saltspring became "hot" property, as had Galiano Island although Mayne and Saturna islands still slumbered in the sun — but their day of so-called progress was coming.

Slanting off to the west we passed low over Cusheon, Blackburn and Ford Lakes and climbed and circled up over our old farm, since subdivided into acre lots selling at $50,000 to $70,000, to look down on the place where Mother had lived during most of her younger years. Dad built a bigger farm house for his growing family and here her two middle daughters, Pearl and Edie, came into the world with only the help of her neighbours. Most pioneer women were capable midwives.

Pearl arrived on August 29, 1914, then Edie on February 29, 1916 — a leap year child and barely 18 months younger than Pearl.

Mother was very excited and talkative as we flew quite low over the hilly old farm and the buildings and trees she had known for years, but never had seen as a soaring eagle does.

"See those big old fruit trees down there. Those are the same trees that Ted Akerman brought all the way by boat from England to Victoria before the beginning of the century. He bored four small holes about half way through a large potato, then tucked a little sprout in each hole. He packed the potatoes snugly in metal boxes filled with moist sawdust. This kept the little tree upright and alive, you see. All they had to do when they arrived here, was slice the potatoes through and put each sprout directly into the soil so the roots that had already started to grow would not be disturbed. Now just look at them, Joe. Sprouted in England, now so tall and straight here."

Over Wakelyn Creek I pointed out the little shack where Tom had been born. We knew it as the Duke's house, named after a deaf old pioneer that lived there.

"You know, Joe, we had been snowed in for almost a month that year. Four feet deep outside that little cabin. Dr. Beach rode his saddle horse all the way up from Ganges after Oland went down to get him. Tom was born about two o'clock in the afternoon. I remember that, but I never did know if it was the

128

Community picnic at Cusheon Cove, Saltspring Island in 1916.

A sketch of the farm house where Joe remembers seeing his mother jump eight feet from the verandah roof after drinking a mixture of turpentine and sugar in hot water to try to bring on a miscarriage.

day before New Year's or the day after. I thought it would be nice to have my first son born on New Year's Day, so that was the way he was registered."

I remembered the big fight she had with Dad over Tom. He and I were sitting outside by the door.

"I'm agoin' to take Tom to Mass at the Blackburn's house this morning," he said to Mother. The Blackburn home was used as the Catholic Church and Sunday School.

"No, you're not goin' to do any such thing as long as I'm here. He can choose his own church when he gets old enough," Mother snapped back. She then took hold of both of Tom's hands to pull him into the house. Dad reached down and picked Tom's feet up off the ground and a tug of war began. I started crying because it looked as if they might pull out his arms.

Dad, beaten for once, let go and started off alone down the trail to the Blackburn's. But he turned and shouted, "There'll be another day, Lona. Just you wait and see."

Mother locked the door and picked up Tom who had started crying. Naturally. There would be no more Catholics in this family. Let Tom choose was her decision. And a good one.

Mother was Baptist. Dad was a devout Catholic. Tom was six years old and I was just four at the time. A year earlier I had been baptised by Father Sheiland at that same house. It's one of my first clear memories. Mother wasn't there. She refused to go inside a Catholic church. I remember she warned Ethel to always keep her distance when Father Sheiland came visiting. This plane ride was bringing back plenty of memories for both of us.

"Do you remember, Mom, when the big tom cougar chased me down there. I guess that was the first time my sense of survival hit me and my subconscious mind came to life. I was only eight years old, and I'll never know how I found strength enough to jump over a gate higher than my head while running full speed up that hill towards home. Do you know that 40 percent of North America's recorded attacks on humans have occurred here on the West Coast of B.C.? I read that in *Time Magazine*."

Then we flew higher up the mountain over what was left of the small log tool shed where I was born. Only the foundations could be seen.

"Never even had a floor in it," she said, looking down. "Just dirt. You're a pioneer boy, Joe."

"We did have a good little wood stove for warming water, though. That was a cold February. We didn't think you'd make it, you know. You only weighed about three pounds. That's why your father refused to pay to have you baptised or circumcised. To keep you warm I'd tie a towel under your arms to hold you upright and dip you in a pitcher filled with warm water and put the pitcher into the big pot of water on the stove. When I took you out I'd wrap you in a blanket and put you back on the bed. At night you'd sleep between my breasts."

"Those must have been rough times for a young lady from South Carolina."

"Sure were," she replied, in the easy drawl she had never lost. "And you know, Joe, just now I'm missing your father a bit. Remember his storytelling? You kids used to enjoy his Uncle Remus tales."

"Yeah," I chuckled. "'Brer Rabbit' and the 'Briar Patch'. Stories about cotton fields and other such things."

"And do you remember his banjo and his singing? Oland knew so many songs: 'Pretty Red Wing,' 'Casey Jones,' 'Nellie Gray,' and that song about the James boys. I still remember that last line: 'The dirty little coward, who shot Mr. Howard, and laid poor Jesse in his grave.'"

At Christmas time he'd often give Tom a mouth organ and me a Jew's harp, so we could join in. We weren't very good, but we learned enough to help the younger children who would be trying to make a noise using tissue paper wrapped around a comb.

During the cold winter months our neighbours, the Seymours, would walk over the bush trail to have supper and spend the evening. Clara Seymour would usually bring a cake or a couple of freshly-baked pies. Wilfred would bring his mouth organ to help boost up the rhythm as Dad played his banjo and sang. Ed Wakelyn often would be there with his mandolin. He had a crush on our oldest sister, Ethel, and was up at our house several times a week.

Because of his singing and banjo playing, Dad was always in demand at the Christmas concerts and at the village "dos" he would call the square dances. These were family affairs and the children learned to dance by watching and copying their parents. If the small ones got into too much trouble the music would stop and the adults would straighten them out. Then off they'd go again. I was able to square dance when I was only five years old.

Over the drone of the plane engine Mother spoke again.

"Your father was quite a tap dancer too. You remember, Joe, how they'd always ask him to get up at school concerts and do a demonstration of "Cutting the Chicken Wing"? Told me once that he learned it in Charleston, down in South Carolina watching some Negroes."

I didn't say it aloud, but I was thinking that this musical side of my father's character could well be one of the reasons why Emily Carr was so attracted to him. They used to have a meeting place at a small cabin on the beach near Sydney where she sometimes worked during the summer. Little did we know she would become one of Canada's most famous painters.

"I had to leave him, son. He was a difficult man to live with; sometimes very domineering. I knew, too, that you and Tom had to get away if you were to make a life of your own. But the main reason was that, after 10 children, my doctor warned me the next pregnancy would likely kill me. Then none of you would have a mother. I just couldn't take any more chances."

"We understood, Mom. That's why Tom and I went and built a house for you and the kids in Vancouver."

"I certainly appreciated that, Joe. Always remember that. And I'll never forget the beautiful fur coat you bought me at Eaton's the following year when you went fishing at Bella Coola. I know it cost you half your summer's wages. Lawsie sakes, it was fit for a queen. When the house got cold I even

Small sailboats being towed out to fishing grounds by company launch from the Tallheo Cannery at Bella Coola, 1927, where Joe and brother Tom earned about $600 each that season.

slept in it. More than a few times too."

"Well, Mom," I said, patting her knee. "It would have been worth a whole summer's pay to see the pleasure it gave you." Then, gazing again at the ocean and forest below, she said, "I know it's about time we headed for home but I'd sure like to fly over Maxwell's Peak. Is it too far out of our way?"

We'd almost circled the island while we talked, and the peak was close. A high mountain to prairie folk, but a small one to West Coasters. We first flew along the south side, about 200 feet below the top and then flew over Demains Lake where we could see the old Rogers' log home with its orchards and hay fields. Mrs. Rogers had acted as midwife when Margaret was born.

"All that don't seem to be a very long way when we fly," Mother said, smiling at her memories. "It used to take more than two and a half hours from Maxwell's Peak to Demains Lake when you walked it. We picnicked up there many times when you were a little boy, so I know," Then, almost as an afterthought, she added, "Joe, no matter where life takes you, you must never, never forget the good times!"

I banked west and we flew over The Narrows between Saltspring and Vancouver Islands and began our descent towards Quamichan Lake and home. Mother was tired but happy, a return as an eagle, to the scenes and memories of days long ago. Me, too.

Joe's sisters and mother in 1951. Standing from left, Edie, Dorothy, Pearl; seated, Ethel, Mother and Margaret.

The Garner boys with their mother at a New Year's Eve family gathering December 1957. Standing from left, Ollie, Al and Lloyd; seated, Tom, Mother and Joe.

Before Mother moved back to Vancouver again to live out her later years with Ethel, there were several other trips. But always, when I took her up she wanted to see again and again the Saltspring Island areas where her children were born and grew up, where she had lived as a true pioneering young woman. For more than 20 years she gave us everything we needed, even if it meant doing without herself. She practiced the Golden Rule: "Do unto others as you would have them do unto you."

"Live by that and you will be happy," she said to us again and again.

She had a wonderful way of praising us for almost everything we did: cutting wood for the stove, milking the cows, feeding the calves or hunting grouse so she could fry them with home-cured bacon. Her fresh milk gravy on hot biscuits with a pinch of curry gave it a special tang.

"That's southern style cookin'," she would say as she gave us a second helping and a pat on the back.

"Lawsey sakes, I couldn't do all that unless you boys brought in those grouse," she would tell Tom and me.

I remember how proud Tom was when he got his first grouse when he was only eight. I got mine with a sling shot when I was just seven, and that took skill. But then maybe I was just lucky.

It doesn't matter now, but then we hunted for the "pot" and not, as so often now, for the dubious thrill of killing. Even today, when I knock over a grouse it is for the pot — for mine or one of my children's or for a friend's.

DALL LAKE

THAT AUTUMN Tom and I planned a hunting trip into the north country where the rivers flow towards the Arctic Circle. We hoped to bring home a trophy ram. At dawn on August 15, 1951, we headed north for Dall Lake, just over 800 flying miles from home. On the way we stopped twice, once at Quesnel and again at Finlay Forks, where we fueled up before flying the 217 miles to Dall Lake — up the Finlay River through the Rocky Mountain Trench, through Sifton Pass which links the Kechika and Fox Rivers, and over the divide. Back then the slow flowing Finlay River had not been dammed up and flooded to form what is now Williston Lake.

A week earlier we had arranged to have two barrels of fresh 80-octane gas delivered to Finlay Forks from Prince George. If we ran into trouble with poor quality gas where we were going we would be helpless. We also filled up our two five-gallon containers to ensure we had enough gas to make the return trip from Dall Lake.

At Finlay Forks their parting words to me were, "Isn't that Pacer a bit small to be taking into that country? Better watch out for Sifton Pass. It can dish up bad weather in a hurry."

Ted Robson came along with me, Bill Auchinachie went with Tom. They were two of our regular hunting gang.

Tom had his 180 Cessna tied up in plain view when I arrived at Dall Lake. We pitched our tents and collected wood for a smoky fire hoping to keep the big, hungry mosquitoes at bay. We were camped on a pack trail leading into the higher mountains from the south end of Muncho Lake Park, Mile 446 on the Alaska Highway. Close by we found a cache for storing rations out of the reach of grizzly bears — four trees fairly close together with a split plank platform about 20 feet off the ground. Each of the trees had huge fish hooks spiked to the trunks facing out so that any bear or wolverine trying to climb up would soon change its mind.

That night we zipped up our sleeping bags leaving only a small hole to breath through, but these holes soon plugged up so solid with mosquitoes you couldn't even see out. We each used our spray can of repellent in the hope of clearing them away, but it didn't take long before the hole was plugged tight again and we had to use some more of our precious spray. This kept up until three in the morning when the wind came in over the lake and blew those blood suckers away. Sleep was practically impossible. One night of this was certainly enough for us.

After an early breakfast we took our guns and headed out to different mountains where we had seen herds of Dall's sheep the previous evening. We agreed to be back at camp no later than three in the afternoon. I started off for the top of a mountain to inspect a stone cairn we had seen on the way in. Once up there, just over 7,000 feet above sea level, the view was breathtaking. Endless miles of high mountains — the feeling of utter freedom and awe I find impossible to describe. I felt about as small as a church mouse in a big hay field.

On the highest peak I found the stone cairn. Carved into a split piece of cedar sticking up in the middle were letters and figures which had been worn away and were illegible. But it was probably the original and only survey mark.

Close to the top I spooked two young grizzly bears apparently trying to dig out a colony of marmots. From half a mile away I could hear the rocks rolling down the mountain side and decided to make a detour and find out what was causing all this commotion. As I got closer I could plainly hear the high-pitched whistle of the marmots. Keeping my distance I saw several of these greyish brown, furry little creatures, the largest of the ground squirrels, sitting straight up on their hind legs whistling frantically, trying to draw the bears away from their burrows. But the bears just kept right on digging, rolling out boulders almost as big as themselves.

Further down I came upon a small alpine meadow where there were a dozen or more beautiful snow white ewes and lambs grazing. On a rocky knoll not more than 200 yards away there were several full curl rams watching me. I could see none that would really classify as trophies, so I just walked on.

Hoary marmots live as far north as Alaska and the Northwest Territories. They are found in areas so remote only hunters and hikers are likely to see them in the wild.

Lower down I watched several bull moose feeding in a swampy area. They showed no fear whatsoever, only curiosity. Pieces of tattered velvet were hanging loosely from their huge antlers. This was a sure sign the rutting season would soon be starting and the bulls would be sparring to see who was boss.

As the day progressed, dark clouds began forming to the north so I headed for camp. Walking around a dusty hillside I came across what few people, even hunters, ever see — a flat ledge packed down hard from constant use where the sheep lie facing the high side and slap their front hoofs continuously on the fine dirt to keep up a constant cloud of dust to keep away the mosquitoes. Over the years this procedure wears away the dirt directly in front of them and eventually at the base of the bank a ledge forms over their heads which helps contain the dust around their faces. This ledge must have been over a hundred feet long and reached at least 18 inches into the bank. The sheep come back to the same place year after year in the

Tom Garner with his Dall's sheep — not quite a trophy, but a beautiful specimen.

late spring, waiting for the snow to melt when they head up to higher ground to feed.

We were all back at camp before the agreed meeting time. Only Tom had got his ram. We grabbed a bite to eat, then quickly packed up and set off for Finlay Forks. Tom was soon out of sight in his bigger and faster plane.

Ted and I had not been airborne for long before we ran into a terrible thunderstorm with lightning flashing all around us. Then we ran into hail stones almost as large as golf balls. I felt quite sure the fabric cover on the body of the plane couldn't withstand such a pounding for long without suffering serious damage.

Visibility was poor and the air so turbulent I feared we would find ourselves flipped upside down at any minute. Ahead and to my left I saw a small lake and prepared to make a forced landing. As I lost altitude and circled to land, the hail turned into wet snow that was so heavy it became impossible to see out the windshield. Managing to keep the lake in view by looking out my side window, I put the plane in a side slip and to my relief made a perfect landing.

We tied up under cover of some trees by a dilapidated old log cabin. Carved on the log walls was the name "Fox Lake" and dozens of messages. The one I can still remember said: "I have finished eating my last dog. Temperature around 40 below. Three feet of snow outside. Heading S.E. Feb. 11, 1892. I doubt if I will make it. B.Collison."

This had been one of the stopping places on the trail going through into the Yukon during the gold rush days.

As we covered ourselves with our sleeping bags and got as comfortable as we could, me in the front seat, Ted in the back, we wondered how Tom was faring.

By morning the storm had blown over and I was pretty sure I could take off with no passenger, but I was doubtful about being able to do so with Ted aboard. I taxied to the far end of the small lake, less than half a mile away. I took off into the wind and barely cleared the tree tops. I knew now I could get off on my own but there was no way I would try it with my passenger.

As we cooked breakfast and sipped hot coffee, we heard the welcome whine of Tom's Cessna approaching from the north west. I dug out my red shirt and tied it to a long pole, and, waving it, walked into the clear so Tom could easily spot it from a distance. As he came into view he dipped his wings to let us know he had seen us. He circled the lake once, then landed in a tight side slip.

When he had tied up, his first words to me were, "What in hell are you doing here? There's no possible way you can get that thing off this little lake with the load you've got."

"Did you get lost?" I asked him. "And where did you spend the night?"

"About 40 miles from here on Johiah, a lake about twice this size, with a cabin to spend the night in."

"I can tell you one thing, Tom. I've already been out of this lake once this morning. But I know I can't make it out with two people."

Ted was already adding more bacon to the pan and I scrambled up half a dozen more eggs. As they ate, we discussed our situation. Finally Tom suggested, "Well, you take all the guns and I'll take Ted with me. But Joe, remember before you try to take off you'd better go behind a tree and lighten your load a bit."

At the windy end of the lake Tom tied one end of a short nylon rope around my left-hand back cleat. With the other end in his hand he walked around a small tree growing right at the edge of the lake and tied that end to the cleat on the other pontoon. As soon as my engine was warmed up I opened the throttle wide and gave Tom the signal for Bill to chop the rope, which was by now singing tight. My Piper Pacer leapt forward and was up on the step almost immediately. Even with all the guns aboard I was airborne before I was halfway down the lake, the short pieces of rope strung out behind. Keeping the engine at full throttle I again barely cleared the tree tops. I circled and watched as Tom, in his more powerful plane, took off with apparent ease. Without delay I headed straight for Finlay Forks and gas.

As Tom passed by minutes later, he dipped his wings and waved. I was close enough to see a big happy smile on his face.

I landed at the Forks and immediately removed the two pieces of rope and inspected the plane. I found a small tree top about as big as your finger stuck in between the left hand float and the metal guard. I had clipped the top of a tree coming out of Fox Lake. Three feet lower and I could have crashed.

When Tom walked over to shake my hand I asked him politely to check my hair for any grey ones. You see, he was already grey since his first flight into Chilco Lake years earlier, when his little Cessna could not take off at that high altitude and he had to leave his passenger behind and next day send a plane in from Vancouver to pick him up.

PART IV

FRIENDS, FAMILY AND COMMUNITY

O N THE MOUNTAIN each step was torture. I was barely able to take two or three at a time without stopping to rest. Because of the lack of food (which my diabetic condition required), and the excruciating pain, I was wondering if I was even rational. I had no way to judge. Just keep going. I had been in tough spots before — but nothing quite like this. Had my luck run out?

The Nanaimo River, fed by snow melt and rain at higher elevations where I'd left the vehicle, was close by on my left, bouncing along in the darkness. The only other sound was my aching feet scuffing chunks of gravel.

Slowly, fearful of every step, I inched my way along.

But something else was helping me.

Looking up through the trees that had been cut away when the road was built, I imagined I could actually see Virginia watching me from above. It was as though she was an angel guiding my every step. Otherwise I would surely have stumbled and fallen over the edge and onto the rocks below and I'd be finished. These thoughts gave me the strength and courage to keep going. Her presence kept me from the worst thing of all — panic!

Memories of family and friends passed through my mind.

FLYING AND FISHING FRIENDS

I FIRST MET my mother's cousin Ralph Edwards, the legendary pioneer made famous by several books, in Bella Coola. Tom and I were salmon fishing for the Tallheo Cannery and he was fishing for the Carlisle Cannery across the bay. That was 1927, when salmon were plentiful and you could fish five days a week.

Years later, when Tom and I had both got our pilot's licences and we had been appointed flying game wardens to look out for poachers in those back areas, we would occasionally fly in to visit him at Lonesome Lake. There his family fed and cared for a flock of rare trumpeter swans. He was so isolated we encouraged him to learn to fly. But to fly, he needed a plane. So, being Ralph, he built one, in itself an incredible accomplishment. He used whatever parts he could get hold of and on his own lathe he built those he couldn't get. It wasn't very well done, but it did fly.

When he figured he was ready to get his licence, he radiophoned Tom from Bella Coola to tell us he would be at the Vancouver airport the next day. Somehow he'd taught himself to fly. He flew down without a licence, without a Certificate of Airworthiness for his plane, without anything. The authorities didn't know how to handle this fellow.

He went up with an instructor while we watched and waited from the floating dock. He went through all of the flying tests, including spins and stalls, and at that time he was over sixty years old. The instructor got out, shaking so bad he had to walk around for a bit. As he walked we saw him shaking his head.

"I don't know what to do about this," he told us.

"Why don't you just give him a Certificate of Airworthiness after you go over the plane," I suggested. "He took you up, did all those things and came down and you're still very much alive."

"We've never seen anything like this one. And we've never checked out a pilot who has not had any instruction or training."

We took Ralph back to Tom's for the night and returned to the airport first thing the following morning. They had him do his written test and be checked over by the doctor at the airport. He passed his written test and his medical examination with flying colours. His eye test and physical test were equal to or better than ours, even though he was almost twenty-five years older.

They made him do another flight to be doubly sure he could land and take off in a safe manner. After they got through with him, the chief instructor thought it over and finally said, "I think the best thing to do is for Mr. Edwards to get into that plane and go back to where he came from. We'll give him his licence and his Certificate of Airworthiness. We don't know how to check the plane. It's homemade. We don't know how to check him, but he can certainly fly. We've never seen or heard of anything like this before, but we'll give him his papers and gladly let him go back to where he came from."

As we watched Ralph disappear through some clouds to the northwest, navigating only by his compass and altimeter, to fly back home through some of B.C.'s roughest mountains, the instructor turned and made this startling statement: "We don't want to admit that we've even seen him or his plane."

Soon after, we flew into Lonesome Lake again, hoping to go fishing or hunting grizzly with him. Ralph was there to help us tie up. His plane was spanking clean and looking good.

"How are you getting on?" we asked.

"I have no trouble if I don't try to buck the weather. If it isn't clear I stay put. Between here and Bella Coola at the coast, there's a thousand places I could crash. Even if they knew I'd gone down it's unlikely they'd ever find me."

JIM GILLESPIE was another wild guy we encouraged to fly, but unlike Edwards, who was quite a bit older and much more bush-wise.

Jim was logging on the east side of the old Youbou Road on a steep sidehill. I was logging on Bald Mountain across the bay to the west. I had just tied up to our float when Jim walked up.

"I'd sure like to go up for a flight and look the countryside over from the air," he said. "I've been thinking of buying myself a plane."

"Get in and I'll push off." When we were airborne I pushed a button and swung the controls over to his side. "Take her where you like. I'll be here to help if you get in any trouble." We crossed over the Youbou mill and circled back just above his spar tree.

"Why don't you fly down to the foot of Cowichan Lake and take a look at the village," I suggested. He needed no encouragement. Twenty minutes later I had landed back at our float. "You don't seem to be having any trouble flying, so why don't you get yourself a plane?"

Jim eventually owned five different types of aircraft, but his favourite was the old workhorse, a Beaver on floats. He equipped it to haul logging crews in and out of camps from the isolated islands north of Campbell River. Some of them had no other means of dependable transportation. The Beaver was also a flying ambulance. It had radio equipment costing $6,000 — an enormous sum — and it was the first float plane on the West Coast with a two-way Worsberg radio. He borrowed the down payment from the Bank of Commerce.

He flew in and out of camps, hauling crews, power saws, light machinery or injured men. He also did some falling, but there wasn't much money in that at the time, and he was in serious trouble with his loan payments. His bank finally agreed to let him make payments of $50 a month. They wrote a letter explaining that things were bad in the logging industry, so they'd let him make these token payments to show good faith.

He had only just started working steady for a gyppo — a small logger — in Boogey Bay when the outfit went broke, as so many did, victims of up-and-down log prices. Now the bank wasn't getting even its $50 a month. Apparently they lost faith. One morning he went out to check the floats for water and found the plane had been seized. There was a sheriff's sticker on the windshield. Before he could fly it to Victoria, the weather turned cold. His Beaver was frozen in solid. For the rest of that hard and unusually cold winter he was to be paid $100 a month plus board for looking after the busted camp.

In early March after breaking the ice he took off for Minstrel Island to pick up coal oil for the lamps and some stove oil to keep the cookhouse warm. After all, this is where he had to live.

"Where the hell did you come from?" he was asked after

he had tied up at Minstrel. There was ice and frost all over the plane.

"Boogey Bay, fifteen minutes away," Jim replied. "How about some kerosene and stove oil, and charge it to this Boogey Bay outfit?"

"Yeah, we'll help you out," was the reply, in the true spirit of the coast where goods were given and payment made as soon as money came in.

He flew back with 40 gallons of stove oil and a four gallon can of coal oil for the lamps.

That night the temperature dropped sharply again!

Next day a big blue police launch, on patrol out of Alert Bay, came crunching in. Jumping off onto the frosty planks of the dock in their shined boots and pressed uniforms, Gillespie counted seven officers. Someone had squawked, thinking he was chisel chartering. His log books weren't up to date. His medical had expired. His Certificate of Airworthiness had expired. Just about everything had expired except Jim's courage.

All bundled up and looking like Davey Crockett, wearing one of those raccoon hats with the tail hanging down his back, he met the Law and said, "You fellows are wasting your time in this bay. The Indians are all friendly in these parts. There hasn't been a scalping here for years."

"Is that your aircraft?" an officer asked.

"Yeah, I suppose you could call it mine."

"Constable Smith here is very interested in airplanes."

Not knowing quite what they were up to, Jim invited them to have a look around. Then the officer in charge said, "Gillespie, you're under investigation."

"Oh, am I?"

"Where's your log books?" he asked.

"I don't know where they are at the moment."

The policeman jumped in the back seat, and like a pack rat, was into everything.

"They're not in here," the officer snapped.

"Nobody said they were," Jim replied, getting tired of all this. "The reason they're not kept in the plane is because of the mice. They're paper-eating mice in this bay. They're very bad. You can't leave any loose paper around, 'cause it will be chewed up to make a nest in no time."

"Where's your medical?"

"It's not here either."

"Where's your pilot's licence?"

"Well, I don't have it with me at the moment. It's not kept

in the plane unless I'm flying," Jim answered, weary of this nonsense.

"We want to see these things," the officer said.

"I'll tell you what, sir. As soon as the ice goes, I'll fly right over to Alert Bay with them and save you people a long trip and save the taxpayer a lot of money for diesel, and save wear and tear on your nice big boat. How will that do, sir?"

"Thank you," he said ignoring the sarcasm. "We'll be waiting for you."

The big launch took off slowly, breaking the ice as it plowed out of the bay. When they were out of sight Jim just burst out laughing. They'd fallen for it.

As soon as the ice cleared, he flew out to Pat Bay. No point in waiting around. He probably wouldn't see a pay check anyway. At his hangar he found a letter from the chief inspector of the Department of Transport threatening to put him in jail for breaking air regulations. Without delay he phoned to tell them he'd be on the first ferry for Vancouver next morning.

With his log books and other expired papers in a briefcase, he strode into their office as soon as it opened.

"We're glad to see you," they said.

"It's a surprise to see you guys up so early in the morning," Jim said, smiling. "Now listen! I want to tell you people something. The plane was frozen in up there. As you might know, when things get that tough it's hard to live up to the letter of the law. I'll tell you something else. You can have a look at my log books. You can have a look at anything in here. I'm already in the process of getting a Certificate of Airworthiness at Pat Bay. I'm getting my medical fixed up this week. And something else, I'll bet I'm the only guy in the world that ever owned and flew a Beaver while on welfare."

"Bring your log books up to date," the chief inspector said and left the room. Left alone, Jim wrote down ten hours of local block flying and when they returned the chief inspector blew his cork.

"What did you do that for?"

"You asked me to bring the log books up to date. Now you're mad because I've suddenly turned honest. There's another thing you're suspicious of. You think I'm crazy, don't you? Let's bring a doctor in here right now."

They did, from another department in the same building.

"I suppose you've got me under surveillance too," Jim said to the doctor. "Do you think I'm crazy?"

"No, no, not a bit." he spluttered.

148

"Well then, state here that I'm fit to fly for sixty days. I'm having my medical checkup in Victoria this week."

He wrote out a special permit that declared Jim fit to fly. This was just what was needed. With the permit and his log books, Jim went downstairs and got a pilot's permit, a ferry permit and a test flight permit, all in one.

"You owe me $37," the clerk said.

"I've only got $17 to get the bus back to the ferry and on to Victoria. Would you take a man's last dollar?"

"No, I wouldn't. I'll just send you a bill."

That evening, Jim put the Beaver inside the hangar. Next morning another sticker was pasted on the windshield, but the sheriff didn't have the keys. The once friendly Bank of Commerce was getting mean.

That night, with the help of a mechanic, Jim stripped the Beaver of all its moveable parts. Out came the engine with the propeller attached. Next the seats, doors and all the radio equipment. By morning the plane was stripped bare and the parts were hidden in an old barn.

Jim went to the bank and gave the manager a letter stating that he had his half of the Beaver in safe keeping. They couldn't charge him with theft. Airport security, of course, took a very dim view of all this.

Jim was hauled into court four times. The Beaver and Jim became a major topic at the Bank of Commerce regular meetings in Vancouver. They had people searching everywhere for the missing parts. The bank was screaming mad. They demanded the equipment and the log books.

Jim, canny and cunning, moved the engine several times. Once, when it was on top of a flat-roofed building, everyone thought it was the fan for the cooling system.

Jim told me once, "You should never fly a plane with the log books in it when you have it heavily financed. Unless the log books and registration papers are with the plane it can't be transferred without going to court. You see, if they seize the plane, you're still the owner. The log books are the key."

Judge Cashman held an examination for discovery on Jim.

"You had a discovery on Mr. Gillespie last year?" Jim's lawyer pointed out.

"Yes," replied Mr. Johnson, the bank manager.

"Did you ask for the parts back?"

"No, we didn't."

"Mr. Johnson, have you ever considered that if you give a person enough time, matters can correct themselves?"

149

Jim and his lawyer went over to the bank for a talk with Mr. Johnson

"Mr. Johnson, I'll tell you what I'll do. As soon as I get that plane back together, I'll fly it up to camp and work off the debt I owe the bank."

"I'll tell you something," the bank manager countered, "If we ever get our hands on that plane we'll take our losses and get the hell out of this mess."

When they got outside, Jim told his lawyer, "I'm going to do something behind your back."

"Christ, what are you up to this time, Jim?"

"Well, anything else I've done behind your back has worked out all right. I'm going over to the head office of the Bank of Commerce in Vancouver and ask them for $20,000 to put this plane back together. They can cut the old loan in half, write off all the interest, and I'll make four lump sum payments in four years."

"You've got to be nuts to try that. They'll throw you out."

"Just you wait and see."

He arrived at their Vancouver head office unannounced. They brought down Mr. Quinn, their regional manager.

"He looked just as I figured he would," Jim told me. "Nice white hands and dressed like a pallbearer."

He took him up to his private office where Jim declared, "You know, Mr. Quinn, fraud is a very serious offence. I'm over here to try and save you from going to jail. You tried to collect $60,000 from your insurance company over the loss of half that plane when you knew that I had my half of it in safekeeping. I personally brought you a letter to that effect. I stopped the insurance company from paying because I felt sorry for them being defrauded out of their money. They've cancelled your insurance since then and you know that."

Quinn sat there, stiff as a statue.

"What I want from you, sir, is $20,000 to put this Beaver back together. Cut the old loan in half and take the interest right off. Then four lump sum payments over four years will clear my debt."

"I'm going to have Mr. Graham come in here," Quinn said, as he picked up his intercom. Graham was the guy who had refused to even talk to Jim a few days earlier.

Graham, looking none too happy when he saw Jim, listened and then Quinn walked out of the office.

"I'll phone you my decision in the morning," the loan manager offered, knowing he was in trouble.

Next morning he phoned, "We've agreed to pay you $15,000, cut the loan in half and have you make four lump sum payments, with no payment the first year."

Back in his lawyer's office, Jim told him about the deal. He looked at Jim for a full minute before saying, "There's no way you could ever do that."

"Phone him and see."

He did, speaking to Johnson, who at that very moment was signing the cheque. It arrived later that day at the lawyer's office. He phoned Jim to come right over. Now!

"Take three grand and keep your hands off the rest of it," Jim told him. He made out a cheque for $12,000 and Jim immediately took it to The Royal Bank. He walked in, signed the cheque in front of the teller and asked for cash.

"We're not authorized to hand out this amount of cash over the counter," the teller told him. "But wait."

Three important-looking men came to the counter. All Jim wanted was his $12,000, made out on the account of a respected city lawyer.

"You want to make a deposit?" one asked.

"No."

"You want a draft?"

"No. Hell, I just want the cash. Just $12,000 on a perfectly good cheque. This is a bank, isn't it? Haven't you got that much money?"

"Can you come back in twenty minutes?"

"After you give me a receipt for the cheque," Jim said.

On his return they asked him to follow them into a back room. There must have been a million dollars stacked up like bundles of wood on one table and a woman in a cage with a round-shaped window that looked like a toilet seat. She put two bundles on a machine and it just spun around with numbers flashing, looking like a chicken-plucker.

She pushed the money down under the window and Jim just kept pulling it out and stuffing it into the little onion bag he'd brought along.

"I'd do the same thing if I ever won the Irish Sweepstakes," Jim told her, annoyed at all this foolishness.

"Well, make sure you don't come here," she quickly responded.

Jim went directly back to Pat Bay airport to the hangar where they had his stripped down Beaver.

"Would you move her out of here, please?" Jim asked.

"Sure, Mr. Gillespie."

151

He and his mechanic put a big tent over the Beaver, then went to the old barn and collected the missing parts. The engine had to be completely rebuilt. It was much worse then anyone had expected.

"No sane person would even consider flying with that engine," they told him at the repair shop. "It has over 3,000 hours on it. These engines are required to be completely rebuilt after 1,400 hours of use."

But what the hell. Jim decided he'd try and get a partner with some money. As luck would have it a guy from Alaska named Steve Butler put up $25,000 and the engine was completely rebuilt piece by piece. They put the whole thing back together and got a Certificate of Airworthiness.

Then Jim went to work at Jackson Pass — for another gyppo who went belly up. Back to Port Hardy. Back on welfare. But word got around town. There was a bush pilot on welfare who was flying a Beaver float plane. The local welfare officer got word of this and held up Jim's cheque. They brought an inspector up from Victoria.

"You know this is fraud," he accused Jim. "I understand you own a Beaver aircraft."

"Yes, that's almost right. I'll take you down and show it to you. But do you know what's owing against it? More than it's worth. That plane is not an asset, it's a goddamn liability."

Jim had the loan documents with him. He showed the inspector what he owed the bank, his lawyer and his partner.

The inspector seemed not only puzzled but nervous, as he handed Jim his welfare cheque. That afternoon Jim walked uptown looking for work. No luck. Tough times. When he went back to the dock to check his plane the next morning, all he saw was dock space and two ropes floating in the water.

Someone had flown the Beaver out at daylight. The island bailiffs had had it flown to Vancouver and locked it in a hangar.

After sixty days he transferred that plane, still seized and locked in a hangar in Vancouver, because he had the log books and the registration papers. He conveyed it over for one dollar to his partner, Steve Butler.

Steve phoned the bank, saying, "I own that Beaver, I'm coming down with a certified cheque to redeem it." For $80,000 he got himself a $150,000 airplane.

Then another guy who'd heard about this Beaver flew down from northern B.C. in his rebuilt twin 310 Cessna worth at least $50,000. He gave Steve his Cessna and a cheque for $90,000 and flew the Beaver north.

So Steve had a twin 310 Cessna and $10,000 in the bank. Not a bad return on his original $25,000 investment. Jim was out from under his debt. And the bank had their $80,000.

THEN THERE WAS Bud Cloake. I met him at Harrison Hot Springs in 1960 when he was chief of the Pacific Indian Trapshooting Club. Much later he told me, "I was one of the three pilots considered when President Truman's military advisors had to decide who was to fly the Enola Gay and drop that first atomic bomb on Hiroshima. I'm certainly grateful it wasn't me they chose," Bud admitted.

STEVE TREMPER, a helicopter specialist, was also involved in historical high drama. He joined our regular group on big game hunts in the B.C. interior. In the early fall of 1962, Steve called me to confirm that he'd be flying in to join us. As things turned out, he would arrive a bit late.

On October 25, 1962, Steve was in Washington, D.C., with other top advisors as President John F. Kennedy faced the Cuban missile crisis. J.F.K. had informed Soviet President Nikita Krushchev that if his missile-laden ships crossed a specified line in the Caribbean Sea the United States Air Force would halt them, one way or another. At 10:20 a.m. on the 28th, a few minutes before the deadline was reached, the Russian convoy commander turned his fleet around and a potentially catastrophic conflict was averted.

Within two years, Kennedy would be assassinated, and Krushchev would be removed from office by his enemies in Moscow.

Steve Tremper arrived the day after the crisis, a nervous wreck. I met his small plane at the short air strip just south of the town of Clinton with our 4-wheel drive jeep. As well as his rifle, he had his hunting bow and arrows with him and he placed them carefully on the back seat within reach, saying, "Just in case some big buck gets curious on the way in."

"I can't get the whole thing off my mind," he said. "The world was just that close to a nuclear war." He talked of little else on the way back to camp.

At daybreak the rest of the gang took off to hunt higher up the mountain. But, because Steve was obviously upset and nervous, I stayed with him. We scouted along a side hill not far from camp to a big fir tree overlooking the valley below. I told him, "Just sit here with your rifle and rest while I swing around through this valley. I'll try and drive a deer or sheep up your way."

It took close to an hour and a half to make the circuit down over the rocks, through green meadows and trees and back up towards Steve, and then I spooked a big buck out of a thicket. It took off straight up the mountain. A few minutes later there was a volley of shots. I was certain Steve had got himself a good one. When I got there Steve was sitting under the tree where I'd left him.

"You missed him?" I exclaimed, amazed.

"Yeah, I think I was nowhere near him, Joe. Couldn't keep the rifle steady."

For the next few days Steve just sat under that big fir near camp, seeing nothing, alone with his thoughts. When he combed his hair each morning great clumps came out in his comb. The man was in worse shape than we'd originally thought. But he pulled himself together, shot his deer and felt much better.

By now the Russian fleet would be far out in the Atlantic headed for home. I've often wondered, based on Steve's actions, if the media really knew how critical the situation had been. Perhaps they did not know everything about the ins-and-outs of this ride to the brink of annihilation.

Steve certainly knew. He was there. But it was top secret and no subject for fireside chat after a day's hunting in our magnificent wilderness — as far from the corridors of power as it is possible to get.

WHEN THE STEELHEAD were running up the local rivers to spawn, George Syrotuck would drop whatever he was doing, sometimes to later face the displeasure of an irate housewife who had counted on her floor being finished yesterday. He would head for one of his favourite fishing holes, oblivious to the woman's concern for her furniture stacked on the porch.

George would take a skein of salmon roe, and cure it by alternately sprinkling it with salt and brown sugar, and then chuck it into his freezer. Properly cured roe in flowing water trails a "smoke", smelling like freshly dropped salmon eggs.

He'd impale a gob of roe on a hook and secure it by winding some fine red thread around it. This would help hold his bait together for at least a dozen casts. He called these "Syrotuck sandwiches", and many a steelhead was fooled into thinking they'd make a delicious snack.

George has been dead now for twenty-five years. He suffered a heart attack while he was fighting a huge spring salmon at Cowichan Bay. He was in the back of the boat with his wife, Hilma, up front. Suddenly he slumped over. A nearby fisherman who saw what had happened hauled in the salmon and towed his boat to the wharf. From there an ambulance rushed him to the Duncan hospital. He was pronounced dead on arrival.

He was luckier than most, he died doing something that gave him great pleasure. I miss the man. We had fished and hunted together for over thirty years.

DENIS HAGAR was another close friend who loved fishing and hunting. He was a partner in the financial firm of Hagar & Swayne. Denis and I would meet for lunch at the Union Club in Victoria, and always the conversation got around to our annual hunting trip. We would normally pick a day in November.

I've noticed that men spend an awful lot of quiet time on hunting trips thinking and talking about women. Sitting with Denis one sunny afternoon on a ridge overlooking Sheep Flats, he obviously had something on his mind, so I asked him, "Anything wrong?"

"Joe, you're looking at a bankrupt man, but a happy one."

"You want to explain that?"

"Just last week I finally got my divorce. The courts have given my wife just about everything I own. On the other hand, I'm now free to marry "Highpockets", the woman I've loved for years."

Denis was well over six feet tall and he gave Carol her nickname; when they stood side by side her pockets were level with his.

"Well, it seems to me you're pretty lucky, Denis," I told him. "Making money has never been a problem for you. You've just got to go out and make some more. If "Highpockets" makes you a happy man, you can't lose." Denis just smiled as if to thank me for listening.

Denis phoned one day, in 1981 according to my diary, and asked me to join him for a day's fishing. We headed out from the Maple Bay wharf into Sansum Narrows. He didn't look at all well and we did more talking than fishing. Within a week, he was dead, a massive heart attack. I'll always remember one story he told.

One autumn his partner's son brought home to their estate in Ireland an Indian prince who was a fellow student. His friend really wanted to catch a big salmon.

The gamekeeper, a master of profane language, would guide the prince. He had been carefully instructed on how to address and handle himself while in the presence of this visitor.

"You must, at all times, address him as "Your Majesty". He has done very little fishing. Be patient, and, above all, don't swear," he was told.

Few words passed between them as they walked down the well-beaten trail to the fishing hole.

"Your Majesty, you see that big boulder out there. The salmon are lying in a deep hole just below it. You must cast your bait above and on the far side of the rock, and then let it drift down into the hole. When the fish strikes, Your Highness, you must set your hook and keep your rod tip high." On his second cast a salmon struck. The prince set his hook as instructed. It was one big fish, and even the gamekeeper became excited.

"Your Majesty, keep your rod tip high."

As the fish leaped out of the water, the excited gamekeeper yelled, "Keep you rod tip up, sir, up, up, or you'll lose it."

On the second time around the pool, the salmon again leapt and shook the lure free. Exasperated, the gamekeeper shouted, "You black son-of-a-bitch, you lost it," and he walked away in disgust.

The prince has told this story in many places around the world. A good sport, if not a good fisherman.

THEODORE VINCENT SANDYS-WUNSCH, who would be our neighbour when we moved onto Maple Bay Road, was an interesting fellow and a fine fisherman. When Sandy retired in 1946, he was the assistant commissioner of the Mounties in Manitoba.

Sandy's marksmanship with a handgun was legendary. He was twice named to represent the Canadian team to the Bisley competitions in England. He did well against some of the British Commonwealth's finest shots. Returning from one of those competitions, he astonished the ship's passengers by shooting the spots off playing cards from about thirty feet away. He also set a world record with his .45 calibre revolver for consecutive bullseye's, which to my knowledge, has never to this day been beaten, but has been tied.

Sandy's passion was fly fishing. He would study the insects the trout were feeding on and then go home and tie some flies that looked as much like them as possible. He'd then go back to the river and usually bring home his limit. As far as I know, he never used anything but his own homemade flies. Some of you may remember the photographs of dry flies on the back of Sportsman cigarette packages in the forties and fifties. Some of those flies were tied by Sandy and he was proud to show them to anyone who might drop in.

He was convinced most fish feed both day and night contrary to many opinions. Sandy would fish the Cowichan River in the pitch dark. He normally used a jet black fly and most always came home with as many trout as he wanted. But Sandy's wife didn't like trout, so their three big house cats were fat and happy.

At first he was opposed to using Quamichan Lake as an air base, but a few trips over to St. Mary's Lake on Saltspring where the bass fishing was excellent soon changed Sandy's opinion about float flying.

MAPLE BAY ROAD

ON JUNE 1, 1951, we moved to the big house where Bob Whittome had lived and raised his family — the one I'd got with a low offer and a lot of patience. Located on seven acres it bordered on Quamichan Lake to the north and the land extended a short distance across Maple Bay Road on the south where it shared a common boundary with St. Peter's Anglican Church. The one-acre piece across the road I later gave to the church.

Our next-door neighbours were the Thorpes on the east and the Sandys-Wunschs on the west.

The house was close to the road with the driveway along the south side. We always drove in the east gate and drove out the west gate. There was a short, steep hill just inside the exit and that autumn we put a steel gate across it to stop the kids from sliding out onto the road if it snowed.

The easterly end of the driveway passed by a small barn with three stalls, just big enough to hold one horse and a couple of milk cows.

As soon as we were nicely settled, Pat wanted to start a major remodelling job of the kitchen and dining room — women always do. Both were finished in 1 x 4 V-joint stained a dark brown. The dining room had only one small narrow window on the east wall which we closed in and put in a new 4 x 8 plate glass window facing north out over the garden and on down to the lake — a beautiful view all year.

Pat was pregnant again, and our second son, Edwin, was born early in December, six months after we moved into our new home.

I built a brick fireplace in our living room with big wood-

The young Garner family: from left, Joanne, Pat, Eddie, Dana and Tom, taken in 1952.

boxes, one on each side. Joanne and Tom, then Ed when he was older, would sneak in through an outside door, open the inside door and jump out into the livingroom. They played for hours on end in those boxes.

WHILE ALL THIS was being done I brought in our TD14 bulldozer and the Insley shovel and built a good road between the barn and the house and on down to the lake. With the backhoe attachment on the shovel, we dug a channel deep and wide enough to bring our float plane into a hangar at all times of the year. The lake could be more than three feet lower by the end of summer. The hangar had to be constructed over this wide excavation so that the aircraft could be turned and backed in. This would leave our little plane facing out and ready for takeoff.

My best foreman, Bill Brown and I looked the job over before we started.

"It's not going to be easy with one side on solid ground and the other out in the muskeg," I told him.

"Now, Joe, just go away and leave us alone if you expect me to build this hangar. Just get lost for a while."

Bill Brown worked all weekend putting up the hangar walls while his crew built the roof trusses. By next afternoon he not only had the trusses up, but the metal roofing on and nailed down. I taxied the Piper Pacer over with a couple of log floats in tow. Bill put the specially-built floats in place along one side of the channel and into the hangar. He stood on the float and turned the plane around, then backed it into its new home. The wing tips cleared each wall with less than a foot to spare. Everything fit perfectly.

THE NEXT DAY I flew out to Brentwood Bay. General George Perkes, who became Minister of National Defence in John Diefenbaker's Progressive Conservative government, lived there. He told me they needed a complete water system for that community near Victoria and he asked if I would look the job over.

He met me at the Brentwood Bay boat basin. I studied his drawings covering the project and he showed me the six inch wood stave pipes and all the other equipment on site. He offered a cost plus ten percent contract and I told him we would start the job that same week.

Brentwood Bay was rough when I taxied out for takeoff. The seas were so high the propeller was actually touching the water at the bottom of the trough. I had to take off diagonally across the waves and at an angle to the wind rather than head directly into them. I made it, but more by good luck than good management. It was fortunate I didn't have a passenger with me because I'm sure the extra weight could well have swamped the plane. When I told this to Tom he looked at me with his crooked smile: "Better smarten up, Joe, if you want to live a bit longer."

THE NORTH END of Indian Road had become a favourite parking spot for young couples and the clubhouse had twice been ransacked by local hoodlums.

I had never charged the Aero Club for building it, so in the interests of safety I decided to move the clubhouse onto my property, less than 100 yards away. We slid two big timbers under the jacked-up building and put two heavy cross timbers at each end and bolted them solid. Two cable straps the same length were hooked to these timbers. The following morning we hooked the cable straps onto the drumline and as we tightened up we drove ahead with the bulldozer. The clubhouse followed like a well-trained dog.

Our neighbour Sandys-Wunsch, or Sandy as we called him, had given us permission to cross his property, which he had bought in 1946 from Bob Whittome's parents. This was the only private land between ours and Indian Road. It took less than an hour to drag the building over and put it in place.

We had earlier brought in our logging crew to take out all the big trees that looked dangerous. They loaded the logs and hauled them out over the new road down to our log dump at Cowichan Bay. I had the stumps cut off near the ground at the exact same height. The clubhouse, which was to be our new gardner's home, was carefully lifted onto its new foundations with the shovel. These fir stumps made a mighty solid foundation.

There were no more worries with the clubhouse and the aircraft now safe on our property. The land the flying club had leased from Mrs. Leather is now the Kinsmen Park, a credit to the community. It is a popular place for family picnics. Children and adults alike get a thrill when the wild swans, geese and mallards come right up and take grain or bread from their outstretched hands.

WE MOVED the Whittakers from their house at the north end of Quamichan Lake into their new quarters at our place. Mrs.

Whittaker helped Pat with the housework and did our babysitting. Her husband acted as watchman for the aircraft, looked after the chickens and the sheep, and did some gardening. I remember he always carried some candies in his pockets to reward the youngsters when they helped him with some small task. It was a lovely place to live and everyone seemed happy doing their own thing.

Mr. Whittaker loved his radio. If Walkmans had been available back then he would have been plugged in as he did his chores. One year he got very interested in contests that required you to send the answer to the sponsoring company with a box top, soup label or some other proof of purchase. I always bought case lots of supplies for our logging camps and stored them in our old chicken house at home. One weekend I checked inside the little building and found a whole case of soap boxes, Rinso I think it was, which he'd cut the tops off. At least once a month he'd walk into Duncan to check the contest results, and send in more.

"Anything this week, Mr. Whittaker?" I'd ask.

"Not this week, Mr. Garner. But it's fun you know, an 'armless 'obby.''

Every member of our family remembers the six years on Maple Bay Road as some of our happiest years together — especially the three older children. They had rabbits, chickens, sheep, dogs, cats and various other critters.

Since we had the barn and grazing land we got Dana a riding horse. She had learned to ride as a day boarder at Queen Margaret's private school, and she was thrilled when we bought her a big brown gelding she called "Kitimat". He was a well-trained and good-natured horse that any of the younger children could enjoy.

Kitimat usually chose to cooperate with his rider, but he was getting on in years. Dana was young and full of energy and wanted to ride for hours at a stretch. She wanted to train for hunter trials which meant a lot of jumping. The jump we constructed on the Sandys-Wunsch's property was not more than two feet high; no great obstacle for a young horse. But old Kitimat, after a few jumps, would tire and balk, planting his feet firmly in front of the bar and Dana would sometimes fly right over his head. A yell of "No, Kitimat!" usually indicated her horse had done it again.

Dana spent many hours grooming and caring for this gentle animal, but the other children didn't dare go into the barn and mess around with her horse or she would get furious.

Dana on her horse "Kitimat".

The neighbourhood children came over in the spring to watch the lambs, their little docked tails wiggling while they happily nursed. But if a strange dog came near, the mothers nudged their lambs behind them and started stamping their front feet. It was quite a sight, and a good nature lesson.

The tree house was a constant source of pleasure to our boys and their friends. I helped them put up a solid floor. Then they took over and put up the walls, not very straight or square but they managed to put a roof over it. At their age it was quite an accomplishment. It was about seven feet off the ground, so we made a rope ladder that went up to a little hatch door. It seemed frightfully high to the smaller children, yet they always managed to scramble up somehow.

Bobby Low, our minister's son, lived across the road and spent a lot of time up in that tree house with Tom and Joanne. His sister Penny was Dana's friend and, like Dana, she also liked horses and riding more than a tree house.

I encouraged the children to plant a garden each year by giving a prize of one silver dollar for the best garden and fifty cents for the second prize. Our big family garden was well fenced to keep the horse and sheep out and Mr. Whittaker gave each child a plot close to the path. The soil was jet black and would grow almost anything. They planted carrots, radishes, green peas and always a few pumpkins. They'd start with all kinds of enthusiasm, but when the weeds, which did better in the soil than the vegetables, got high and the sun got hot they never quite worked their "land" the way they should. Understandably, our gardener got fed up when the kids lost interest.

I OFTEN took the children up in the plane to do a couple of circles over Quamichan Lake and the house. Tom and Joanne were a bit nervous when I'd side-slip it down for the landing. I occasionally took Joanne and Tom on trips up over the mountain ranges to the West Coast where we could fish in the little lakes rarely visited and full of trout. The flight took about forty minutes and was a very big deal. On the other hand, Saltspring Island was only ten minutes away, and in the evenings we could catch half a dozen bass and be home before dark. We'd park the plane on St. Mary's Lake and rent a boat. We always cleaned the fish before heading for home. These were great outings for our children, always learning more about nature. I guess they were luckier than most youngsters.

Sometimes I took Tom's friend, Chuck Coleman, with us. He was a good rower, whereas Tom couldn't handle the oars without splashing and likely scaring the fish. Occasionally we dropped in at Ganges to buy chocolate bars to eat on the way home. The kids thought nothing of it. They seemed to think everyone did this kind of thing.

Later, when we took trips into Chilco Lake far up in the remote Chilcotin country, I taught Tom and his friend Bo Reynolds, who was the youngest son of our accountant, to spin cast. These well-planned trips usually lasted about a week and gave us memories we'd never forget. When all the kids were along we took the station wagon, giving them another view of the wonderland of forest and mountains we lived in.

I REMEMBER one trip into Chilco Lake with Sandys-Wunsch. We were at the "Blue Hole", just below our lodge where the big trout usually gathered. They were rising but not taking any fly we offered. We could see they were going for the black ant hatch, and I didn't have any. Sandy dug around in his tackle box and handed me two black flies, saying, "Try them."

"Maybe I'd better tie both on at once!" I joked and made a two-hook setup on my three-pound test leader. First cast, nothing. On the second, two big trout came up from the bottom and each grabbed a fly. Securely hooked and mad, they tore around the pool like a team of wild horses.

I tightened the drag, keeping my rod tip high, but I was helpless, or hopeless, against their strength. Eventually, tired, both trout dove to the bottom, and burned out my reel on their way down. They just lay there sulking. With a bum reel I could do nothing, but we had the last laugh. Carefully, very carefully, pulling the line up hand over hand, we eased the exhausted fish to the surface and netted them. We now had all the fish we wanted, so we packed up our gear and headed for home.

It was a clear, smooth flight down the Homathko River and across the top end of Georgia Strait, to Campbell River and on down the coast to Duncan. On that trip home Sandy told me, "My son, John, tells me he's planning to go into the ministry. I don't know what to think about this, Joe."

"Well," I said, "if he's sure that's what he wants, it will probably work out. I've noticed when people get a chance to do what they really want to do, they are usually successful at it."

John went on to obtain a Doctorate in Theology, and become President of a liberal arts college in Sudbury, Ontario. I'm sure Sandy would have been proud of his achievements. Several years later, when he was at St. John's Anglican Church in Victoria, Reverend John Sandys-Wunsch conducted the burial service for Mr. Whittaker, a man he loved to chat with when he was just a teenager.

BILLY HANSON, who lived just down the road, was one year older than Tom and a year younger than Joanne. They played together most of the time.

When I got home from work January 19, 1954, I was met at the door by Joanne and Tom. I knew something was wrong. They didn't do the usual "sack of potatoes" greeting, wrapping themselves around my legs and riding down the hallway on my boot tops. They could only talk of Billy. In a flood of words, it all came out.

Tom and Joanne had been sleigh riding behind our house. The snow was thin so they decided to go to Billy's and slide on the little private road outside his house. That hill wasn't very steep so when Bobby Low joined them they decided to go to a short, steep hill that ran from St. Peter's Church past the rectory and down to Tzouhalem Road which went through the Indian reserve to Cowichan Bay.

"We were sliding right across the road," Tom told me. "When we got to the bottom we could have turned into a little field to the right, but instead we just kept on going till we hit the snowbank on the other side of the road.

"Joanne had been riding with Billy and I was riding with Bobby, but this time, when Billy asked her, she said 'No, it's getting too cold, I don't want to go. I'm going home.'

"It was just starting to get dark as I watched him go down," Tom recalled. "I had my sleigh ready, 'cause it was my turn next. Then an Indian girl at the bottom of the hill screamed, 'Look out, there's a car coming.' But Billy didn't hear her, or couldn't stop. He slid right out onto the road and into the front bumper of one of Kyle's taxis. We ran home and phoned Mum. She was up at a friend's."

Tom has never forgotten the image of Billy lying there perfectly still on the road. His little dark brown hat with a chin strap that was still buttoned up was laying on the road.

Billy never regained consciousness. He was transferred to Vancouver General Hospital where he died almost a month later on February 17. After the autopsy, a verdict of "accidental death with no blame attached to anyone" was handed down by the coroner's jury. The thought that we had been so close to losing a second daughter was a real shock to both Pat and myself.

OUR YOUNGEST SON Gerry was born November 13, 1954. We named him after Pat's nephew, Gerry Howe, who was an R.C.M.P. officer. A few year's earlier Gerry had come to me with a special problem.

"Uncle Joe," he said, "I need a job."

"Thought you had a job, Gerry. You tired of police work already?"

"No. I love it, but I'm in a very dangerous situation. I've been working for a year undercover on the drug squad and we've recently made one of the biggest busts the province has known. When the court case is over I've got to get out of Vancouver. Probably best that I get out of the force altogether. Some underworld characters would like to see me dead. There's a bounty on me dead or alive."

"Are you good with numbers?" I asked. "Our bookkeeper needs some help."

"I was good at math in high school," Gerry replied, "and I guess I could learn a lot about business from Earl Reynolds. I know I could work with him, no problem."

Gerry proved to be an excellent student. With a sound understanding of logging economics he moved to Quesnel a few years later and bought into my brother Al's logging business and did very well.

Pat, meanwhile, had decided she would like to have our Gerry christened by Reverend Low. On the big day, we got the kids all dressed up, marched them across the road to St. Peter's Church and sat in a pew near the front. Pat and I went up to the font with baby Gerry.

Eddie, who had been bored and fidgety since we arrived, slipped away. That little rascal found a rope to swing on. There was now, of course, no secret about where he was. In the middle of the christening the church bell started pealing. We always like to believe Eddie had chosen his own way to announce that, in the eyes of the Church, his little brother now had a name.

I STARTED TO TEACH the children about guns. Always keep a gun pointed at the ground and never under any circumstances do you point it at anyone. They got mad because I wouldn't even allow them to point cap guns at each other. Perhaps I was a bit paranoid, but I had reason to be.

I bought Tom a 20-gauge shot gun for his eleventh birthday. He liked shooting at targets and was good, but he never liked hunting. Years later Tom recalled a duck hunting trip to Brooks, Alberta. "You know, Dad, what I enjoyed most about that trip was watching those flocks of ducks, hundreds of them, flying into the fields. I still remember the sound of their wings whistling as they came in to land. I would have been happier with a camera, but I didn't tell you that at the time."

When there was a fall of fine dry snow, which doesn't happen often on Vancouver Island, I would bundle up the children and take them tracking coons. These furry and wise beggars will rob any nest of its eggs and can clean out a chicken house overnight. We'd head up the Cowichan River until we hit fresh tracks. If the trail split, Joanne and Tom would follow one way and Ed and I, with Gerry on my shoulders, would follow the other.

Sylvia, our German pointer, would follow along at my heels. Eventually we'd track a coon to its hideout in a hollow log, or maybe up a tree.

The tracking of the animals through fresh snow in the silent beautiful forest was both a pleasure and an education for the kids. But Joanne and Tom both found the shooting of these animals quite upsetting. Joanne was often shedding tears as she reluctantly dragged her "trophy" back to the car. On one occasion we had the skins cured and made into coon skin hats by a taxidermist.

UNFORTUNATELY Pat didn't enjoy flying. She once took a bumpy ride with me to Vancouver and made the trip home by ferry. But she would sometimes wave when I circled the house before landing and send the kids down to the lake to welcome me. She recalls seeing me leaving one morning for Lake Cowichan where I had breakfast and attended to some business. I had a luncheon meeting in Vancouver with Jack Sexton, the log comptroller for MacMillan Bloedel. From there I phoned to tell her I'd be having supper with brother Al at Quesnel, another Cariboo Country town which was beginning to boom as the logging, lumber and pulp industries were all working around the clock.

I was away quite a bit during our married life due to the spread out nature of our businesses. Home on weekends I wanted to take Pat and the children on hikes or fishing trips and I became annoyed when Pat would never be a part of it. She'd willingly pack a lunch, but hiking and fishing was not her thing. I feel she missed a lot by not joining in with us. One of the excursions the kids especially enjoyed was our annual Easter lily hunt. They'd bring along their friends, and usually their cousin Wendy English would come along. We'd head up Mount Prevost west of Duncan and pick bunches of lilies, then make a fire and eat our lunch.

On one of these lily hunts Joanne saw a black bear cub scooting up a smallish fir tree. The youngsters were excited but I was anxious. There are few things nastier than a mother bear who thinks her cub is in danger, and I had spotted her in some salal not fifty feet away. Trouble with a capital "T".

"Hustle back the way we came," I shouted. "Now, and I mean right now. Get going. Fast. Mother bear's getting angry."

Bobby Low was usually a bit of a cutup but he was really scared and headed down the muddy trail fast. The other kids followed. In fact, Bobby ran right out of both his shoes when he ran through a muddy spot! But he kept right on going. When I got to the station wagon carrying his shoes, the kids were having a big laugh at Bobby's expense, and they didn't stop giggling until we were home.

But they'd all learned a good lesson about mother bears. They don't run away if they feel their cubs are in danger. You run.

BY THE EARLY FIFTIES, Garner Bros. was virtually out of the construction business. The boom days were dwindling down. We now had over half a dozen logging shows operating in various parts of the province and Garner Builders' Supplies was expanding monthly under Joe Gergel's management. Joe and his wife, Lea, had bought our house at the corner of

Alington and Sherman roads.

Five years later, pleased with his management of the store business, the possibility of him buying me out seemed right. Nothing down, and a monthly payment which the bookkeeper worked out to be the same as the store telephone number. In those days it was only three figures — 694. We signed the papers in 1960 and that ended another successful business chapter in my life. The marriage of Garner Builders' Supplies with Beaver Lumber in 1993 saw the demise of our old store and the opening of a big new store and warehouse on the Island Highway just north of Duncan.

But I seemed to be kept busier than ever because of community activities. There was always something more to do if we were willing to make the time to do it. Life was full. Too full, perhaps. I never stopped running.

ONE COULD GO back to the late 1940s when the directors of the Cowichan Exhibition couldn't borrow the money to hire a contractor to enlarge the showing area and improve the parking lot. It had to be completed fast or there would be no exhibition that year. The exhibition buildings were on Indian Reserve land, so the banks wouldn't lend them more money. Garner Bros. volunteered to help the district out of a tight spot. Late on a Friday afternoon we moved our bulldozers in, and our experienced operators got the job done that weekend.

I'VE ALWAYS believed that the Rotary motto "Service Above Self" conveys a powerful message for its members to live by. I joined the Duncan Rotary Club in 1948 and was acting president three years later.

Jack Long was elected president and I vice-president. After his first meeting, Jack was hospitalized for the entire year. I went with his wife to pick him up from the hospital for the final meeting and I sat beside him as he took over the chair. Jack was a wonderful Rotarian and I'm sure he treasured his president's pin. My year as acting president meant I was unable to carry on as president the following year since Rotary regulations state you cannot serve as president for more than one term.

ON JANUARY 28TH of 1954 I got a call for help from Ron Harper, the president of our Duncan curling club. The roof of their new 190 x 82 foot wide rink was caving in under two and a half feet of wet snow and it was beginning to get dark. A serious blow to the area's enthusiastic curlers was in the making.

Duncan curling rink, caving in from wet snow, before rescue by Garner's logging crew and bulldozers.

They had tried to wash the snow off the roof with a fire hose, but this just added to the immense weight. The building was beginning to heave and strain, shuddering like a sinking ship. Many of the beams supporting the center of the building were shifting dangerously. The city engineer and a couple of local architects had inspected it and said the situation was hopeless. That's when the emergency call to me was made. I carefully looked the structure over. With ingenuity and some gyppo logger muscle and resourcefulness I figured we could save that poorly designed Quonset building. The experts left. "No hope," they still said.

Never having faced anything quite like this before, I came up with an impromtu plan. I explained to Harper what I had in mind.

"Go for it!" he said.

"We haven't much time," I replied, "Every minute counts."

Our office was just across the street. I got our crew boss, Bob Paine, on the radio phone. "Start walking two cats off our now snow covered logging show on Mount Prevost," I ordered. "And send the crew to the rink with tools and power saws immediately."

It took less than an hour to walk the bulldozers out to the nearest blacktop where they were put on two waiting lowbeds and escorted by a couple of police cars, one in front and one behind, sirens blaring and lights flashing. Quite a sight as they came rolling in through the falling snow.

In the meantime I had scrounged six 12 X 12 timbers, forty feet long from an old dismantled bridge nearby that I would use later to support the sides of the building. I was guessing we had no more than half an hour at the most to save that buckling building. The whole thing would surely collapse in a tangled heap of broken lumber and smashed equipment, as another four inches of wet snow had fallen during this frantic hour.

First, we had to stop the roof from settling further.

We used four 20-ton jacks to lift four steel uprights into position, two on each side of the center rink. The jacks sat on 5 x 10 railroad ties to spread the weight on the ice. The uprights were five-inch boxed angle iron about 20 feet long which had been fabricated and delivered to the site by Sanderson's Iron Works. Two layers of ties were added to make a square crib, with the ties resting on the jacks. The men worked fast as I directed them. All the while we were alert to the fact the roof might cave in — and we were working under it!

Using a fork lift we stood the four uprights, capped and held in position with 8 x 8 timbers, on the four corners of the cribs, directly over the jacks. The travel available from the jacks was more than the thickness of two 5 x 10 ties, so we jacked them up, in pairs, far enough to slip two fresh ties underneath. We now had the uprights two tie-thicknesses higher. We repeated this process until the tops of the uprights, capped with the 8 x 8s, were supporting the sagging roof. It was crazy, and you had to see it to believe it.

Glen Harper, Ron's son, was in charge of ten four-man crews working in relays shovelling the wet show off the collapsing roof. I was "general" of about a hundred volunteers, from high schoolers to merchants to loggers, working to save their curling rink. Such a community effort is perhaps impossible today in this "me-me" world.

Karm Singh, the sawmiller who had supplied the lumber for the roof trusses, came up to me, looked and shook his head.

"Let it go, Joe. You can't possibly stop this from collapsing. Somebody could get killed!"

I wasn't ready to give up just yet. As soon as the two cats rolled into the parking lot, I directed the machines to opposite sides of the rink and to back up against the logs other volunteers had rolled up to the base of the building. I was still

171

sticking to my plan and I intended to play it out to the end. The cat men dropped their blades, and ran the drum lines off the winches through the holes previously cut in both sides of the sagging roof. Looking back I can see why the engineers had thought I was nuts.

When their hooks were through the wall, we attached them to a bridle around the center of the three lapped 12 x 12s that extended the full length of the bowed-out portion of the building on both sides. If we could create equal pressure on both sides of the Quonset, the sagging center would have to rise as we tightened up on the lines. We would use the jacks and our vertical supports inside the building to hold the roof in place as it went up.

This was instant engineering, in high gear!

The trusses in the center were twelve to sixteen feet below their normal height. Those must have been very tense moments for Bob Paine, who was giving all the signals and orders to the cat drivers and the rigging crews, when simultaneously both cats cinched up their lines and the roof started to rise. Some "wows" rang out, mixed with sighs of relief, as the volunteer workers and town spectators watched their curling rink being once again reshaped. In the darkness of the nastiest night of that year I smiled and wondered what the inevitable wreckage would have looked like if it hadn't been for those two cats.

When the roof arc was almost back up to its original height, with the steel uprights supporting it, we welded in angle irons to hold our supports in place. The job was done. A video camera covering all angles showed what logging savvy and luck can do when civil engineers walk away saying it's hopeless. And really it was!

The following afternoon the cables were released. All was fine, so I sent both cats back up the mountain. The snow had stopped and the heavy fall was already melting in the pouring rain. The building was reopened for curling on February 7th, with six steel supports on either side of the center rink. The Duncan community could now relax and enjoy its curling rink for many years to come.

Did I get credit? Yes. A month later they put on a party for me in the repaired curling rink.

I WAS NOW also very active in the Duncan Chamber of Commerce. These were some of the good times — meaning high lumber prices — for this part of Vancouver Island. We had plenty to do. While Hector Stone, manager of Hillcrest Lumber, was the Chamber president, he asked me to start building an up-to-date office for our organization. A lot on the west side of the new Island Highway had been given to the Chamber tax-free by the Duncan council, provided we included a tourist information bureau in the same building. It was completed the following year during my term as president. Most of the materials were donated by local suppliers.

EARLY IN 1954 Will Dobson, then editor of *The Cowichan Leader*, and a past president of the Chamber, came to me with a great suggestion. All smiles, he said, "Joe, I attended college with John Grieves, the current local manager of the B.C. Forest Products sawmills in these parts. You know his company has been searching for a suitable site for a pulp mill on the east coast of Vancouver Island. Cowichan Bay, Mill Bay, Chemainus and Crofton are all being considered."

"That's interesting, Will" I replied. "How about arranging a luncheon for the three of us? We'll chat it up, kick it around. You never know."

"Something in mind?" he asked.

"Sure do. I know the perfect spot."

A luncheon followed, lots of talk, and a few days later we walked over the Crofton site I knew so well. I had hunted deer there as a younger man. Grieves was impressed. It seemed to have all the requirements — flat land, deep water and rail and road access.

The business people in the Cowichan Valley were delighted when the word came that Crofton was going to be the site for the new pulp mill. I felt as if I had dropped a running buck with a head shot at 300 yards.

Construction started in February of 1956. A thousand construction workers would be employed on that project. The mill produced its first bleached pulp in December of 1957 and full production began the following year. Their huge pulp mill operates to this day, and it did wonders for the economic well-being of the Crofton area.

It was with great pride that I accepted, on behalf of our Chamber, the "Gavel of the Year Award for Achievement" at the provincial Chambers of Commerce annual general meeting in Vancouver.

DOWN-TO-EARTH talk started about the building of a golf course for the Cowichan District when land south of Duncan was still cheap, compared with today's sky high and climbing prices. For four years I worked with other recreation-minded citizens putting together a parcel of land for an 18-hole golf course. Ten of us put up $10,000 each to buy the land and get the project underway. It was a long haul, but today's first-class course is proof of what can be done when a whole community becomes involved.

We each received a life membership to the Cowichan Golf and Country Club, rather than repayment of our loan. A fledgling club needs to earn money, not give it back, and $10,000 was a great deal of money in those days. It's a gift I never have regretted.

IT WAS the American philosopher, William James, who wrote "a man could do worse than create things during his life that will live on after he has gone." That's always made good sense to me. However, it's easy for "doers" to take on more than they should.

I started thinking about retirement in 1957. Pat and I began talking about moving back to Victoria, where we had lived during the early years of World War II. We made a down payment on a house still under construction. I knew that as long as we stayed in Duncan there would always be more to do than I could comfortably handle. I felt my health was suffering. I was right.

There was a small lake in the woods eight miles up the old Cowichan Lake Road, Tadpole Lake. It had plenty of pan-sized trout and not many knew of it. We hiked in on an old trapper's trail which had been blazed some thirty years earlier.

Joanne, Tom and Ed would scurry on ahead and already be fishing by the time Gerry and I arrived. They might even have a couple of small trout strung on a forked stick to show us. This wasn't so much fishing as just pulling them in.

On this trip I was carrying Gerry up on my shoulders with his legs dangling around my neck as he was not yet three. We were halfway to the lake when I took a dizzy spell and sat down, somewhat bewildered. I shouted to Tom and Joanne to come back. Luckily this time they had not run too far ahead and they heard me and ran back. I stood up and vomited violently. Tom, Joanne and Ed stood there, bewildered.

"I'm sick. Take Gerry and go on back and wait at the car," I told them. Three times I had to stop and vomit. I was getting dizzier by the minute. I had to steady myself against trees to keep from falling over, but I made it. I unlocked the car and got the children in, and still wearing my hip gumboots, headed

174

for home. On the way I had to pull over several times and get out to be sick.

Pat took one look at me, and said, "I'm phoning Dr. Stanley." He told her he'd be right over.

He asked a few questions and put a thermometer in my mouth, read it and said, "I'm getting an ambulance."

I remember waking up in the Duncan Hospital with terrible pains in the chest and Dr. Stanley saying, "You've developed pleurisy with double pneumonia."

Two weeks after that memorable fishing trip I was allowed to go home, but I was still feeling very weak. I told our neighbours I was moving the family to Victoria.

Our Quamichan Lake home on Maple Bay Road — a wonderful place to have lived.

A few weeks later Sandy told me he was having heart problems and would be having an operation.

"Joe, I want you to have a couple of things I've made for you, things I hope you'll enjoy for the rest of your life."

One gift was the most beautifully carved moose-horn cribbage board I had ever seen. Then, he handed me a box of hand-tied flies, saying, "Each of these I have tied especially for the areas you like to fish in most. This one here is a certain fish-catcher for Chilco Lake. This one is for St. Mary's Lake

175

bass. Here's one for Cowichan River brown trout. I've even tied you some Coho flies for Cowichan Bay. Success, and tight lines, my friend.''

Sandy went to the hospital a couple of weeks later. He lived on for another nine years, dying in 1966, 20 years after he had moved into his lovely old home on Maple Bay Road. As so often happens, the opportunity never arose to see him again after we moved to Victoria. I certainly regret this.

I still have most of those flies — a reminder of a wonderful friendship, and the good times we spent together.

While I was in the hospital we had accepted an offer on our Maple Bay Road house. We were leaving that lovely home. What awaited us in the big city?

PART V

CITY LIFE

O N THE MOUNTAIN the sound of the river close by reminded me of happier days when the sun was shining and the trout were rising. I thought of the friends I had fished with. I have always believed that as your life unfolds, you are indeed fortunate if you can use up all the fingers of one hand counting those who are your true friends, those who would be prepared to lay down their lives for you should the occasion arise. Those I have felt this way about were brother Tom, George Syrotuk, Shorty Berkey and later in life Denis Hagar and Bill Heaney. Only Shorty is left now and we don't get to see enough of each other these days. I know that Tom, George, Denis and Bill will be happy to see me again.

I suddenly realized I was thinking about death, now a distinct possibility. While I have no fear of death I was not ready to die just yet. I must stop wandering in the past and start thinking of how to get out of this awful mess.

How in hell could it have happened?

GOODBYE DUNCAN - HELLO VICTORIA

HOW WELL I remember moving day, Saturday, June 15, 1957, as my diary notes. The children saw it as a big adventure, with an earlier summer holiday, a new home and in the fall some new classmates. I was still weak from my bout with double pneumonia the previous month, but I wanted to be as helpful as possible. When the moving van arrived I parked myself on a chair by the driveway and directed traffic as the kids helped, carrying small pieces of furniture and odds-and-ends out to the van.

We closed the door and took a last good look at the wonderful home where the children had spent six happy years. Mr. Whittaker, bless him, had given each of the children a goodbye chocolate bar. The Whittakers would get the house ready for its new owner, Red Moffat, who owned the Tzouhalem Hotel.

Earl and Wyn Reynolds and their two teenage boys helped us with the move. Having them along turned out to be a big help and a great comfort to us. Earl drove my station wagon with the five boys and two dogs in the back. His wife drove their station wagon with Dana and Joanne and our three cats. Sadly, the rabbits were left with the Reynolds because there was no place for them at our Victoria house.

Pat and the girls had put all of our good dishes packed in boxes in her car and stuffed pillows and bedding around them. The trip over the Malahat, then undergoing major relocation, was a bit lumpy but the kids were excited and in good spirits. They were obviously impressed as we circled the roundabout that used to be at the intersection of Douglas and Hillside, a place in memory which still makes me smile. My friend Bill Heaney drank too much Irish whiskey one St. Patrick's Day and ran his Thunderbird over the curb and right into the middle of that roundabout. A young police officer soon arrived.

"Mr. Heaney, how could you possibly end up in the middle of this roundabout?"

Straight faced, Bill queried, "Young man, don't you believe in miracles?"

"Get your car moving," was the officer's response trying to hide a smile. Back then enforcement of drunk driving laws was lenient — maybe even more so on St. Patrick's Day.

"Come back in twenty minutes," Bill told him. "You'll see things have been cleared up." His repair shop was only half a mile away and he had already called for a wrecking truck.

Our caravan of three cars and the moving van headed on down Government Street to our new house. Everyone pitched in and when the furniture was in place and the kids had dragged their belongings upstairs to their bedrooms, there were cries of, "I'm hungry!"

Anticipating this, Wyn and I had picked up a big bucket of chicken and chips and a couple of bricks of ice cream to top it all off. Pat was ready with plates and soft drinks on our big kitchen table. Sitting on chairs and boxes, or whatever, everyone tucked in. We had arrived.

The Reynolds got up to head for Duncan and I was beginning to feel awfully weary.

"Right now Earl, I'm going to hit the sack, but I will see you Monday afternoon, "I told him. "And thanks for all the help."

Joanne asked their oldest son Don to take good care of her big white rabbit she called "Cream Puff".

Home now was at 1054 Montgomery Avenue, just off St. Charles and a block below very fancy Rockland Avenue. We really wanted waterfront property, and continued searching. But our Montgomery home was large enough, comfortable and in a quiet neighbourhood.

Keith and Jean Olson next door, were also new to the district. Keith and his brother John owned the Strathcona Hotel. Keith looked after the day shift and his brother worked evenings. I'd known their uncle, nicknamed "Speed", for years. We had hunted and fished together often.

A year earlier, Dana had attended St. Margaret's private

school as a boarder. She had broken school regulations and was now living at home again, attending the local high school where she was one of the top grass hockey players.

Joanne started classes at Norfolk House as a day girl because her friend Patsy Davie was a boarder there and they had been in the same class in Duncan. It was Patsy's father, the lawyer Jack Davie, and his partner Dave Williams, who were the first tenants of the temporary offices behind our gas station years ago.

Tom and his brother Eddie could walk to Margaret Jenkins Elementary School, one of the oldest public schools in Victoria. They both became active in the Boy Scouts, due to the encouragement of our neighbour Peggy Heisterman. Her son John had earned almost all of the merit badges, and this really impressed Tom.

Gerry, the youngest of our brood, started kindergarten with his friend next door, Craig Olson.

That first summer they decided to do some exploring with our cocker spaniel, Holly. A mile later they were hopelessly lost and getting hungry. They were at the grocery store at Richmond and Fort Streets, kitty-corner from the Jubilee Hospital.

Fruit sitting outside the store looked mighty tempting, so they helped themselves, sat down and began eating. The store owner asked where they lived. Getting few answers from the two little fruit-thieves he called the police. The two constables had no more luck than the storekeeper. Neither could remember the name of their street. Hoping they might recognize something familiar the police drove them slowly around the district.

Back home, each mother had believed her son was playing next door. But at lunch time, no kids. They phoned the police.

A few minutes later a police cruiser drove up with the two little boys sitting in the back looking important. Holly, quite unperturbed, was sitting between them. The boys were smiling as they eagerly ran into their mothers' arms. One of the constables handed a bill for the fruit to Jean and while she was getting the money, Pat told Gerry and Craig to thank the policemen for bringing them home. The two boys are both businessmen now, and they remain good friends.

Eddie has always been attracted to anything on wheels. Shortly after we moved onto Montgomery he got into our car in the driveway, enticing Gerry in with him. They were on the front seat playing with the gear shift. Somehow they got it into neutral and fooled around until they released the emergency brake. Away they went — rolling backwards down the driveway across the road and crashed through the fence. A fine way to introduce yourself to your new neighbours! We were just plain lucky that neither of the little guys was hurt.

I was now describing myself as semi-retired, but as my health returned I was commuting almost daily to Duncan to keep track of our logging operations. Like any workaholic, I thought everything would collapse if I wasn't there. Driving home late one Friday I started wondering why I was still this way — was it an escape from part of my family life?

IT WAS BACK IN 1950 when I got into salvage logging and became busier than ever. John Hemmingsen and I talked about going in on it as partners, but he was offered such a good job with MacMillan Bloedel in Port Alberni that he changed his mind. He joined them as general logging superintendent, and I went into pulp salvage on my own under contract to MacMillan Bloedel.

I told H.R. McMillan we would have to spend a substantial amount to get started with the proper equipment. With that quick, decisive manner I admired and which put him on top of the heap, he said, "Don't worry and don't bother me unless you get into serious trouble." He backed me on the initial purchase of the equipment and we paid him back as we logged. Fair to him and good for us.

Our first contract was at Stamp Falls, just northwest of Port Alberni. It had been logged the previous winter, yet we got nearly as much out of the slash after the snow went away as they got on their first logging of the area.

We devised a system that worked very well. We sorted the logs right in the woods. Sometimes we had as many as six different sorts at the landing. Species, size and quality varied greatly from place to place.

Hemmingsen and I decided that if we could get away from scaling (measuring each log) and just weighed the whole load it would save time and be much safer for the men. We put one big set of scales at the log dump. We'd just pick the whole load off the truck, weigh it, number it and drop it into the water at the north end of the Alberni Inlet. We were paid on an established cubic scale by weight. This simple procedure had not been tried before.

We had one air tong shovel loader and two cats at each landing, the site where the timber was all brought together. We wrapped heavy wire around each end of each bundle to keep them together. Instead of having to sort the logs at Port Alberni, the mill just sorted the different bundles. The biggest percentage of the logs went for pulp as much of the wood was not of lumber quality.

We used one portable slack line spar on wheels — the first ever used in B.C. We tried to have it built up at Madill's machine shop in Nanaimo, but they were too busy. So we went down to Sedro Wooley, a village in Washington, to an old steam donkey engineer. He knew exactly what we wanted and I asked him if he could build us one.

"Sure," he said. "When do you want it?"

"Next week."

"Well, it will take a bit longer than that," old Syd said with a knowing smile. He knew gyppo loggers. To make sure everything was done right he supervised the operation himself. The mainline would have to come in at 30 mph and out at about 40, because we were yarding such long distances. In rough country we usually rigged a back spar to keep the logs from hanging up. We had to work fast and have good equipment to make money.

A truck could be loaded and heading back to the log dump in about 10 minutes. At the sawmill the bundles would go up the jack ladder and be sent to the various locations. Cedar didn't make good pulp so the sorting was very valuable and necessary to the mill.

All this was agreed to on a hand shake and I told Hemmingsen, "We don't need any help out here. We know what you want us to do, but the day we can't make money we'll be gone. This has to be a mutual thing. We both have to make a profit."

The sorting and weighing was the key and there was a lot of interest in what we were doing. We put out about 10 loads of pulp and 10,000 board feet of saw logs every day.

Hemmingsen rarely bothered us. I had to phone H.R. only once, when his foreman began putting us where the timber and slash was poor, a lot of cedar, no more than a bunch of slabs. He said, "Don't worry about it, it will be fixed by morning. Go back to work." And we did, for the next several years.

Bill Clarke and I had accumulated some 4,000 acres of old E & N logged-over land by keeping the yearly land taxes paid up. Clarke was an old timber cruiser and we began selectively logging the bigger and better stands. We put in a log dump at Cowichan Bay and started buying logs from all the gyppos in the Cowichan area.

We were acting as an agent for MacMillan. A licenced

scaler scaled the logs on the trucks before they were put in the water, where they were bundled and boomed. We put a big swinging boom on a spar tree and it could pick up a whole truck load of logs and gently lower it into the water. MacMillan's log buyer Chick Qualley would come over and look at what we had in the water, then take his copy of the scale sheets back to Vancouver and send us a cheque so we could pay the loggers. We were paid every second week, so it was good for everyone. We did this for a couple of years and averaged 150,000 board feet a week.

Then we got orders for piling, six-inch tops and 20 to 60 feet long. These were towed around from Cowichan Bay to Crofton Harbour and loaded on ships for Japan. We left a growing crop of timber on over half the acreage, most of which was along the Cowichan River. We took out some 25 ship loads of fir piling and then had to give it up because we were running out of that type of timber. Through selective logging, we had just about cleaned out our 4,000 acres which was scattered throughout the Cowichan District.

I would be dead before the timber was of merchantable size again, but I thought it would be in perfect logging shape for the children. However, they showed absolutely no interest in it, so in 1952 we decided to sell Clarke and Garner Timberlands Ltd. — C & G — to H.R. MacMillan. He sent Chick Qualley to handle the deal.

"We'll buy your shares including the land and timber for $160,000," he said. A fair price then. Today it would be worth ten times that. Clarke and I split the proceeds down the middle.

I bought up several old timber licences in Howe Sound in the Foulger and Potlatch Creek areas. I wanted to make it all into a small Forest Management Licence. I had it mapped and had satisfied all the government requirements when I was asked for a $20,000 bribe, nothing larger than $20 bills and delivered in a box. I wouldn't go for it. Then they called the timber "immature" and said it was more valuable standing. I believed I would have had one of the best little timber management licences on the coast. It wasn't large, but the timber was good. It was 100 years old and more, and there is no doubt in my mind it was ready to be harvested. As far as I know, after I didn't come through with the bribe, they sold all the government timber in that area to Bay Lumber Company and it was clear cut within the next few years. We sold our privately owned land, including Foulger Creek Logging Co., to George Whittaker, another Cowichan logger.

I continued salvage logging and pre-logging for a few more years.

Over the years I had as many as 20 different logging shows on the go at any one time. There were at least four different shows at Quesnel, where we contract logged for Western Plywood. These operations I eventually sold to my brother Al.

We were the first people to use a fifth-wheel in the woods in the Cariboo. It had the same hook-up used by highway trucks but had to be bigger and stronger to withstand the rougher ground. After setting up and disconnecting his empty trailer the driver just backed the truck in under another pre-loaded trailer, hooked on and away he went. The turn-around-time was cut to a minimum. We kept several extra trailers at each of our landings.

Having my own plane made it possible to spread out in all directions. We had several camps up the B.C. coast, four at Knight Inlet, two at Redonda Island, one in Bute Inlet and three at Jarvis Inlet. They were mostly old timber licences we had picked up years earlier.

My logging shows were usually small and the bosses were often partners. We would supply the money and the equipment and they would supply the know-how to get the timber out for the best possible price. When I decided to sell, the first person I would usually go to was the man who had been bossing the show.

Over the years I had up to 300 men working for us at one time. We paid good wages in order to get good men, usually better than union rates. I don't say we always had better men, but we had good men and they had an interest in what we were doing because there was always a bonus if their production was good. It worked out well.

Brothers Tom, Ollie and Al all logged on Galiano at one time or another. Tom found and bought the timber and land, then sold it to them. There was a lot of timber on those Gulf Islands and Tom could easily see from the air exactly where it was. If it was for sale, he bought it and had another logging show going.

In 1950, when Tom finished logging on Galiano Island he offered all of his land to Ollie for $1,000, but Ollie decided he didn't want it. That same day he sold it to the Powell River Company for $5,000. MacMillan Bloedel later amalgamated with Powell River. Now in 1995, they're selling it off as residential building sites for millions.

All this is such a long, long way from my childhood on

Saltspring — when a "misery whip" was another name for a swede-fiddle or falling saw, so called because it was hard to pull and keep going for any length of time. It took tough men, not necessarily big men, to get the rhythm of working that saw and keep it up all day.

I remember Dad using an ox team for logging on several jobs. In the morning, when the four beasts pulled the first load of logs to the salt water, we unhooked them at the landing and gave them a few handfuls of oats. They just put their heads down and ate greedily. When they were finished and had a drink of water we started them back up the skid road to the spar tree. Again we'd have some oats and a bucket of water waiting. The only thing they seemed to really want was food and water. It was a simple and humane way of keeping them working and going in the right direction. Behind the logs was a sleigh called a "pig" about 20 feet long and up to 4 feet wide, on which we carried a few logging tools and some skid grease. My first job in the woods was greasing the skids, by dipping a two-handed mop into an old wooden bucket of stinking whale oil. I was barely eight years old.

The forest industry of today, highly mechanized with improvements coming along each year, has changed unbelievably as it must as our timber supply diminishes. But I will always remember my many years in the woods with a great deal of affection and satisfaction — as a kid, as a man, as an employer, and yes, sometimes as a gadfly to government and to the huge operators.

Thank you, Oh Lord of the Tall Timber, for letting it happen.

BUT NOW, in 1957, I was looking for waterfront property in Victoria. I found it quite by accident. Or luck! Our spaniel needed her toe nails clipped so I took her to the nearest vet.

"You new to Victoria?" Dr. Cranston asked, as we shook hands.

"Yeah," I replied. "We're over on Montgomery but looking for waterfront."

"You should have a look at my place, Mr. Garner, five and a half acres right at the end of Haro Road."

Surprised, but keeping my business cool, I asked, "What about tomorrow?" We agreed to meet and I left, not showing the elation I felt.

The next day I saw the property. This could well be it. It had potential and plenty of it. The land sloped down to a gravel beach and at each end of the little bay there was a rocky point. The tide was out as we walked along the beach and Dr. Cranston pointed out the best spots for digging butter clams. Then we walked the treed area to the south of the house. I knew my search was at an end. Dr. Cranston explained that the property had its own foreshore lease but he did not believe it could be renewed.

"How much for everything, as is, where is?" I asked.

"I want $85,000," he replied.

"I will pay you $75,000 cash, if I can get the foreshore lease renewed," I told him. He left to discuss my proposal with his wife. He'd tipped his hand by telling me he had already made an offer on another property on Lansdowne Avenue facing the Uplands Golf Course, so I was feeling hopeful.

Within five minutes he came back into the living room, and said, "We'll accept your offer, Mr. Garner."

"I'll write you a cheque for $5,000 now and give you a post-dated cheque for the balance once the foreshore lease is approved," I assured him. It was ours.

The minute I got home I phoned the office of Ray Williston, who was then the Minister of Lands and Forests in the Social Credit government. When I got through to him I said, "I would like to see you about a foreshore lease out in Saanich."

"I'll be here all day. Come by at two-thirty. Would you happen to be the Joe Garner that flies a float plane?"

"Why, yes."

"If you remember, the last time we saw each other I was wading two feet deep in the waters of the Fraser River in Prince George. It was in flood, muddy, a mess and you showed up out of nowhere."

Tom and I had been flying over one of our timber operations south of Quesnel and heard on the radio that the only bridge over the Fraser in Prince George was unsafe and closed to traffic. Parts of the town itself were under a couple of feet of water. We decided to fly up and see if we could be of any help. We landed and taxied the Cessna 180 up 1st Avenue! There was Williston, then a school principal with a yen for politics. He had just sent the school buses, loaded with teachers and students, to higher ground.

At his office Ray greeted me with his usual friendly handshake and we talked briefly about that day in flooded Prince George. I had Dr. Cranston's foreshore lease and after looking it over, he said he could see no reason why the lease could not be reinstated, or just extended.

"One good deed deserves another," he said as we shook hands.

That evening Pat and I drove to Haro Road. She seemed to like the place as much as I did. Next morning I gave a post-dated cheque for the full amount of the balance due to Dr. and Mrs. Cranston.

On December 18, 1957, six months after we had moved to Victoria, we got possession of 4071 Haro Road in Saanich, a suburb of the city.

I arranged to camp with the kids on the beach the following night. Sputnik was to pass overhead. Two and half months earlier, the Russians had launched the first space satellite. It was big news everywhere and shook the vaunted American NASA space program to its very core. I pitched our large tent on the lawn a few feet above high water. We were in luck. It was a beautiful clear night. I got a fire started at dusk and the kids lay in their sleeping bags, using logs for pillows, watching the flames.

"What do you know about those groups of stars, Dad?" Joanne asked.

"Well, I know a little about constellations. Sailors have navigated by them for centuries. Why not shift yourselves a bit so you're facing north."

"How do we know where that is?" Tom asked.

"Just find the Big Dipper. The two stars on the dipper opposite the handle point to Polaris, the North Star. Keep watching and maybe we'll see Sputnik."

We all stared up at the star-studded night. And then it happened! As if I'd ordered it up, a steadily blinking object slid across the sky.

"Look, a flying saucer!" Joanne shouted.

"No, Sputnik," I corrected.

"Now, you can one day tell your grandchildren you saw Sputnik. Before long it'll be burnt up and gone forever when it falls back into the earth's atmosphere. But you have all seen the dawn of a new age."

The following day I started looking for a contractor to begin the renovations, that inevitable next step after buying a house. I had met Carlos Bellagente at a trap shoot. He was a very good light-heavy weight boxer and trained many of the young upcoming Victoria fighters. He also enjoyed rye whis-key and was generous with it. I made arrangements to meet him at Haro Road.

He was in a sharply pleated shirt, looking very dapper. To

my disgust I was to learn that he still looked dapper at the end of the work day! His carpenter foreman Ron brought a drafting board and we stood at the kitchen counter and drew a plan of the house and the work to be done. By noon we had the planned renovations roughed out. I told them I would have all the materials needed by the time they arrived the next morning.

Carlos turned out to be a better boxer than a contractor by quite some bit. I was disappointed to find things were not being properly supervised. Carlos was hardly ever there. But fortunately his foreman was excellent and knew exactly what had to be done. We were able to start moving our belongings into our new home at the end of March. I asked Carlos to get his equipment and workers off the job as we would finish the outside work with our own men.

We made a rental-purchase deal for our Montgomery house and realized a nice profit.

BILL HEANEY loaned us a big truck with a driver and helper to move the piano and other heavy furniture. I first met him in the mid-forties when he was establishing his heavy equipment business in Victoria. I remember looking out my office window in Duncan in 1952, when Bill's two big cranes were lifting the trusses in place for the ill-fated Duncan Curling Rink. He had volunteered his machines, even though he didn't live in the district.

Bill liked swimming in the cold north Pacific waters. "Stimulates your blood circulation, Joe," he shouted once as he leaped off his launch at River's Inlet, where we were fishing. He was a frequent visitor to Haro Road. He would walk across the beach into the bone-chilling waters of Haro Strait. After 20 minutes he'd swim back, toss on his robe, and say, "Invigorating!" Pat would have a hot cup of rum-spiked coffee waiting for him.

Bill was the fellow who got the first low-bed trailer licence on Vancouver Island, shortly before Garner Bros. got its licence for the Duncan-Cowichan area.

Bill and his father had started with horses and wagons before they got into the trucking business and they soon became one of the largest freighting outfits in the province. Bill's slogan was: "Big or teeny, just call Heaney". His only real competition was Bray's Transfer and on his office wall was a framed sign:

"BIG OR TEENY, JUST CALL HEANEY"
"SHIT OR HAY, JUST CALL BRAY"

The Garner home purchased in 1957 on five acres overlooking Haro Strait in Saanich, north of Victoria.

MONDAY, MARCH 24, 1958 was the first night we spent in our renovated home, on its beautiful site. Later, son Tom would say, "Dad, I never once thought about us being rich until we moved to Haro Road."

The next job at Haro Road was to repair the cottage adjoining the garage so we could move the Whittakers in again to assume gardening and housekeeping duties. They had been working at the north end of Quamichan Lake since we moved south, and were delighted to be once more part of the Garner household. Mr. Whittaker would say, "Nice to be 'ome again."

Shortly after we got settled in Dad visited. The moment he walked down to the beach he recognized the little bay. "Right here is where I pitched my tent when I was fishing for the market. Imagine, that's over forty years ago. Just over that way Emily Carr had one of her many shacks where she came to paint during the summer," he said wistfully, pointing to the mossy mound to the south.

"We had many a good meal of butter clams dug right out there at low tide," he mused.

He showed us the spot where he pulled up his row boat when he stayed for the night. Like all the others he sold his fish for cash to the fish buyers that daily plowed up and down the coast. Back then there was no ice to keep the salmon from spoiling. Most of these packers belonged to the Todd family, which also owned a cannery and the salmon traps on the southwest coast of Vancouver Island near Sooke. I hunted with Ernie Todd, one of the older sons, and was with him when he lost his right eye, speared by a short branch while tramping through thick brush near Lake Cowichan. I rushed him to the hospital in Duncan but they could do nothing to save his eye. I was most impressed with the patience and determination he demonstrated while learning to shoot from his left shoulder. Even with this handicap he was good enough to win the B Class Singles at a trap shoot at Cowichan Lake only a couple of years later.

I remember his car with two holes cut in the top of the trunk so his hunting dogs could put their heads out and look around. The lids were hinged so that when the dogs pushed them open they lay back flat.

ON WEEKENDS I frequently went to trap shoots at the Victoria Gun Club in Metchosin and my shooting actually seemed to be improving with age.

In 1958, the Island Championships were held on the Sunday of the Victoria Day weekend in May. When I drove over, John Olson started towards my vehicle. He and I had been having a friendly rivalry over the previous few weeks.

"Hello, Joe, I'd like you to meet Jimmy Pattison. He's big in the automobile business in Vancouver. Has a dealership, and other things. Like you, always busy."

"Hi, Jimmy. Come over to see John lose another bet?" I joked.

"Nice to meet you, Joe."

"Hop in guys, and take a load off your feet," I suggested, as I reached across to open the doors.

"Sounds like you feel lucky today," John said.

"Lucky enough! Maybe you'd like a drink to steady your nerves," I offered, taking a bottle of Crown Royal from under the passenger's seat.

"Not concerned about the whiskey dulling your reflexes?" Jimmy asked. He was a teetotaler, a generous donor to his Pentecostal church. He eventually built an empire of companies worth $1.5-billion. Liquor never figured in his plan for his life.

"Probably won't trouble me as much as it troubles John," I responded, and passed the bottle over to my main competitor.

The booze went back and forth and there wasn't much left by the time we went up to the firing line. I was pretty sharp that day, breaking 96 out of 100 at 16 yards, 91 of the 100 handicapped at 20 yards and then hit 45 doubles out of 50. By day's end I was pretty proud — a top day despite the rye whiskey. My overall score gave me the Vancouver Island Championship. What would my score have been without the Crown Royal? Of course, maybe Olson's score would have been better and he only lost by two birds; still remarkably good as we were handicapped by a brisk wind. But we both believed the whiskey had helped us. And guess what? We each poured ourselves another drink.

THAT SAME weekend Dana won both second and third place ribbons in the hunter trials on her Arabian mare, Coco. This little mare, unlike Kitimat, liked to jump and showed well in front of the horsy crowd. At first, she kept this spirited horse at Carley's Stables and rode at the Victoria Riding Club. Later, she rode at the Bar S. Ranch on Blenkinsop, over those lovely country trails that are now streets in the classy Broadmead subdivision.

PAT ALWAYS was busy with her own life, and her own circle of friends. We were drifting further and further apart. She had lots of free time and her new friends were mostly party types. She was particularly fond of Elaine Crump, twice married and no longer tied down with family responsibilities. Pat called Elaine the "Butterfly" which seemed like a pretty good description.

THE BOYS had started school at Frank Hobbs Elementary, up Haro towards what would later be the University of Victoria campus.

Tom and Eddie played soccer and other sports with the neighbourhood kids, but they were really more interested in baseball. I gave some thought to coaching their team the following year, when I planned on selling off many of my logging operations.

A major protest had begun about the opening of a doe shooting season on Vancouver Island. Dennis Hagar and I, and most of the old timers who had hunted for years, were adamantly opposed to does being killed. I was invited by CHEK TV to discuss the issue on their public affairs program, and give my reasons why this slaughter should not be allowed to continue.

"If you want to build a herd of cattle, then you don't kill the cows!" I declared. "You want to maintain deer herds for future generations? Then you don't kill the does. It's as simple as that."

I had asked my three boys to come up and stand beside me. With my hands on two of them, I said, "These are the three best reasons I know of for stopping the shooting of does. The future of our young people."

Those of us from the fish and game club who had worked hard on the campaign were able to stop the doe shooting for only two years. Then it was open season for anything that moved in the woods. No need to identify the sex or size of an animal. Just aim and fire. It actually became unsafe even to be in the woods under such regulations, particularly on weekends. I still believe that killing does is wrong and I'll never change my mind.

SHORTLY AFTER moving to Haro Road, I met Shirley. Her low-slung little Dachshund used to wander down the street to our place to play with our spaniel and Shirley would walk down to retrieve her pet. I liked her immediately. She was attractive and she had a good sense of humour. I began to look forward to our meetings. Things started to get serious a few weeks later, when John Olson and I attended a $50-a-plate gun club fund raiser out at the club's new location where Goldstream runs into the bay. John's wife, Pat, and Shirley drove out to join us for a drink at the end of the evening. Then Pat and John left for home. It poured rain that evening out on the Goldstream Flats, but neither Shirley nor I paid much attention to the weather.

Pat and I were seeing less and less of each other. Pat was usually out with her friend Elaine and the Victoria crowd, or with Trixie in Chemainus. My business interests were keeping me away from home more than ever. Looking back, maybe I just didn't want to argue with Pat about her activities so I kept finding other things to do.

I ALWAYS enjoyed the challenge of organizing fund raising projects. The most satisfying was in Victoria where the first Goodwill Industries Sheltered Workshop for handicapped persons was started by the Rotary Club. I worked with George Grey on that project for several years. We both put up considerable personal funds to raise the down payment for the original building at 560 Yates Street in Victoria.

We put on one of the first ever Klondike Nights to raise funds for this worthwhile project. The event was held in the inner harbour on one of the CPR ships moored within a long stone's throw of the parliament buildings. It was a $100-plate dinner affair, a big event and unique in those days. After dinner we held a draw for $10,000 in prizes. Maurice Green, who loved to gamble, was in charge. We had sold 100 duplicate-numbered tickets at $100 each for the draw. As the ticket holders entered the ship, Maurice tore the perforated ticket in half and returned one half to the owner. The other half was tightly rolled and inserted into a cylindrical container. The numbers and names of the owners were written on a blackboard. The containers went into a closed barrel. Just before dinner, the blackboard and the barrel were brought to a platform behind the head table.

After the dinner dishes were cleared away, Maurice Green announced over the loudspeaker that the draw would commence, explaining, "The first ticket drawn out of the barrel will be returned to the holder and his name will be wiped off the blackboard, as will the next eight tickets. The tenth ticket will be returned to its owner, along with a brand new hundred dollar bill. This person must now draw the next ten tickets, with the tenth holder getting his money back, and so on until ninety tickets have been drawn.

"At this point in the procedure, the draw will be stopped for fifteen minutes. Then you may wish to visit the bathroom, refill your glass, or maybe better still, have another cup of coffee. Then the remaining ten ticket holders will be asked to come to the head table while I ask them whether they wish to auction their tickets off or keep them. When a ticket is up for auction, I will call for bids and the new owner of the ticket will take his or her place up here.

"I will then draw out eight of the remaining tickets. These will have their names wiped off the board. So there will now be just two tickets left, and one will win $9,000. But! Big but! The two holders will have the choice of either splitting the prize money or again have their tickets sold by auction. Do you understand? If you don't, I do. Now, ladies and gentlemen, get set for an exciting time."

Between each draw the barrel was spun around like an old-fashioned butter churn. In the end one man won it all and donated it back to Goodwill, demonstrating the true Rotary spirit. Then the dancing began. It was a great evening.

The official opening of the first Goodwill store on the

island took place three years later in 1962. Over the years Goodwill Enterprises expanded its operation, selling low cost goods to the poor and often the not-so-poor. They provided pickup services, education and training for the handicapped and had their administration offices at 220 Bay Street in Esquimalt. The retail store at 560 Yates Street is now a huge outlet.

Later, in 1965, the Nanaimo Rotarians would open a receiving depot and store in downtown Nanaimo where they trained and gave employment to many handicapped people of the district. Over the years similar outlets have been started elsewhere on the island.

I TRIED TO SPEND as much time as possible with Joanne and the boys. They still enjoyed flights to St. Mary's Lake on Saltspring Island, and looked forward to the motor trips to Chilco Lake, where they had tons of fun and caught lots of delicious trout. Chilco Lake has some of the finest dry fly-fishing in the world, with rainbow trout ranging from two to six pounds. I always took the station wagon in the summer because, if it got too cold or the bugs were too bad, we could close up the windows and sleep in it.

Bud MacLean bought our shares in the lodge at Chilco Lake. Eventually he sold the lodge to a German syndicate, but kept his house and 25 acres on the Chilco River at the outlet of the lake. Bud had a daughter Gerry's age, another daughter Ed's age, and a son Tom's age.

On the day we left for the Cariboo, I'd say to our gang, "Those MacLean kids will outrun you if you don't watch out. The air up there is much thinner. You won't be able to keep up with them. So you better practice."

"Aw, Dad!" one would shout, "We'll be ready for them."

The boys trained hard on the road that ran across many open grazing meadows from Alexis Creek to Chilco, running alongside the station wagon when the terrain was suitable, accompanied by Holly, our spaniel, and Sylvia, my pointer.

There was a silver dollar for the winners and 50 cents for the losers. They ended up pretty even, though Gerry usually won his race. He was quick for a little guy.

"But you're running against a girl, Gerry." Tom always reminded him.

On these trips I taught them that wild animals are not pets. At Chilco they saw animals unlike those on Vancouver Island. If we came upon a porcupine I did not give my usual "Fetch 'em out!" command to the dogs, but called them into the car. A porcupine cannot throw his quills, as some people believe, but a flick of his tail can leave a curious dog with a mighty sore nose. The kids only had to touch the waddling creature with a stick to end up with lots of quills embedded in it.

One year, a red fox came scrounging around the lodge. When the kids tried to chase him off, he would go only so far, then turn around to face them, and make a hissing sound that stopped them dead in their tracks.

I taught them how to clean and smoke fish, and how to shoot my .22 target revolver.

"Some day you might want grouse stew instead of fried trout for lunch," I told them.

IN AUGUST, 1958, brother Tom phoned me from Vancouver, saying, "I'd like to come over for a visit."

"Sure, when would suit you?"

"I'll be over in an hour."

"Okay, I'll be down on the beach waiting for you. The tide is close to high so there won't be a problem," I assured him.

After tying up Tom's Cessna, we sat on the front porch and enjoyed a cold beer. Tom suggested we drive up to Duncan next morning. I asked why.

"I'd like to visit some of our friends and look around Old Angus again."

At the time he bought the old house back in 1943 he had been looking for a place in the Duncan area. He and his first wife, Marie, had been living in Westholme.

He found this property when he and George Syrotuk were driving around looking at several other places they knew were for sale. George had bought a bottle of Old Angus Scotch to lubricate their spirits. It was George's favourite whiskey.

The property Tom liked best had a long straight driveway leading off the highway up to the big house. There was a row of bishop oak and horse chestnut trees bordering the driveway. Tom was at the wheel of his station wagon. I suppose they were talking and gawking around at the fields and fences as they slowly drove down this impressive driveway. Maybe it was the whiskey, but Tom drove head on into one of those huge oak trees. The jolt knocked the engine hood crooked. It had been fastened with only two small bolts which had sheared off. They just lifted the hood off, backed up and drove on up to the house.

As they walked around looking the place over, they finished the rest of the Scotch. The house had eight rooms of

Rustic lane shaded by chestnuts and bishop oaks leading to Old Angus, Tom Garner's home.

varying sizes. There were two huge old barns and a caretaker's cottage, which was big enough for George and his wife Hilma to live in. In return, Hilma helped Tom's wife with the housework.

A large acreage went with the house extending from the highway east to Grieve Road, about half a mile away. They paced off a field near the house and Tom figured it was long enough for an air strip if he tore down one of the barns.

Tom and George drove back through town to the real estate office. Tom wrote a cheque for just under $5,000 as payment in full and he named the property "Old Angus". He had a keen eye for a bargain and this house and land was certainly one to boast about.

On this trip Tom and I looked around Old Angus and then visited several of the baseball players we had played with and against so long ago — the two Berkey brothers, Glen and

196

Old Angus, named after a favourite Scotch whiskey, was in disrepair when purchased in 1944.

The new Old Angus, photographed in 1993, but still in fine condition as it was when it was restored.

Shorty, Charlie Stroulger, Sonny and Gillie Bruce, Joe Gergel, Don Pitt, big Tom Krall and Frank Craft and George Syrotuk who had long since moved out of the cottage. It had been a wonderful day of reminiscing with friends.

As we were about to head home Tom said, "Let's drive down and look at our old air base on Quamichan Lake."

By the time we got back to Victoria it was getting dark.

"Plane looks safe here. Mind if I stay the night?" Tom asked.

"Stay as long as you like." I said. I noted he just didn't seem to want to leave. Next morning there was a wind from the southwest.

"Looks like I had better be ready to take off soon as the tide gets high enough," he said.

My three boys, Tom, Ed and Gerry, came down to the plane and Tom explained all the instruments. He idled the motor so they could see what it would be like to be a pilot. Each one sat on his knee to feel the varying pressures the propeller wash had on each different setting. He even let Tom, his namesake and my oldest son, change the propeller pitch. He explained why it was better to have the fine pitch for takeoff and the coarser for ordinary cruising.

By now the tide was high. Tom handed each of the boys a two dollar bill, quite a bit of money for a youngster in those days. Then he came over, shook my hand, looked at me intently, and said, "If anything should ever happen to me, I hope you will look after Sally for me." Sally was his daughter.

"I'll do that." And we said good-bye. That was August 19 of 1958, my Tom's tenth birthday.

Saturday, September 6th, started well enough. I'd stayed up in Duncan the night before so I could be deer hunting west of Lake Cowichan by daybreak. I bagged my limit of six blue grouse and a nice buck deer, then headed down island for the weekend arriving at Haro Road in the mid-afternoon. Pat had just got home. She had stayed, I assumed, in Chemainus the night before.

Dana and her boyfriend, Jim, were sitting outside enjoying the late summer sun. After supper I asked Jim if he'd like to go fishing. Not only did we come back without a salmon, but we got a line fouled up in some kelp and I lost one of my favourite flashers. The loss would be truly insignificant on that day.

We dragged the boat up on the beach and Jim offered to put the gear away. I walked up past the goldfish pond to the back door and Pat met me: "Joe, are you ready for a shock. I've got some bad news for you. Your brother Tom has been killed in a plane crash."

I didn't know what to say. Just like that, Tom was gone.

"Where? Was he alone?" I finally managed.

"No. Another man was with him. Up in Desolation Sound."

The kids were there staring at me. I asked them to go to their rooms. My first reaction. Later they told me they thought I'd sent them to their rooms because I was angry at them. It wasn't anger, just all sorts of emotions. I wanted to be alone. I'd just lost my brother, my longtime business partner, my best friend. Even now, 35 years later, I wonder if he really knew he was going. Had he come over two weeks earlier for just one reason — to say good-bye? A premonition? A hunch? A feeling? Who knows? No one ever will.

My brother Lloyd and I made funeral arrangements at the Roselawn Cemetery in Vancouver. Brother Al and his wife Barb drove down from Quesnel to join the rest of the family. Tom's wife Helen had to be hospitalized in Vancouver for some time. Old friends, people I hadn't seen for years, showed up to pay their respects.

After his will was probated and his business affairs settled, his widow and daughter moved to South Carolina. Tom's estate was largely tied up in his Bute Inlet company and I am certain that Helen, in ill health and an alcoholic, was taken advantage of by some of Tom's so-called friends. I was surprised his daughter, Bunky, from his first marriage was not even mentioned in the will. But these things can happen sometimes when death is sudden.

People who do not fly small planes have often asked me how an experienced pilot like Tom could crash on landing under apparently ideal weather conditions in the middle of the day. Most crashes are caused by pilot error, including "glassy water" landings. This is when there are no ripples on the water, and it is like looking into a mirror. In these situations pilots normally judge their height by looking towards the shoreline. Some have on occasion thrown something out on the water to judge their altitude before circling again to land.

I have never accepted that a "glassy water landing" was the cause of Tom's accident. I'm sure I know what really happened. He simply neglected to reset his altimeter, affected by barometric pressure, after leaving the interior. A pilot's expression is "High to low, look out below." He had failed to make his instrument adjustment after his takeoff from the mile-high Chilco Lake, so when he looked at his altimeter as he made his approach for the landing at Desolation Sound it read well above sea level, when actually his pontoons were almost touching the water. This oversight cost both him and his passenger their lives.

AFTER TOM'S DEATH, Pat and I seemed to get along a bit better for a short period, and we actually started talking about things we might do together with the children. In early December I bought an older model Cadillac sedan for a family trip to Disneyland. I booked rooms for seven at the Anaheim Hotel, near the famous park we'd visit during the Easter school holidays. Everyone appeared to be excited about the prospect, at least initially.

THE BREAK-UP

OUR CALIFORNIA TRIP began on March 24th, exactly one year after we'd moved to Haro Road. But it did not turn out to be the pleasant family excursion we had hoped for. From the beginning it was a fiasco: Pat got the ferry schedules all mixed up and we missed the last ferry to Anacortes in Washington. We sped over to catch the Blackball Ferry that left for Vancouver within the hour. We got there early and it seemed like an eternity to the three boys.

"When's the ferry coming, Dad?"

"When it gets here," I replied. Seattle was as far as we got that first night but everyone enjoyed a clam dinner at Ivers Seafood, the famous fish restaurant overlooking Puget Sound.

Next morning Dana put on a teenager pout that lasted 'til we got back home. Who can understand teenagers, or ever hope to? I certainly couldn't.

We did the usual tourist things at Disneyland and Knott's Berry Farm. We all enjoyed the heated swimming pool where there were lots of kids. Everyone, except Dana, seemed to be having fun. But we did notice that she quit pouting when boys her age or older gave her a lot of attention.

On the road it was different. When you have five children, from five to 17, it is impossible to settle the petty disputes that arise continuously. I must have swatted each of them on the bottom a good many times. It was a relief to drive back into our yard two weeks later. The garden looked lovely with some of the rhododendrons in full bloom, the daffodils nodding their heads and everything neat and tidy. Inside, Mrs. Whittaker had the house spic and span.

IT WAS NOW time to get out the baseball equipment and begin practising. I had decided to coach the team for their first year. Little league baseball was just getting popular around Victoria. There wasn't much of a diamond or infield at Penrhyn Park, so many of our neighbours worked with rakes and shovels and in about two weeks the field was in fairly good condition.

Our team was a ragtag bunch. Little experience but lots of enthusiasm. Ed wasn't yet nine years old but he badly wanted to play with the 11 and 12-year-olds, and we could certainly use an extra player. The little guy would chuck pebbles around out in right field while he waited for a fly ball to come his way. When he was at bat he would go into his invented crouch, his elbows almost resting on his knees. The pitcher wondered what had happened to the strike zone. When Ed sometimes took a wild swing at a ball up over his head, his teammates groaned.

"Hang in there, Ed," they'd shout. "Wait him out!"

He usually did and then he'd trot down to first with a big grin. He became our resident "walker".

My first game as manager was not very successful. Our boys dropped the opening day contest 14-6. However, we made adjustments and in three weeks this new Cadboro Bay Little League team won its first ball game 15-8. Tom pitched most of that game. He and his brothers had been throwing rocks since they were big enough to walk, so the transition from rock-thrower to pitcher was not all that difficult. Tom usually played third base or caught when he wasn't on the mound. He could whip the ball across the diamond with lots of speed.

I ended up coaching and managing, and the boys actually won their league the second year. Who would have thought it, after that first game?

Tom pitched a game the following summer that he hoped "would never end" as he put it. It was the biggest game of his life. He'd been chosen to play for the Cadboro Bay All-Stars, who were to play a top team from an American league just south of the border, in a playoff game. The field was in downtown Victoria and there was considerable excitement around town.

I had promised to take the family to the logging sports at All-Sooke Day that Saturday, but I told Tom I'd be back to watch the final innings.

We left and Ray and Kenny Baker came by to see Tom. They walked over to the vacant lot next door. Tom had a magnifying glass I'd given him so he could get a closer look at the many bugs around our yard. I also had shown him how to hold the magnifying glass and focus the sun's rays so you could burn a hole in a dry leaf. By noon it was hot in the lot next door and it was covered with dry grass. Fascinated, they watched the long stalks smoke and then catch fire and topple like falling trees.

"Let's build a little bonfire," Ray suggested, dragging in some loose grass and tinder dry branches. Away she went! In no time a brisk breeze blew the flames across the field. The boys raced over to the house and grabbed an armful of towels and wet them with the garden hose. At least they were thinking right. But they didn't have much success. The proper thinking would have been to call for help, but they were scared.

Instead, our neighbour called the fire department. The truck arrived and the fire was put out in minutes. Not much damage had been done.

Tom went into the house and put on his baseball uniform and waited for the coach to pick him up. He thought he was really in for it. We'd come back to the house and see the blackened field and know immediately what he'd done.

But we didn't go to the house. We went directly to the ball park. I was surprised to see Tom pitching. He'd been scheduled to catch. But the starting pitcher got in trouble early on and the assistant coach had put Tom in.

He saw us arrive and thought we had been home and seen the burnt field. Surely we could see the guilt all over his face?

He pitched a good game and the whole team played well defensively but the Cadboro Bay boys couldn't overcome the early mistakes and lost 4-1. When I walked out to congratulate the kids on a good effort, Tom was noticeably subdued. Furthermore, he didn't say a word on the way home.

In our driveway I saw the result of the grass fire and asked, "What happened, Tom?"

"You mean you don't know?" he responded. "Every time I looked at you in the stands, Dad, I was sure you knew."

"Well, I didn't know, but I do now. It was a pretty silly thing to do, Tom, whatever you did. Go have a shower and we can talk later," I said, knowing Tom had already learned a valuable lesson.

THAT SAME SPRING Louvaine Bailey came to me for help. Our family had known "Bain", as we called her, for many years. She'd been like a sister to Pat and me since our Chemainus days and she had worked in the cookhouse for Hillcrest Lumber to support herself and her teenage son. In fact, I had been expecting to hear from her since I knew the Lake Cowichan operation of Hillcrest would soon be closing down.

"I've got no house and no job after the end of the month, and I really would like to get Jimmy away from this area," she said.

Her son fancied himself as a race car driver and he used the road between Duncan and Lake Cowichan for a speedway. The police were not amused and they picked him up every chance they got.

"Would you like to move to Victoria?" I asked. "Why don't you come on down and we'll see what we can work out. Maybe you could start a boarding house? That could solve most of your problems."

"You better believe it would!" was her enthusiastic reply.

A week later she came down and we went to look over several houses in the Fairfield area that I had picked out for her to look at. It didn't take her long to decide which one she liked best. It was a pre-World War One house located at 19 Cook Street right across from Beacon Hill Park. We went in, talked to the owners and agreed on a cash price. I bought the house and put it in Bain's name.

"You'll need no money down and there will be no interest charges," I said. "Once you get operating you can decide on how you want to pay me back. For now we'll just say you pay me what you can when you can."

The children were delighted to have Bain to visit. She had been like an aunt to them, and she always found the time to teach the girls what young ladies should know and how they should behave.

Yet through years of listening to loggers' language, she'd developed her own amusing but terse way of talking and didn't respond kindly to obvious falsehoods.

"Oh yeah, I've heard ducks fart in shallow water before this!" she would say, then add, "If you don't like it here, then pack your duds, gather up your gear and clear out."

Bain's boarders loved her and there was much good-humoured bickering around her table. She enjoyed her life in that old house on Cook Street. Her son Jim settled down, finished Grade XII and moved to Alberta to start a successful trucking business.

I WAS STILL involved in a couple of logging shows up coast. Some associates and I were discussing the possibility of starting up a major helicopter logging operation. Our plan was then considered new and startling, but now it's common practice around the world.

In the early summer of '59, Denis Hagar and I flew to Philadelphia to meet with Steve Tremper, the world salesman for Vertol helicopters. In the parking lot near their manufacturing plant six 50-foot telephone poles had been shackled together with two slings as Vertol's biggest machine idled nearby.

"Are you ready to go for a ride, Joe?" Steve shouted.

"Sure am," I shouted back.

When the chopper lifted its load at the end of a 100-foot pick-up line with ease and swung away out over the river, I was convinced the potential for helicopter logging was here.

We spent the next three months cruising timber and talking to the right people. We had to convince our government that our scheme would work. I did the flying and aerial work while Mauris Ayers, a professional forester, did the ground work. He selected the trees, and by boring into them with a small auger he could obtain weight, volume and age. We flew over each area to roughly estimate the volume of timber, and Mauris mapped the trees on terrain that could be reached and logged

Largest Vertol helicopter, with Joe as passenger, demonstrating log carrying capabilities in Philadelphia.

only by helicopter. This was the key — accessible only by helicopter.

After much research, we had in excess of one hundred million board feet of timber set aside by the B.C. Forest Service, specifically for helicopter logging in areas as far north as Knight Inlet on the mainland, and up beyond Port Hardy on both sides of Vancouver Island.

Vertol Aircraft had offered to bring in two of their powerful experimental 107 twin-turbine transport choppers at their expense. The forestry department was offering sufficient timber to keep us operating for at least 10 years. Without sufficient timber the plan would surely fail.

Our company was known as Pacific Helicopters Ltd. and when it came to the final vote as to whether we should go ahead with this unique logging scheme, a meeting of our five directors was called — J.D.Storie, chairman and president and a major shareholder, Denis Hagar and Bruce Samis who were stockbrokers and the two loggers, Bob Kincaid who was a big truck logger in Prineville, Oregon, and myself. Bob and I voted "yes", but the other three voted "no". Months later Bob and I had a chat and decided perhaps it was a good thing they had voted us down. It was all so new and expensive. It would have cost around seven million dollars to buy the helicopters and get started. We could have gone broke and after all, we were both supposed to be retiring.

Today the chopper option looks better than ever. With all the current environmental battles over clearcutting, and the contravening argument from the big forest companies that selective logging is too dangerous on most steep ground, moving trees to salt water by heli-logging makes a lot of good common sense. At that time, however, Vertol's biggest helicopter was only able to handle 7,000-8,000 pound loads. That's four tons under perfect flying conditions. Since then, of course, the size of helicopters and their capabilities have increased greatly. Moreover, the price of logs has risen dramatically. Did our foresight and research help speed up the beginning of this airbound industry of today?

Hindsight is wonderful, but we had foresight. Thirty-five years later, I know Bob Kincaid and I were visionaries in a logging industry which is now in deep trouble, due to years of over-cutting and environmental concerns, not to mention aboriginal land claims.

The Honourable Ray Williston, Minister of Lands and Forests in the Social Credit government, realized the enormous

MINISTER OF LANDS AND FORESTS

Victoria

September 3, 1959

Messrs. J. E. Garner and J. Denis Hagar
Directors
Pacific Helicopters Ltd.
Vancouver A.M.F., B. C.

Dear Sirs:

This will acknowledge receipt of yours of August 27th, concerning
the acquisition of timber for logging by helicopter.

As requested, I would advise that your understanding is correct
concerning the acquiring of 100 million f. b.m. of inaccessible, mature
timber in the Vancouver Forest District on a salvage basis.

Since you desire flexibility of operation, it may be that you will
want the 100 million feet in several separate Timber Sales in different
parts of the Vancouver District. This is approved in principle, and can
be worked out in detail between representatives of your Company and the
District Forester, Vancouver.

As regards use of your machines for fire suppression, my idea was
not to enter into a seasonal charter, but, rather, to hire these machines
at a Department-of-Transport-approved, hourly rate for use on individual
fires as they occur and when the machines can be spared from their
regular logging activities.

I trust the above is satisfactory.

Yours faithfully,

(SGD) RAY WILLISTON

Minister

**Joe's "million-dollar-letter" from B.C. Forest Minister Ray Williston
approving plans for huge timber cut on Vancouver Island and the mainland
coast.**

possibilities of heli-logging. He put it in writing, making it government policy.

The hundred million board feet could have been worth at least one million dollars. When we were voted down by our partners, two or three other companies were waiting to jump in and begin logging this inaccessible timber with both Vertol and S-61s. The irony behind all our work and time was that these companies were backed by American money.

This whole episode was a great disappointment for me.

In 1960, an article in the Vancouver Sun featured me as one of the successful gyppo loggers, those independent and innovative entrepreneurs who work hard and play hard. I had hoped the interviewer would focus on the efficient ways these small logging companies could and usually did operate.

Instead, it featured that now famous poker game at Old Angus some years ago. It was written by Paul St. Pierre, as good a writer as B.C. or Canada has ever produced. The story grew as it travelled around the coastal logging camps. Some swear one man won three airplanes that crazy night. Not so. Only one airplane actually changed hands, even though at one point there were three IOU's in the pot for a Beaver, a Cessna 195 and a Stinson, all on floats.

Following are some excerpts, with minor editing, from Paul's article which appeared on the front page of the *Vancouver Sun* on February 16, 1960:

> The way to be sure was to talk to the man who was there, so I wheeled through the brick gateposts and down the paved driveway to the Garner mansion on the shore of Cadboro Bay and saw Joe, the herd bull of the Garner enterprises, a medium-size man with a nose like a camel, 51, millionaire he guesses, straight as the grain in a cedar tree.
>
> He is a man of a vanishing breed.
>
> Pays higher wages, logs steeper side hills, and gets more production per man-hour than any big logging corporation in British Columbia, they say.
>
> "Sure, I remember the game, the crazy so-and-sos," he said, as we settled ourselves in one of the living rooms.
>
> "The funniest thing about it wasn't the size of the pot. It was that after the show-down we still didn't know who'd won. It was at my brother Tom's house. There were five of us, Tom, Ted Robson, Jack, George Syrotuk and me.
>
> "Ted and I dropped out of the big hand as George did. I guess I got out of the game five, six hundred

208

up. Maybe a thousand. Tom and Jack kept raising each other.

"Finally, with cheques and cash and IOU's of one kind and another there was $162,000 in the pot, including one airplane, and one whole logging camp.

"Then one of them called and we couldn't figure who was the winner. Tom held an ace, king, queen flush. Jack held an ace-nine flush, but he held the joker.

"Jack said he figured he could call his hand a double ace flush, but he admitted he could be wrong. Tom didn't think there was such a thing as a double ace flush, but he wasn't positive either.

"Finally they shook on it this way. They split the cash on the table down the middle. All the cheques and IOUs were burned. I burned them myself, stack about 10 inches high. And Tom gave Jack his Stinson float plane."

"What happened," Paul asked, "when Tom checked Hoyle's book next day and found that there really wasn't such a thing as a double ace flush?"

Joe was startled. "Why he gave him the plane, of course. What else? The deal had been made, they shook hands, it didn't matter what any rule book said the next day."

That's gyppo loggers for you. And that, too, is gyppo logging. The name gyppo is confusing. Many of the small contractors avoid it now even in casual conversation but Joe says it's a good, proud name.

It has nothing to do with gypping. The gyppo's boast is that he will still do business on a handshake, poker games included. Neither does it denote shoddy equipment. There's another name for that — the haywire outfit.

Sipping his beer, Paul asked about the way we were logging and the equipment we were developing for salvage logging. Here are more excerpts from his article:

"I am maybe the first logger in B.C. to give the guaranteed annual wage. Fifteen percent of my staff get 10 months wages a year whether fires or strikes shut us down or whether they don't.

"The guaranteed annual wage runs from $5,000 minimum to $12,000 maximum. My men are all union men but I pay more than the union wage." said Joe.

"My outfit was the first in the world, as far as I know, to develop the portable slack line spar tree.

There's still only two — one on my show north of Ladysmith and one in Africa.

"We pioneered the Burger air tongs and the pre-loading trailer, with the oscillating adjustable steel reach. Recently, our outfit welded together a D8 Cat with an integral arch, with which we can log 45 percent grades.

"With average-size timber on a good show I'm willing to bet I can get 20 percent more production per man hour than any big corporation on the B.C. coast," he said. "I'm not bragging. I'm just telling you."

"The public," said Joe sorrowfully, "have come to associate bigness with efficiency, but it isn't so."

"The big get too big," he said. "The big get a bloody big pile of executives, non-producers, who spend all their time correcting one another's memos and arguing about which end of the egg to open first."

"Now we got the tree farm licence, designed to protect the inefficiency of the big boy, and maybe the race of gyppos is going to be wiped out."

It may be that only the B.C. coast of a generation ago was capable of producing men like Joe Garner.

"Did you ever go broke?" I asked.

He considered.

"Are you broke as long as you're working and have got ideas?"

I was very concerned even then about how successive provincial governments had turned the forests over to the big corporations, the largest being MacMillan Bloedel. Thirty years later not much had changed, and I would write a book on the subject, *Never Under the Table*.

I HAD NO INTEREST whatsoever in getting into politics and people wondered why. After all, I was recognized as a leader and I was supposed to be "semi-retired". In Duncan I was approached a number of times to run for mayor. When the North Cowichan municipality was formed I was told I could run as reeve, unopposed. But I've always believed, and I still believe, I could more effectively serve the community through such organizations as Rotary clubs and chambers of commerce.

I've known a lot of politicians, both federal and provincial. There are some good people involved. Forests Minister Ray Williston comes first to mind, but many are just in it for the power and the money and what they can get out of it. In the legislature there are numerous lawyers and other professionals, and I felt that if you want to compete, you had better have some university education, although some will say honesty is far better than professional training. Besides, I communicate much better with individuals and small groups.

HOWEVER, I was not having much luck communicating with my wife. My semi-retirement plans were not working out as well as I'd hoped they might when we moved to Victoria. Our marriage was falling apart.

"You're running around too much," I'd say. "Spending too much time partying, away from home and the children."

"How would you know?" she'd reply. "You're never home!"

And that just about summed it all up.

The stress on the children was beginning to show. Nevertheless, I continued to try to build trust in the children. If I told them I would pick them up or be home at a certain time I would do so without fail.

One day Mr. Whittaker met me in the driveway. "Mr. Garner, I'm afraid someone has broken all the windows in our cottage."

"You know who?"

"One of the boys, I guess. But I don't know which one."

At this time, I was pretty edgy myself, and I wasn't as patient with them as I would normally be. I didn't spank my kids very often, but without fail, I would if they told a lie. Tom and Ed denied it. I didn't ask them a second time. They each got a good whopping. Little Gerry probably didn't take part in breaking those windows but he wouldn't "fess up" to knowing anything so I gave him a few on the butt as well.

I was hurting too. Several months earlier, out duck hunting, I jumped across a ditch and landed on the edge of a piece of lumber buried in the mud. I went down hard, and felt a sharp pain in my right knee. Dr. Joe Tassin, who was hunting with us, told me he didn't think I'd ever walk on that leg again. We could see the knee cap was damaged and out of place. It continued to deteriorate as I limped around on crutches over the next couple of months.

I was fortunate in St. Joseph's hospital to get a specialist with lots of knowledge and experience. The following day he came to see how I was recovering and told me he was leaving for Hawaii the next day to take over the running of a new hospital. I was kept in St. Joseph's under intensive therapy for three more weeks.

They must have done a good job because thirty years later, ON THE MOUNTAIN that same knee was now painfully carrying me down a rough logging road on the toughest walk of my entire life.

I was rather short tempered as I hobbled around the house. Pat and I were drifting further and further apart. Then on April 24th, I wrote in my diary:

> *Decided to leave home.* I can't stand any more lies and bitching! Our home is becoming more and more an all night party house. My two best guns and most of my fishing tackle have somehow vanished out of the den. Even the beer and hard liquor have walked away.

There was no official separation. I simply moved most of my personal belongings up to Duncan, and spent many nights sleeping on the couch in our office.

In the autumn I started looking at farm land in Saanich, thinking that if we moved out of the city it could be good for the whole family. Pat showed no interest.

In the spring of 1961 I made one last attempt to get her away from some of the people she was associating with and particularly one named George, a salesman who spent a great portion of his time in the Legion. But without success.

I was spending more time with Shirley, who was in the process of separating from her husband. We even talked about moving out of town together to get away from two unhappy marriages.

A young lawyer named Bob Hutchison, whom I met steelheading on the Cowichan River, advised me that I'd better be prepared if I was thinking of separating from my wife.

"I keep hoping we can work something out without anybody getting hurt," I said.

"You can hope, Joe, but it doesn't usually work out that way. Has she got a boyfriend?"

"I'm quite sure she has more than one."

"Better have them followed. I can make arrangements. We must have reliable evidence if it goes to court," he said, already appointing himself as my lawyer, which was fine with me.

Pat became aware that I was seeing someone else about the same time. She chose her own way to show her displeasure. I had taken Shirley home, and was driving slowly south towards

212

Haro Road when I felt a jolt. Something had hit the back bumper. In the rear view mirror I could see Pat behind me in her car.

Not wanting to stop and cause a scene, I speeded up. Thump! She hit my bumper a second time, just as we got to our driveway. I drove down the driveway, past the house and just kept right on going around and out again. Pat jumped out of her car, slammed the door and went into the house. I spent the night in my office in Duncan again.

Shirley later told me Pat had phoned her, saying, "I want you to know you're welcome to my house and you're welcome to every bloody inch of him. But if you try to lay claim to any one of my kids you'll be the sorriest woman that ever lived!"

This was assuming one hell of a lot on Pat's part.

The following evening I went back home and told Joanne and Dana I'd soon be moving out. I moved into an apartment on Newport Avenue with Laurie Burt, our chartered accountant who was also separated from his wife. It seemed like a match box after Haro Road. I often wondered if I was doing the right thing, but every time I talked to Pat it was clear that reconciliation was impossible.

IT WAS DURING this period I made my last flight as a bush pilot, two years to the month since brother Tom had died in the fatal plane crash. I flew from the logging camp at Doctor Bay on West Redonda Island to Duncan. I had sold that camp to brother Ollie and we were going over the final details. I found I didn't really need the plane for business any more and I no longer had Tom for company in the north country where we always flew as a team. And I'd had my share of close calls.

A bad one occurred in the Fraser River just south of Quesnel. On the way north I had dropped in at Williams Lake to fuel up. This day I remember they had to open a new barrel to finish filling my tanks. To my dismay the motor started spluttering even before I got to Quesnel. I landed on the river. Fortunately I had been forced down across from Western Plywood's booming grounds. Once down, I had enough power to taxi over and tie up to their boom sticks. When I got the gas filter out with a small crescent wrench it was practically plugged solid with dirt.

After draining out all the dirty gas and cleaning the lines and filters I filled up with four gallons of clean gas and took off for Dragon Lake five miles away, where I knew there was plenty of clean fuel and a good aviation mechanic available.

While I was there Al drove out to join me and we later did an hour's flying to locate some new logging roads.

Before taking off for Duncan the following day I had the mechanic help me thoroughly clean all the fuel lines and screens again. Back safely in Duncan I had Jack Griffiths make a light funnel with a chamois leather lining to carry with me for straining any gasoline I was unsure of.

MY SECOND forced landing was in Ladysmith Harbour where I was bucking a head wind of just over 30 miles an hour when the motor quit. A log buyer named Dennis Binstead was sitting beside me. In the sudden quietness he looked over and asked, "What now?"

"Just watch," I said. I had plenty of altitude to glide down and land alongside a tie-up float.

"Now what?" he asked.

"You take those two gallon cans from under the back seat and get them filled up at the first gas station you come to," I told him.

This set us back less than half an hour. At Quamichan Lake we filled both tanks, then I flew him home to Vancouver. This must have had quite an effect on Dennis because he phoned two months later from home and asked if he could come over for a visit. "See you in about twenty minutes," he said proudly. "I have my own plane now."

Dennis told me it was that easy dead-stick landing in Ladysmith Harbour that finally encouraged him to get his flying licence.

THEN THERE WAS the day I left Chilco Lake alone with a strong southeast wind blowing directly head on. I had enough gas for three and a half hours flying. Normally it would take less than one and a half hours to reach Doctor Bay where we had our logging camp on West Redonda Island.

After leaving the inlet near the south end of Chilco Lake I flew over the Homathko ice fields, 10,000 feet above sea level. It's an eerie sensation when you look out your side window at the ice only 150 feet below and see the plane standing still or even slipping backwards, when your air speed indicator tells you you're doing over 100 miles an hour. That means one thing: a 100-mile an hour head wind. After a few minutes of this, a quick decision had to be made. Do I keep trying to go ahead or should I turn back?

I decided to head in a more southerly direction, for Re-

Homathko Ice Field west of Chilco Lake in the Interior, where Joe's plane flew "standing still". Picture taken on a later trip.

donda Island. I slowly turned into the Southgate Valley where I knew the winds should be lighter. Cattermole and Trethewey had a logging camp and plenty of aviation gas at Sonora Island at the entrance to Bute Inlet.

The wind had dropped by the time I reached their camp. First thing Bob Cattermole did was hand me a mug of steaming coffee. He then suggested we sit up a bit closer to their big wood stove. The temperature had been 10 below the old zero coming over those ice fields. After a bit of chitchat I bought 30 gallons of gas, said good-bye and headed on down to Ollie's camp at Doctor Bay, only 25 miles away.

I was exhausted by the time supper was over, and I stretched out on Ollie's old couch in the kitchen for some much needed shut-eye. It was late the next afternoon before I left for Duncan. After talking it over with brother Ollie, I decided to sell my plane.

Though I loved it, flying was getting a little too hectic. My luck might not hold out much longer. I now had three strikes against me, not to mention the flight out from Dall Lake and the time the two eagles attacked my plane as I flew over their nest on Samuel Island. One collided with the leading edge of my right wing and the other struck and jammed the elevators at the tail assembly. I had been lucky. And I wasn't getting any younger.

THE KIDS were at an age when I thought they'd enjoy boating, so Grant Hawthorne, the skipper of our 45' diesel camp tender brought it down to Brentwood Bay from Redonda. I spent the better part of that winter cleaning and painting her and would often sleep aboard. The "Skeena Bell", which I moored on Finlayson Arm, north of Victoria, gave us good fishing and weekend trips that spring and summer of 1961.

In the meantime, lawyers were working out the details for a divorce. I bought a house on Montgomery Avenue which Pat picked out and I paid for. I put it in her name. It was next door to 1054 where we had lived when we first moved from Duncan in happier times.

I now moved my Duncan office to Haro Road where I intended to live until I sold it. By now I had disposed of most of the logging camps and equipment.

Decisions had to be made about where each of the children would live, with Pat on Montgomery Avenue or with me at Haro on the ocean.

We both tried to be reasonable, I'll admit that. We wondered what would be best for each of the children.

In the midst of one of our last family meetings, once irrepressible Ed went upstairs. Minutes later he returned wearing a crude sign: "EDDIE'S FOR SALE - 10 CENTS." I guess this was his way of saying he really needed to be wanted.

Tom, who was boarding at Shawnigan Lake Boys' School, decided he wanted to stay with Ed and Gerry and their mother on Montgomery Avenue when he was home from school.

But the boys would usually spend their weekend with me, so it was a saw-off. I didn't approve of George moving in with Pat while the children were living there and Pat would get angry if Shirley and her three children visited me when the boys were over. She eventually got a restraining order preventing me from visiting my children. Eddie phoned me one afternoon, saying he would like to go to the Jaycee Fair downtown.

"Can't do it," I said. "I'm not allowed to go to your house. Maybe you should ask your mother?"

"I have. She says she and George have made other plans for the day."

Eddie phoned twice more that afternoon and the second time he was crying. This was a most upsetting situation and I could do nothing about it.

Joanne, showing good sense beyond her thirteen years, later said, "Dad, there's just no use ever trying to get back together again with Mom. Too much has happened."

Joanne has always watched people in her own quiet way and her observations of the social gatherings at Haro Road were certainly thought provoking: "The guests seemed to have more fun discussing the party the next day than they did at the time." She believes it was because of what she saw and heard there as an adolescent, that she never became a party goer.

Tom probably had the most difficulty handling the separation. He didn't talk about it and we weren't a religious family, but when he went back to Shawnigan Lake after a weekend I was told he always went into the chapel. He would get down on his knees and pray that somehow, some way the family could get back together again.

It was a difficult time for every member of the family. Even our cocker spaniel Holly seemed uneasy and confused. The children she loved were living in two houses. She wasn't sure where she belonged.

One morning Pat called me, "Joe, we can't find Holly anywhere. No one has seen her since yesterday afternoon. Dana didn't pick her up, did she?"

I put my hand over the mouthpiece and checked with Dana, and then said, "No. She hasn't seen her. Should I go looking for her?"

"Guess you better, the kids are really upset."

I got into the station wagon to drive the six miles across town to begin the search in the Rockland area. But as I pulled onto Haro Road I saw Holly walking slowly towards our gateway. She was tired and hungry, but was obviously happy to see me. I'd swear that little dog was smiling. She had previously travelled that route across town only by car, yet somehow she had found her way through all that heavy traffic and other hazards. It was the Haro Road home she obviously preferred, so when it was sold we moved her up to the farm near Nanaimo where she had lots of room to enjoy the last years of her life.

PART VI

CINNABAR VALLEY

O N THE MOUNTAIN I shuffled along the stony, washed out road sometimes aware of what I was doing, and sometimes aware of other things, at other times, in other places. Mostly, I was aware of wet — the rain around me and at times the water up to my knees in the freezing cold. Leaning heavily on the cane with both hands I was able to take as much weight as possible off my aching hips. Even taking just one step had become extremely painful.

I remembered a family get-together in 1988 for what would have been Pat's and my 50th wedding anniversary had we stayed together. We had remained friends. This was to be one of those good time gatherings where we could all reminisce together. I presented Pat with an engraved gold watch and I lifted a glass of water, or "Adam's Ale" as I call my favourite drink, and asked my children to join me.

"Please raise your glasses and join me in a toast to your mother, to 25 years with, and 25 years without. Best wishes, Pat, on our 50th anniversary."

I wondered what the family's future might hold, and if I would be around to be a part of it.

MOVING TO THE FARM

WHEN I FIRST flew over what is now known as Cinnabar Valley, it spread out below me in varying shades of green. I banked the plane around and came in at a lower altitude to get a closer look at China Lake, sparkling in the sunlight. What a wonderful place to live, I thought, as I flew off to pursue life's activities elsewhere. But in the summer of 1961, I thought again of this secluded valley less than three miles south of Nanaimo. I'd check it out.

Shirley was with me that afternoon when I turned west off the Island Highway onto Extension Road and drove in the general direction of the farm I'd remembered. We found it and as luck would have it, the owner was in front of the little white house at the end of the long wagon road. I introduced myself to Mr. Blanco. I was looking for some land, I said, trying not to be too eager. Just scouting the area, I emphasized.

"Might your farm be for sale?" I asked.

"It is," he replied, "You got here at just the right time. Had someone else interested but his option ran out at noon today."

Talk about the gods being with you!

Over tea we talked about the property, and before we left I gave him two one hundred dollar bills as down payment — all the money I had with me. We wrote out an agreement stating he wouldn't talk to anyone else until after the end of the following week, when I promised to come up with the rest of the money. It was all I had wished for, near the city but away from it all.

It was 300 acres of mostly logged-over land and the house and a barn. The price was $48,000. The price of land was very low in those days but even then his asking price seemed ridiculous. Thrown in was an old Fordson tractor, a mower and a dozen head of Hereford cattle. A good deal. I could recover part of that price by selectively logging the treed area and open up more grazing land in doing so.

I am quite sure the price of the farm was low because it was overrun with the noxious weed known as tansy ragwort. This weed in England is commonly known as "stinking willie" or the "yellow peril". A University of British Columbia professor of agriculture, in a letter to me a couple of months later, would describe its effects on cattle:

> Poisoning from the alkaloid contained in ragwort is cumulative and small amounts ingested over a period of time may result in eventual death. The alkaloid works mainly on the liver. Several weeks or even months may pass before symptoms like loss of appetite, staggering gait and sometimes walking in circles occurs. Post-mortems usually show cirrhosis of the liver (hardening due to an abnormal development of connective tissue). Cattle may develop a tendency to attack anyone nearby. Horses can also be affected, but sheep are not poisoned to nearly the same extent.

Certainly I was surprised the first time a steer took a run at me. Now that we knew ragwort had that affect on cattle, the kids would shout, "Stay away from that one. He looks like he's been into the ragwort!"

Fortunately eating the weed does not effect the quality of the beef and, given a choice, cattle prefer to eat other vegetation.

This weed likely travelled from Britain around the turn of the century mixed in with the hay the donkeys fed on when they were brought over to work in the Nanaimo coal mines. Dr. Adam Szczawinski, formerly the British Columbia Chief Botanist and an author of several books on weeds, stated, "The logging of the Nanaimo River Valley and adjoining areas encouraged the spread of tansy ragwort, since the small dry belt created was ideal for the growth of that particular weed." Cinnabar Valley was part of this dry belt.

Broom was also clearly out of control. Broom was first introduced to Vancouver Island in 1850 by settler Walter Colquhoun who planted several of these shrubs on his acreage. Those few shrubs are believed to be the ancestors of all the south island broom which is found everywhere, even over the Beaufort Range despite the prevailing westerly winds.

But my immediate concern was making the most of the farm so the children would want to join me there. It certainly had a lot of potential to offer.

THE FIRST owner was named Richardson. He preempted the small valley in the last century for about a dollar an acre. It wasn't unusual, when we started fencing the property, to find the line to be out as much as 30 feet in places, so it all had to be surveyed again. When the surveyors found the pile of stones that had held the all important corner post —long ago rotted away — they had to dig almost three feet deep before finding the upside down square gin bottle that accurately marked the southwest corner of the farm.

Richardson seemed to be an eccentric fellow, as indeed many pioneers were. An old timer, Ed Torkko, once told me that when Richardson first moved onto his land he lived in a big, hollow cedar tree down near the creek which was the outlet of China Lake. There were no roads south of Nanaimo. So to pick up his mail and supplies, he would walk down Hong Kong

In 1955 — what remains of the huge hollow cedar tree where Richardson is reputed to have lived for several years. It now graces the front yard of Gordon and Lucy Gerrard and their family at the south end of Richardson Road.

Creek, as it was called, to the south end of Nanaimo Harbour and then make his way north along the beach to the village of Nanaimo. It was a full day's travel and his packsack would be heavy on the return trip.

Richardson and his wife had several children. Then, for reasons I've never known, they separated. Perhaps the hard toil of a pioneer's wife became just too much, or he was too cantankerous, or demanding. He built a house for her on a block of land on the other side of the ridge and she moved out with most of the children and all of the furniture. The two would meet once a year, on Christmas Day, and exchange gifts. Then they would go their separate ways again. The agreed upon meeting place was a moss covered knoll on the top of the ridge overlooking the valley below. The ways of pioneers were often strange.

During the first world war Chinese market gardeners expertly tilled the soil in the valley around the lake. Their horse-drawn wagons would roll out from China Lake across the little bridge that spanned Hong Kong Creek. On alternate days they would head north to Nanaimo or south as far as Ladysmith, both mining towns, to peddle their vegetables and strawberries as they came into season.

I WAS EXCITED about "the farm", as we called it, but which would later be known as the G Bar N Ranch. My life was more than a little mixed up that autumn. Pat came up a couple of times to look around and talk reconciliation, but it was just not meant to be. I didn't really care any more, and she decided she preferred life in the city with George.

Shirley, on the other hand, was enthusiastic about the prospect of living on the ranch and we talked about building a house nearer the lake. Bob Sidell, an architect in Victoria, drew up the house plans with ideas we both thought important.

I listed the Haro Road property for sale in July of 1961, and the next day left with the four youngest kids for a holiday at Harrison Hot Springs, a very nice hotel at Harrison Lake up the Fraser Valley. Shirley, who had recently moved into her own house, joined us with her three youngsters and we had a very enjoyable time.

Pat was furious. Shirley's husband also showed his displeasure, since their divorce was not yet final. So we decided to see less of each other for a while.

For my last Halloween at Haro Road I invited Shirley and her three children over to share our fireworks and a bonfire on

223

the beach. The kids played on a trapeze-like contraption, strung between two trees, while Shirley and I sat on a log and talked about moving all the kids up to the farm. My divorce was five months away, and in thirteen months Shirley would also be free. In the meantime, many things would happen.

ON NOVEMBER 4th, 1961, Mother died while staying with my sister Ethel in Vancouver. She was 77. She never got a chance to see the ranch. I know she would have loved the place.

I WAS SPENDING more and more time up island even though Haro Road, where I still maintained an office, had not yet been sold. The logging camps were now sold and most of the equipment disposed of. My financial position was, one could say, comfortable. I moved one D6 bulldozer onto the ranch to do some much needed road work, clear more grazing land and get some necessary fencing underway. Now I had a backhoe, dump truck and a bulldozer at the farm. I was enjoying working with the machines again but I knew that I would have to hire a man as I had already started preparing a plan for a subdivision some time in the future. The farm and the subdivision were to be my next big projects.

The children came up regularly on weekends. Joanne bought a horse in Saanich, half Clydesdale and half thoroughbred, which we stabled. It was a beauty, but not easy to handle. That didn't matter. Joanne always had a way with animals. "Corey" would gallop across the field to greet her as soon as she parked her car and gave a single whistle.

She later decided Corey needed a friend — and horses do need companionship — so we bought "Copper". Half quarter horse and half Clydesdale, a strange mixture. Copper was a big easy-to-handle fellow who would tolerate as many as five kids on his back at any one time.

I showed the boys how to halter-break and work with their calves, a challenge they enjoyed.

There was always something new for the youngsters to discover in that quiet and lovely valley. Wildlife abounded around China Lake. The kids would take tadpoles from the lake in buckets and watch them develop into frogs. We saw mink, raccoons, beaver, snakes and even a couple of otter. One day Ed came running, saying, "There's some bark chewed off one of the big cottonwood trees below the house. It looks kinda weird." We walked down to take a look.

"Those beavers have worked half way round the tree, Ed."

"Do they eat the bark, Dad?"

"Some of it, but generally beavers like to strip the tender bark off the young willow and alder branches for food. These big fellows obviously intend to bring this huge tree down, take it apart and then drag the limbs over to add to the house they've built where the lake empties into the creek.

"Beavers build their lodge on three levels, Ed. Underwater tunnels usually lead to the living space, which is above the water level. Their dining and sleeping platforms are separate and up another level, with an air hole left on the top of the house. The baby beavers, called kits, are born in the spring about four months after the adults mate. I've stood down there on that dam and listened to the kits squealing in their sleeping quarters.

"The father moves out of the lodge when the kits are young. He keeps working, however, building up the dam, which also becomes a part of the family's winter food supply. Looks like that big fellow has designs on this cottonwood, all right. It's old, but it shouldn't die that way."

"I like this tree. Can't we stop 'em?"

"Could trap them I suppose, although we don't really want to injure them. But I've got some ideas, if you'd like to help."

"Sure!" Ed responded.

We did some experimenting. We painted the bottom of the tree with creosote, but those beavers found ways to get at the bark from underneath. We spread moth balls around because most animals shy away from that smell. But that only worked for a few days.

"Well, I guess this calls for tougher measures. Let's go get some electric fencing. We can hook the wires up just above the water, and give the leader of that beaver gang a message he'll never forget."

"Won't kill him, will it, Dad?" Joanne asked with genuine concern. Wild or tame, every animal was a potential pet for my youngest daughter.

"No. I don't think so, Joanne, but he'll probably get such a jolt, he won't be in a hurry to come back."

We hooked up our electrified fence and watched. That evening the big beaver arrived on schedule, slid up out of the lake and up on the bank. He sniffed around the base of the tree suspiciously. Whap! He really got a jolt when his wet nose touched the bare electric wire. He plunged backward into the water and didn't reappear until he was half way across the small lake. His huge tail began slapping loudly, the danger

225

signal to every beaver within hearing distance. "Stay away! Stay away!" the message said. And that ended that.

They did fall two of the big cottonwoods much later, but the third is still there. So are the beavers. Last time I checked, the tree was listing heavily across the creek. All the bark was chewed away on the side leaning over the water and they were eating away at the roots. It's just a matter of time before they have felled the last one. They never give up. They and their descendants have been chewing away on that one remaining tree for over 30 years, generation after generation.

CLOSE TO CHRISTMAS I went to Montgomery to pick up the boys. I was very upset when I found them building forts in the basement with empty beer bottles. Our private detective had reported to my lawyer, "There's absolutely no doubt about it. George and Pat are drinking far too much for the good of the children."

I spent New Year's Eve 1961 alone, and in my pocket diary I recorded, "Hope '62 will be better and things will get more settled."

The children continued to enjoy their visits to the ranch, and I looked forward to moving up there permanently.

Sister Ethel had been very lonely since our mother passed away. While I was in Vancouver at the annual B.C. Truck Loggers Convention I visited her and asked if she would like to come and live with me. She moved fast and within two weeks she was all happily settled in at the ranch. It was very cold that February but she was happy watching the kids skate on China Lake and in the early spring she felt well enough to help them put in their gardens. She picked the tender young nettle stalks and boiled them. The leaves were eaten as a vegetable and the water put in a cup with a few drops of vinegar and drunk as a spring tonic. She taught Joanne how to tell a male squash flower from a female.

"Make sure you never pick the female flower or you won't have any squash to put away for the winter," she cautioned her. She par-boiled the male flowers and then fried them in butter. They were a huge success and certainly the children kept healthy.

ON MARCH 15, 1962, Pat and I ended our stormy marriage which had lasted almost a quarter of a century. The court decided that the details regarding the custody of our children could be worked out at a later date.

Dana would be 21 years old in a month so she could then make up her own mind where she wanted to live.

Joanne wanted to stay in Victoria and finish high school at Norfolk House, even though she loved life at the ranch. She soon would be 16 and I promised her a car so she could drive up island any time she wanted. She frequently brought a friend along with her for the weekends.

Our eldest son, Tom, was still boarding at the Shawnigan Lake Boys School, where they taught young men leadership as well as the academic subjects.

Ed was definitely clear in his own mind where he wanted to live, "I'd like to move up to the ranch for keeps, and go to school up there next September." That settled that. He attended the Chase River elementary four-room school. He started Grade VI there. He soon made new friends and his teacher told me everything was going well with his studies.

Pat and I agreed our youngest son Gerry should stay with her, but frequently Gerry would join Joanne on her trips to the valley.

Despite the quarreling and bitterness during the last few years Pat and I were together, we would in later years be friends again and remember the good times.

For her part, Pat has been consistent, and when one of the boys was critical of me, his mother said, "Look. I was married to Joe Garner for twenty-five years; I've got lots of reasons to criticize him, and I will. But he's your father. You treat him with respect!"

"I'll always be generous with you," I told our children. "But you have a responsibility to see that your mother never goes wanting."

I MISSED having a woman around and was delighted when Shirley brought her three kids, Shelley, Shane and Lonnie to the ranch for weekends that spring. They joined with mine in helping sister Ethel plant a garden, assisting me with a fencing project or just fooling around.

Doug Robinson had the contract for the new house. He sent his crew in to pour the concrete foundations in early March. The school year was coming to an end and the kids, both Shirley's and mine, were anxious to be on the ranch for the summer. There was not enough sleeping space for everybody. Some slept in the little white farmhouse. Others in the barn. Some in tents. Tom and his cousin Randy took their sleeping bags and spent their nights on the roof of the tool shed. The hay loft was a favorite sleeping place. Wherever they could find room, they slept. They were up at dawn and Shirley cooked for the whole crew with Joanne and Shelley's help.

Gerry and Shane loved to drive the jeep and they discovered more ways to get it out of a mud hole than anyone ever believed possible. They might work at it all day using a jack, planks or whatever else they needed. But they always managed to get it out and would proudly drive it up the lane in time for supper. There was rarely enough water in the well to get them clean enough for their meals. But the lake out front took care of all water shortages. They would put on their bathing suits, grab a cake of soap and go for a swim. They always came out clean. Life on the farm was pleasant and fun.

This was the year "The Tea Pot House" on Lasqueti Island, situated in the Strait of Georgia, was the headquarters for the wild set. It was well known throughout the province. Marijuana, in large quantities, was cultivated around the island, served by a crude ferry from north of Parksville. A nephew of mine was one of the big shots and I later found out he used metal milk cans to transport his product off the island by this ferry. I've often wondered if any of it found its way to the ranch. Could that have been the reason sleeping outside was so popular?

Children, both young and old, developed useful skills, not by watching but by actually doing and making mistakes and correcting them along the way. It was at the ranch Tom learned basic carpentry which has served him well in his adult life.

"Son, I want you to build a feed bin in the barn. It has to have a hopper up on the top floor with a sliding door at the bottom. Can you handle it?"

"I don't know," Tom answered, obviously unsure. "It'll take a little while."

"Doesn't matter. Take as much time as you need. Don't rush it. I'll give you advice if you ask. I want you to do it right, so if you come back here in twenty years you'll find that door still opening and closing smoothly." Tom smiled and got to work. Even today, 30 years later that door opens and closes smoothly and any young man could well be proud of having built it.

We moved into the big house later that summer of 1962. I bought a 40 X 8 foot mobile home and moved it in near the two houses for Bert Barkley and his family to live in. I had hired Bert to run the TD9 cat and help clear more land near the lake.

I joined the local Farmer's Institute. Joanne and Ed became

228

interested in the 4-H Beef Club, so called because it aims at improving the Head, Heart, Hands and Health of its members. It is an international youth organization, sponsored by governments, which offers education in both agriculture and home economics. The two Barkley girls were also enthusiastic members of this club.

Joanne got deeply involved right away, and later she remembered: "I had gone to the Pacific National Exhibition in Vancouver several times and watched these kids showing their calves and winning ribbons. I envied them so much. I thought it would be the neatest thing to have my own calf. I remember going to McLeod's tiny house for a 4-H meeting. Grieg was a junior leader and his dad was the senior leader. The Barkley girls were there and they took me into the back yard where Grieg and his brother Rod were leading around some Angus cattle. One was a bull, and I was so impressed that these young fellows could calmly lead a bull around and seemed to know exactly what they were doing. That was the beginning of 4-H for me."

Though Joanne would never have thought so at the time, her admiration of Grieg would blossom into love and marriage four years later. They would eventually build a highly successful dairy herd in the Yellow Point area, just south of Nanaimo.

Joanne smilingly insists that, when she and Grieg were building their dairy, I had the uncanny ability of knowing when they were at a critical stage, like pouring the concrete footings. When my truck appeared in the driveway, Grieg apparently would look up from his work and say, "As expected, right on schedule, the Eagle has landed!"

When they started dating, Grieg would come over with Rod in a one-ton truck to go to the movies. Since they were the oldest, and the only ones with driver's licences, Joanne would take her Volkswagon along too. The whole bunch headed to the drive-in theatre at Cassidy, just south of the Nanaimo airport.

Ed loved a little game he played. He'd take a flashlight and start at one end of a row of cars. When he found a front seat empty, with the occupants in the back seat necking, he'd climb in one front door and out the other, shouting "Hi!" on the way. One could tell where he was from the screams!

JOAN INGRAM had first visited the ranch that spring and stayed a few days and made some good suggestions about how the stone fireplace should be finished. She returned in late summer with her two adopted children, Anne and Bill, to inspect the finished fireplace, or so she said. "It looks real nice, Joe."

I had known Joan since 1957 when I first started travelling to Brooks, Alberta, for what would become an annual duck and pheasant hunt. Bill Heaney, Denis Hagar, John Olson and I made a congenial foursome, having many good times together. I was considered a very good wing shot. Once when we had a bet on, John shot a couple more pheasant than I did. He grinned as he said, "Victory is certainly sweet, Joe."

"We'll see," I replied. A week later I delivered his $25 prize, in pennies, sunk in a large jar of honey.

John and his wife decided to play at matchmaking, not an uncommon exercise. They hosted a game dinner, inviting Joan, who had been a widow for several years, and myself. But I was still involved with Shirley so I declined. I scented their plan. Nevertheless, Joan and I were thrown together periodically over the next year, while Shirley waited for her divorce to come through.

Shirley was free to remarry in November of 1962, but as her divorce date approached I had begun to seriously wonder if we would ever get together. She was a member of a prominent Victoria family and she received a strong message from her mother. Marrying a divorced man with five children would not be acceptable. The funny thing was, she would be divorced with three kids. We were compatible, but the marriage we had talked about so often was not about to take place. I wished her well and our three year relationship ended. Those had been good times.

Joan kept in touch and was obviously pleased I had broken up with Shirley. We got along fairly well and she appeared — I say appeared — to enjoy the outdoors. She even bought an impressive repair kit to do emergency work on hiking and hunting trips.

She invited Ed and me to Calgary, so we spent New Year's of 1963 with Joan and her kids. Anne and Bill were friendly and well-mannered and Ed seemed to like them.

"How would you like to have them live at the ranch?" I asked when we got home.

"Be okay, I guess. Might be fun having a guy near my age around all the time." On January 6, Joan flew to Vancouver and I met her.

THAT DAY, my father died peacefully at the age of 84. Only two days before sister Edie had phoned saying he was failing, so I went over to see him. I brought Ed along and Dad had got so thin and frail we hardly recognized him.

For years he had been carrying his savings around in a brown paper bag because he had lost confidence in banks. Now it sat on the floor by the head of his bed within easy reach. While we talked he asked, "What do you think is the most important thing in this world?"

After a bit I replied, "Being successful in raising a good family and giving them a good education."

"No, son," he said. "The most important thing in this life is love." Then he closed his eyes and fell back to sleep. Before leaving the room, I pulled the covers up over his shoulders.

We buried him at the Roselawn Cemetery, near Mother's grave. I don't know what Mom would have thought of that, their being together again after all those years. Knowing her, she'd probably have told us to remember the good times.

JOAN TRADED her car for a pickup and made preparations to move to the ranch. We set a wedding date.

My sister Ethel's deteriorating health forced her to leave the ranch to get special care at Lion's Gate Hospital in North Vancouver. The cancer had eaten her bones away to a point where they broke if she just turned the wrong way in bed.

Louvaine Bailey had sold her boarding house in Victoria, and she agreed to move up to the ranch as cook and housekeeper.

On April 2, 1963, Joan and I were married in Calgary. Joan was 40, I was 54. It was a quiet church wedding, attended only by her family and her close friends, Harry Jacques and his wife. We spent the last few days of our honeymoon in Las Vegas at the Tropicana, where Joan became ill. Perhaps her illness so soon after our marriage was an indication of things to come.

RANCHING

I HAD LIMITED knowledge of ranching when I decided to get into the cattle business in my mid-fifties. But as a businessman some things were obvious. You must start with good quality stock and care for and feed them properly, and keep up with improvements and trends in an industry more suited to Alberta than wooded Vancouver Island.

We decided to get a good bull and expand our Hereford cow herd. The only hay land we had was near the barn in a five acre field which was really a joke as far as hay yield went. We soon found that buying hay for beef cattle was a losing proposition.

Clearing, fencing and cultivating the land became an early and ongoing priority. Even with our heavy equipment this was labour intensive. Hiring the right kind of help was not easy. What I needed most was a top hand who was good with both machinery and cattle and who could work without a great deal of supervision. If he had a wife who wanted to help part time at the house, so much the better. Some of the men who worked for us on only a short term basis lived with their families in the original white farmhouse and then left. It was not their thing, or they couldn't handle the cattle.

Joan's two adopted children and my five all lived at various times on the ranch, but only my son Ed and Joan's son Bill lived there full time and attended school in Nanaimo.

It was evident early on that Joan was fastidious and somewhat frustrated with all the activity. She liked everything to be neat and tidy and that wasn't always possible.

"There's no satisfying that woman, Joe," Bain finally said. "Sorry, but I'm leaving at the end of the month." It was a great disappointment to my children. Bain had become like a second mother to them.

AS WE CLEARED the land for pasture it became apparent that we would have to deal with the tansy ragwort, that noxious weed. Joan and I joined the Nanaimo-Cedar Farmers' Institute to initiate concerted action for its eradication in our area. I was immediately elected vice-president and was asked to chair the weed control committee. Joan accepted the job of secretary. I was quoted by the Nanaimo newspaper as saying: "Unless we make a move now, we all might as well give up farming around here."

Two of our best heifers died. I contacted John Zacharias, our district agriculturalist and weed control officer. He phoned Professor A.J. Renney at the University of B.C. He recommended: "Mow the weed three times a year, spray with a strong solution of 2-4-D, and graze sheep on the young plants in the spring."

At one of our first committee meetings a member said, "Joe, no matter what we try to do we'll never get everybody to cooperate. We have ninety members, but there are also just about that many people who aren't members and just don't seem to care!"

"Well then, we'll have to get to all of them individually. Let them know how serious the situation is. We'll try to con-

Cinnabar Valley, a paradise just south of Nanaimo, in 1964 after three years of "tidying up" and completion of new home, right, with China Lake behind.

vince them that they should at least look after their own land,"
I said, and when they agreed we laid down a battle plan.

The B.C. Hydro and Power Authority assured us they
would spray all their power line rights-of-way, and Frank
Richter, the B.C. Minister of Agriculture, arranged to have the
Department of Highways do roadside spraying throughout the
district. Our local M.L.A., Dave Stupich, who had a degree in
agriculture and lived in the district, got involved. He was a
great help.

However, our most effective weapon was a small-sized
moth called the cinnabar, so named because it was the same
reddish-brown colour as the mineral. The cinnabar moth had
been used in other countries with some success. It fed only on
tansy ragwort. It ate all the flower first and then came back and
attacked the green leaves. The moth, we were told, would die
of starvation when the weed was eradicated. Dr. Zacharias had
heard of it, but warned he didn't know how effective it would
be here.

Federal government scientists agreed to work with U.B.C.
faculty members and the B.C. Department of Agriculture on
the project over a five year period. This took considerable
negotiating. It would begin with the release of 3,000 moth
larvae. The university agreed to assign a graduate student to
monitor the moth's activities.

"Just what are you going to be doing?" I asked Wren
Green, the U.B.C. student, when he first arrived.

"Observing, Joe, and recording what I see. I'll be marking
these caterpillars with various colours, and then placing them
in specific areas in the fields. They are voracious eaters and
we'll be interested in their movement and rates of consump-
tion," he explained, pointing to some graph paper on his clip-
board. I had high hopes. As his workload increased he hired Ed
to assist him with data gathering, a good experience for any
young student.

Wren, the entomologist, was also trained as a long-dis-
tance runner and was in excellent shape. He ran two or more
miles each day before breakfast, rain or shine. Ed sometimes
joined him and he later got interested in kickboxing. Ed
worked out with Gord Racette, Nanaimo's heavyweight, who
briefly became world champion in 1974. It was Ed's speed that
gave him a win over Racette in more than one kickboxing
match.

Wren spent several months on our ranch in the spring and
on through the summer for two years, and his findings would

be a major part of his Ph.D. dissertation. He then left for Australia to continue his work there, where the ragwort was taking over much of the grazing lands, and costing farmers millions of dollars a year.

In June of 1965 we hosted our first annual picnic. We invited local farmers, politicians and the press to observe our progress with the ragwort project and have an enjoyable outing with their families.

By the summer of 1967 the moth colony had been well established. Federal entomologist A.T. Wilkinson said his crew had counted 69 moths and 5,734 larvae on 324 plants. Dr. Peter Harris, who's specialty was the biological control of weeds, from the Research Institute at Belleville, Ontario, declared that, to date, this had been one of the most successful plantations ever made in Canada.

I was jubilant. The moth's little gold and black progeny had moved more than a mile up over the edge of the east ridge and devoured most of the tansy ragwort plants in their path. The cinnabar moth was well on its way to eradicating the weed. It seemed appropriate I should name the valley after them.

EXPANSION of the ranch continued. Lean-tos were built on both sides of the barn and a service shed was constructed for welding and other repairs. By late spring we put the cows out with the chosen bulls. The calves were tattooed in the ear shortly after they were born.

We continued clearing and fencing more land for grazing. At times I had no hired hands and would drive the TD24 from dawn to dusk. Where had retirement gone? But I enjoyed it.

Some of our clearing fires were spectacular. After several days of piling brush on the far side of China Lake I went to the B.C. Forestry Department for a burning permit.

"Shouldn't be too bad. Just some logging slash," I told them.

"Okay, just keep an eye on it, so it doesn't get away on you, Mr. Garner."

I drove the farm tractor around and dipped torches in diesel oil and, starting in the middle, ignited the piles of brush. There was a light breeze. Zoom! The whole hillside was ablaze. The smoke rolled so high the local forestry branch got a phone call from the mainland asking if the city of Nanaimo was burning up. The nearby Chase River Fire Department offered to bring their trucks to water things down. I assured them that all was well but we would sure be happy to have one of their trucks on standby.

Just about 90 percent of the piles had been reduced to smoldering ashes by morning. The excitement, however, was not over. Bert Barkley took our small bulldozer to push what was left of the brush piles up into the burning piles. A fuel line broke and diesel oil spurted onto some nearby coals. The engine died and Bert panicked. Instead of turning off the fuel valve on the line under his seat he bailed out and the flames flared. By the time I got there the TD9 was nothing but a charred piece of metal. I was feeling a little hot myself — and Bert Barkley quit before he was fired.

THERE WERE USUALLY many young people around, and lots to do. I paid the children and their cousins or friends, whoever came with them, for helping with the various jobs around the place. They helped with the haying or dug fence post holes and the smaller kids picked rocks and piled them up to be hauled away. Haying and rock picking in summer's heat is a rotten job, but they did it.

The boys soon learned to operate most of the machines. Something always needed fixing, most frequently the Honda trail bike they used to scoot about over the rough roads and steep trails.

One summer Ed and Gerry went to a monster truck and demolition show, where drivers send cars flying up a ramp and over the top of old derelict vehicles.

"Can't be all that hard to do," Gerry declared, after thinking it over.

"So let's give it a try," Ed replied.

Richardson Road then had quite a hump, right where Torkko Road now branches off. They took the jeep and after a few tries over the rise at fairly low speeds, Ed said, "Well, if we're going to get airborne with this thing I'm going to have to really wind her up!"

Up Richardson he went and accelerated back down, shifting into high gear as he approached the hump. The jeep flew through the air out of control, slamming up against the roots of a big fir stump and broadsiding as it skidded to a halt. It was a miracle they lived to tell about it. The jeep? It was repaired, but I told them there was to be no more stunting!

LATE SUMMER and fall was my favourite time. The deciduous trees on the hillsides took on their golden hues, contrasting pleasantly with the always green conifers. Everyone around prepared for the fall fairs, and the cattle auctions followed.

Joanne and Ed got their first experience at showing and selling cattle at the Pacific National Exhibition in Vancouver in 1965. By the middle of August their 4-H calves were in their prime. Joan's son Bill had the best looking heifer but he had gone back to Calgary. I wondered if we should send Bill's big heifer along? I asked Joanne, and she smiled and replied, "She's a good looking calf, Dad, but she sure is wild and spooks pretty easily."

"I'll try to show her," Ed chipped in. "I can hold her if she decides to panic." But Joanne was right. On the big day Bill's heifer took a walk. The judges smiled as they watched 14-year-old Ed leaning back with all his might, his hands gripping the rope, his knees locked, and his heels skidding across the sawdust floor of the show ring. They allowed Rod McLeod in the ring to help Ed hold the animal as they pinned the first place ribbon on it. We were astounded. All the rules had been broken, but we weren't going to complain. That was the first of many awards our cattle would receive.

We regularly attended the fairs on Vancouver Island and got to a couple of cattle auctions on the mainland to improve our stock. Kamloops was considered one of the better places to buy calves as there were some fine ranches in that part of the B.C. interior. It was on the way to one of these auctions that I quit smoking. Joan had developed an awful smoker's cough and I decided I didn't want to end up like her. I threw my full package of Sportsman cigarettes on the dash just to prove I could quit despite temptation. It lay there untouched for almost two years before I finally threw it away, my habit licked. I haven't smoked a cigarette since 1965.

Our first herdsman Wayne Johnston, who was with us for only a couple of months, went to a show in Edmonton with the go-ahead to purchase the Grand Champion Hereford bull. Price no problem. "Just buy it and bring it home," I told him. It cost $1,700. Ask any rancher — there is great pride in owning outstanding stock, especially bulls.

JOAN AND I worked hard at raising good stock and building the ranch, but our life was not what I had hoped it would be. Perhaps I stayed away from the house more than I might have, but maybe it was to escape her constant complaining.

It turned out that she didn't enjoy either fishing or hunting trips. Where had I got the idea she had? She did not join me on even one outing after our marriage. Her wonderful mending box never got used again.

She was not cut out for the rather hectic life style we lived, although when I first knew her, it certainly seemed as if she was. My children seemed to annoy her most. "Why is it," she would shout, "everybody expects to be waited on?"

She was understandably upset when Dana, in a fit of temper she must have inherited from her mother, hurled a frozen roast of beef right through the locked bathroom door when one of the boys deliberately showered until he drained the hot water tank. At times Joan was sorely provoked, it is true.

The break-up really began early in 1965. Joan informed me she was pregnant, but was planning to have an abortion. She had been seeing a psychiatrist about her "depression" so I talked to both her psychiatrist and her general practitioner. They both felt that although Joan was 42 and this was her first pregnancy, having the baby might be good for her mental and general health.

One evening, she announced, firmly, "I've made arrangements to have the abortion, Joe. Don't try to talk me out of it."

"Joan, why are you doing this?"

"You just don't understand. There's too great a chance for complications with the baby when you're my age. I've made up my mind. It's going to cost $700."

"Then use your own money! I'm against it. I think you should have the baby," I told her as I walked out the door. After agonizing, I returned and said, "Joan, I think it's all wrong, but I'll drive you there and stay with you until it's over. We won't talk about it again."

Joan had her abortion and I threw myself into work on the ranch, with the Rotary Club and as director of the Associated Chambers of Commerce for Vancouver Island (A.C.C.V.I.).

A year later I took the Dale Carnegie course, thinking that I might sell mutual funds when my hips and knee got so bad I could no longer do the work of a rancher. Something that Carnegie wrote made me think of Joan: "Act as if you were already happy and that will tend to make you so." I guess Joan was never much of an actress, although she sure had fooled me about the outdoorsy bit. It seems people truly are just as happy as they choose to be.

Perhaps I was naive to believe things might change. But we kept drifting apart. When Joan spent a few days in the hospital for nervous exhaustion I phoned her mother. We decided — or did she decide? — a rest in Calgary might help. She welcomed the trip and seemed a bit better when she returned. But it was a repetitive pattern. If she was not with her mother, she was phoning her. In the spring of 1967 Joan decided to move back to Calgary for good.

SEVERAL MONTHS earlier I'd met a pleasant and unattached real estate agent. It was business at first, but our friendship grew. When Joan left, Marge Jenkins suggested she move in. Tom had finished high school in Victoria and had moved to the ranch to live. He later said, "It appeared to me, Dad, that Joan went out one door and Marge came in the other."

That's not exactly the way it happened, but Marge and I did enjoy each other's company. After two failed marriages I wasn't prepared to consider another, and she never pressed the issue. Weddings were for the next generation. Joanne and Grieg McLeod had already tied the knot. Dana would marry a young accountant, Allen Morris.

I was a bit upset when Joanne got married. They were both only 19 years old and she had left U.B.C. midway through her first year.

"I'm just wasting your money," she told me. "Not enjoying university one bit."

"Well, I'm disappointed, Joanne," I said. "As for the money, you know it will always be there for your education. There's $10,000 in the bank for each of you kids specifically for that." I was very pleased when Joanne started classes at the University of Victoria a decade later and finished, not only her B.A., but also earned an M.A. in English. She claimed she "got hooked" on education when her youngest daughter Erica was in Grade II and she was helping her with her homework.

Neither daughter chose to have the kind of big splashy wedding I would have enjoyed providing for them. Joanne and Grieg were married in the legislative registry and Dana phoned me after she and Alan had a quiet ceremony. But I was delighted when Joanne, and then Dana, made me the grandfather of two beautiful little girls in February of 1969.

Many social functions were held at the Cinnabar ranch over the years. Two of the larger annual ones were our summer field day and the Rotary Christmas party and tree sale.

THEN THERE WAS the Chamber of Commerce celebration at the end of a successful campaign by the A.C.C.V.I. which resulted in a provincial-federal agreement on the Island Highway extension to Port Hardy from Kelsey Bay.

After much hard lobbying on our part, and many, many meetings, Premier W.A.C. Bennett announced the North Island

Highway Project would begin within a year, to the utter joy of every municipality and town along the way.

It all began in 1956 when Gerry Furney came to Port McNeill from Ireland looking for a frontier. Port McNeill was just a logging camp back then. Gerry wanted to get the highway extended from Kelsey Bay to Port McNeill. The public road then ran only a few miles from Port Hardy over to the airport and to Coal Harbour. The roadless miles between Kelsey Bay and Port McNeill were known as "The Incredible Gap". Gerry, always thinking, decided to organize a Pot Hole Golf Tournament.

They had earlier held a limerick contest lampooning the road conditions and the lack of ferries.

Three hundred limericks were received and the best were published. Copies of the book were taken to Victoria and given to all the politicians, many businessmen, and the media!

Universities across Canada wrote asking for a copy. Here are three that I like:

Port McNeill was his Island abode,
And his face with intelligence glowed;
But he turned from his book
With a mystified look,
Saying, "Please, teacher, what is a road?"
Mrs. P.M. Barrett

Port McNeill girls are prettier than most;
Of their beauty we really must boast.
Their magnificent rumps
Are caused by the bumps
On the roads of the North Island Coast.
Mrs. R. Moss

A frustrated tour guide named Stout,
Upper Island praises would shout,
God's country is calling,
But the roads are appalling,
So you cannot get in - or get out!
Ida Clarkson

They planned to hold the first tournament on the pitted and potted main road, but the highways department found out about it and did a beautiful job of grading the road the night before.

Ralph James, then president of the Port Alice Chamber of Commerce, blasts golf ball out of one of hundreds of potholes in downtown Port McNeill during the 1968 Pot Hole Golf Tournament.

Undaunted by such political "trickery" the golf tournament was moved into the town. The main road through town hadn't been graded for three weeks.

So began "The First Great International Pot Hole Golf Tournament", and as it was held close to St. Patrick's Day, shamrocks and green ribbons bedecked the "course".

The press gallery from Victoria and Dan Campbell, MLA and Minister of Municipal Affairs, flew in courtesy of Pacific Western Airlines. They even put on a banquet the night before the tournament to entertain the guests.

Next morning, a Sunday, breakfast was Pot Dogs (sausages rolled in green pancakes) and a glass of hot buttered rum. The tournament was played under diabolical conditions and gave the press a good idea of driving hazards "up north".

The aim of the game was to keep the ball out of the potholes. The clubs were supplied by the town — shillelaghs made from small alder trees. They were cut off above and below a branch, thus making a handle.

But long before, while Gerry was working hard campaigning up island, I put as much pressure as I could on the people in power at Victoria. As president of the Associated Chambers of Commerce for Vancouver Island in 1968 I was able to make a difference.

"Two years later, I used some of the letter writing skills I had learnt in my Dale Carnegie course to write to Premier W.A.C. Bennett, and was thrilled three days later when I received his positive reply — on the opposite page."

Premier Bennett, along with cabinet ministers Waldo Skillings of Victoria and Dan Campbell, then Minister of Municipal Affairs, were among those who attended the celebration at our ranch. Everyone enjoyed the surroundings. The premier, B.C.'s most famous teetotaler, sipped tea while others imbibed alcoholic refreshments. Bennett with the characteristic opening words he used to address nearly everyone said, "My friend, you have a very beautiful spread here."

AFTER SIX YEARS of hard work, I knew it was a beautiful piece of real estate. However, the continuing pain in my hips convinced me I should find a buyer. I soon learned there weren't many people who could afford it.

The answer? I would have to go ahead and subdivide the property. I'd leave the lake as part of the ranch and turn it into a U-catch trout farm.

I began carefully putting my plans together. I had done

1 9 7 0

November 26th

Mr. Joe Garner,
P.O. Box 392,
NANAIMO, British Columbia

Dear Mr, Garner:

I want to thank you for your letter of November 23rd, regarding the highway on the North end of Vancouver Island.

I wish to assure you that in spite of a very difficult year, the Government has kept its word, and during this whole year we have spent money on surveying and engineering this highway, and there has been no delay whatsoever.

On November 10th the Department of Highways gave advance notice to alert contractors that they would be calling tenders for the construction for the first portion of this highway (Gazette of November 12th).

The Department of Highways is calling tenders at the earliest possible moment which, they advise me, cannot be until about the middle of December, due to the fact that they are working on specifications, etc.

It is the intention of our Government, even though we have received no co-operation or contribution from the Federal Government, to build this highway, as per my public statement.

Thanking you for writing me, I remain,

Yours very truly,

W.A.C. Bennett

Letter from Premier W.A.C. Bennett, in response to Joe's letter demanding action on improving the road from Kelsey Bay to Port Hardy. Note letter heading!!

property subdivisions for 30 years, beginning with my pre-World War II one in Chemainus. I knew what was involved in satisfying bureaucrats. One has to deal with the highway officials on the roads, health authorities on sewage disposal, the regional district on zoning and planning, and the water rights branch on matters relating to lakes and creeks.

I anticipated another problem after talking to planners and engineers. They demanded that the city water be piped in. A bylaw change in the Petroglyph Water District would be necessary. All this could be one big headache.

I hired the best people I could find to assist me, and amazingly, the necessary papers were signed within a few months.

Ben Wylie with our big TD24 cat was already building roads, while I dug the trench for the water lines with our new Case tractor. Although there were a few delays along the way, deadlines were met and the work was finished on schedule; an accomplishment not to be sneezed at, as every contractor knows.

"My father would get up on that damn cat with his bum hip and put himself in major pain for hours on end," Ed would later tell a friend.

One of the privileges a developer retains is the right to choose some street names within his subdivision. I called upon Joanne and the boys for assistance with the first phase of the Cinnabar Valley subdivision. The names they agreed on were Cinnabar Valley Drive, Ranchview Drive, and Tedwin Crescent.

The prospectus we prepared for advertising and promotion called for 10 percent down, and eight percent interest on the unpaid balance.

The grand opening was Saturday, March 21, 1970. About 800 people showed up — any event was a big event in the Nanaimo area — including Mayor Frank Ney who spoke, praising everyone and everything in his own style. He bought a lot on Cinnabar Drive. The Chase River Fire Department, to which I had donated work on its new hall, arrived en masse. That day we sold 18 lots, and 16 the following day, an amazing jump start. I had been right, believing city people wanted the peace and solitude of the country while being only a 10 minute drive from downtown Nanaimo and the big Harmac pulp mill.

Surprisingly, we also took many orders for the topsoil we'd dug out to make the ponds.

It was evident from the initial response we should move fairly quickly into planning for phase two. Even though I was elated at the potential, I had other matters on my mind.

I UNDERWENT a series of tests with various doctors. The consensus was that my hip sockets were wearing out. One had to be replaced without delay. The best doctor was at the University of Manitoba.

Christmas 1970 saw Marge and me in Winnipeg. My operation was on December 30th at St. Boniface Hospital.

"A fine way to bring in the new year," I said to the doctor as I was wheeled into the operating room.

BACK TO A LOG CABIN

LOOKING OVER MY CHART Dr. Mills asked in his Irish brogue, "How are you doing?"

"You tell me and we'll both know," I replied. "You got me all wrapped up in this body cast, flat on my back, legs braced wide apart. Right now I can't move anything but my head and arms. Most of my body is numb and you ask me how I'm doing!"

Dr. Mills smiled. "Even though you had the toughest set of leg muscles I've ever worked on, the operation went well. But you can expect to be immobilized for some time and you will have quite a bit of pain as you begin to mend. I'm putting you on a strict diet too. You must lose at least twenty-five pounds. We'll start you on a physical therapy program, to help you get around on that new steel and plastic hip of yours."

Ten days after the operation and half way through my convalescence, I stood and put weight on my new hip for the first time. Using two crutches and a nurse on each side I was able to take a couple of steps. Two days later I was moved by ambulance to another hospital in downtown Winnipeg for intense therapy.

Marge visited me daily, but I was surprised when Joanne showed up with her in-laws.

"Thought I should bring you family greetings from home, Dad. I know you miss the kids and the ranch."

"Sure do. I can hardly wait to get home."

"Is it always so terribly cold here in Winnipeg?" she asked. "We nearly froze in the parking lot out there."

"Spoken like a true British Columbian, Jo-Jo. Most of Canada suffers through this kind of weather every winter. We sure take a lot for granted on Vancouver Island."

AFTER THEY LEFT I started wondering just how much of a handicap this artificial hip might be. The work was not a concern. I could hire the help needed to run the ranch. Carrying through with the subdivision would go okay. But a man establishes some lifestyle patterns over time and mine were almost etched in stone.

I would be able to get over to the Annual B.C. Truck Loggers Convention in Vancouver, a week-long business and social affair I enjoyed — chatting and drinking with old-timers I had worked with, as we fought to hold our rightful place in the timber industry.

The mid-summer Pacific Indian Shoot at Harrison Hot Springs might prove to be a problem. Standing unsupported at the firing line long enough to shoot 100 targets could be painful and very tiring. I'd just have to try it when the time came. But it was a very special day seven months later, when Tom and Ed joined me and my brother Ollie, and his son Ken, to enter a Garner squad of five. We shot well, all of us with a score in the nineties. A proud day and a memorable occasion that none of us are likely to ever forget. In spite of the pain I thoroughly enjoyed myself.

What concerned me most was the possibility I might have to cut back on my fishing and hunting, two of the loves of my life. I'd been winter steelheading for more than 40 years but could I still get down those steep trails to the island's rivers and land a big one on opening day? Summer fishing in the saltchuck for salmon or in the Chilcotin district for rainbow trout would not be a problem as I'd be in a boat most of the time. I already knew I'd have to carry a big soft pillow to sit on, but so what? Who ever said life was easy?

My hunting would certainly be curtailed. I'd been told to limit my walking to level ground. I hunted blue grouse in the Nanaimo Lakes area in the early fall and then headed for Brooks, Alberta, for ducks, geese and pheasants. Ducks and geese would not be a great problem as we used decoys to bring in the birds. Pheasants would be a little more difficult, but we'd figure something out. Maybe I'd wait at the end of a fence line while others hunted towards me, driving the wily birds within shotgun range.

In mid-November I'd get out my rifle and line it up until I was able to hit a salal leaf at 100 yards most every shot. There was always great anticipation as our group got ready to head north to the Cariboo for our annual mule deer hunt at the Gang Ranch. There would also be moose and a few bighorn sheep in the area. Augustine, an old cowboy on the Gang Ranch was a big game guide during the fall and early winter. He told us that Tom's Studebaker truck was the first motorized vehicle that had used the wagon road leading to the sheep flats. I well remember we did have to get help from a team of horses to get over the steepest hill that first year.

Tramping the bush had always been a major part of my life, something to look forward to and it keeps a man in touch with nature. I sure hoped to be able to continue this way of life.

ONE MONTH after the operation I was home and the whole family came to a belated Christmas dinner. Marge cooked a turkey and a ham. Later, as we sat around the fireplace, Gerry asked, "Well, Dad, this hip operation, will it slow you down a bit?"

"Not so anybody will notice, I hope. We've got lots of work to do on the subdivision and I sure would like to see you boys get involved. As for hunting, we'll see. I'm going to buy the best 4-wheel drive I can find to get us back out where the game is. Maybe, just maybe, some day you can spook a big buck my way."

But all in all it was certainly tough. When the spring steelhead run was on in the Nanaimo River I couldn't make it down over the steep trails on my crutches. I watched the action below from the bluffs overlooking the river. The spin casters let their red and white lures drift downstream to the deep holes where the wary steelhead usually settle to rest near the bottom, facing upstream. They are not hard strikers. They mouth a bait and will spit it out if you're slow to set your hook. But once hooked, a steelhead will explode with an energy that's unbelievable. An experienced fisherman will make sure the fish is kept headed upstream when this happens. Many a novice, with his drag set too loose, has watched a 15-pound fish strip his reel dry with a single run down river.

But a man of action is never a contented spectator, so Jack Stevenson and Sid Pitt helped me down to the river on many occasions, and I'd try a bit of spin casting. Any wading on the slippery rock bottom was out of the question. These trips weren't as productive as they once were but I always enjoyed being on the river at daybreak. The sight and sound of the rushing river more than compensated for the risks involved.

Hunting was less of a problem. I had a good vehicle and an understanding of game habits and I could usually get to where I needed to be.

I remember a deer hunting trip to the Nimpkish Valley

north of Campbell River in early September with John Heisterman. We'd driven most of the night to be there when the deer season opened. It was a long, slow trip and we took turns driving. We got there just before daybreak and parked at the edge of a logging slash and waited. I was searching the hillside through binoculars when John thought he saw some movement in the scrub on the far side of the clearing.

"There are definitely some deer over there, Joe, but in this mist I can't tell if there are any bucks among them."

"Let's have a look," I said, going to the nearest stump where I was able to rest my elbow and hold the rifle steady. Through the scope I could clearly see several deer moving about.

"You can't walk any further into that bush, Joe. Would you like me to hike around the far side and try to drive them into the open toward you?"

"Won't be necessary, John. There are no big racks over there, but there is one young buck." I flipped the safety catch off, aimed and squeezed off a single shot.

"Would appreciate it, John, if you'd go over and clean it and pack it out to where we can get to it with the truck later."

"Okay, but I wish I was as sure as you are that it isn't a female."

Young John trotted off across the slash and when he returned with the liver and heart, he shook his head, saying, "It's a spike all right. I still don't see how you knew."

"Behaviour, John. When I looked at them through the scope, he had his head up, sniffing a doe's back end. Females just don't do that," I explained. On the way out John got himself a nice fat two-point, so we loaded them in the back and headed for home. Not a bad morning's hunt and we both had some good meat for the winter ahead.

I discovered that hunting grouse isn't too difficult for a guy with a bum leg if he has a good dog to retrieve. Blue grouse are frequently found along logging roads, especially in the evenings when they come out to pick up fine gravel for their gizzards so they can properly digest the berries they eat. Most grouse are stupid. When they spot a hunter they will crouch down, giving you ample time to prepare for a wing shot when they take flight.

After my first operation I trained a young German pointer. He had a good nose and found most downed birds in a matter of minutes. Tippy would gently pick it up, pack it over and lay it proudly at my feet with his tail wagging, and wait to be praised and petted, which an experienced dog owner always does.

That my hip was slowly coming unglued came as no surprise, since I'd pretty well ignored Dr. Mills' orders:

"You've got to take it easy. Stay on level ground," he had warned me. But I had a ranch to run and land to clear. My sons were now busy with their own lives. Tom had finished a B.C.I.T. diploma course in commerce and accounting at Malaspina College, and had taken a job in Victoria. Ed and Gerry had said they would be around for the summer but Ed was moving to Prince George to work in a bank and Gerry was planning on joining him.

JACK AND JOYCE BAKER, with their four children and their cat, had moved into the farm house after the Barkleys left. They had to thoroughly clean the floors and walls of the house, as the Barkley family had a pet monkey that had never been house broken. The stink had permeated every crevice. How anyone could have lived with it is beyond my understanding.

Joyce did the gardening and helped look after our stock, while also taking over from her mother, who had been doing chores around our big house. Jack was a school bus driver and a good mechanic. He had time to help me with jobs around the ranch. I let him bring their two horses for Joyce and the kids to ride. An excellent family to have on a farm.

MARGE was pleased when I gave her son Tom the job of herdsman. He and his wife Lois, with their three children, moved into the 40-foot trailer.

Over the past two years we'd been through two bad epidemics of pink-eye. Tom had just taken over the care of the cattle when we had a real comedy of errors. He got a finger caught in the universal joint of the farm truck and had to just sit around with his arm in a sling for a couple weeks. At the same time, I decided to sell seven heifers that had been bred to our best bull to brother Al in Quesnel. I asked Tom if he felt like making the trip.

"Yeah," he said. "I should be able to get five of them in the farm truck."

"Okay," I agreed. "Put the other two in the three-quarter-ton pickup with the cattle box. I'll send Herman with you. He'll be handy to have around if anything goes wrong."

Tom and Herman loaded up next morning, and headed for the first ferry to Vancouver. I received a phone call a short time later, a surprising one.

"Joe, we've lost two heifers," Tom reported.

"You've done what? How the hell could you do that?"

"Well, it's like this. When Herman got to the ferry I went around to check his load. The tail gate was down and the truck was empty. Herman didn't even realize they were gone."

"Any idea where the heifers left the truck?" I asked.

"Nope. But my best guess is the hill at the top of Richardson Road, right where it turns towards the highway."

"Probably as good a guess as any, Tom. I'll go up there and check for signs. They might have headed into the bush. For all we know though, those heifers could be wandering around downtown Nanaimo! If you two weren't able to load and get the cattle a few miles down the road, how in hell did you expect to get them 450 miles up to Quesnel. Now listen. Both of you take the big truck on up to Quesnel and get back here as soon as you can. Just leave the pickup in the parking lot and put the keys on the right front tire. We'll pick it up."

Tom and Herman got back from Quesnel two days later and we discussed ways we might get the two heifers to come back home on their own. They had been seen in the woods just outside our fence twice. Searching along the power line I had seen them several times but as soon as they saw my truck they bolted like wild deer. I knew the longer those heifers were on their own the more easily they'd be spooked.

"What if we wean a couple of calves early and put their mothers in the field closest to the bush? Their bawling might attract the heifers," Tom suggested.

"It's worth a try, Tom." The plan did work, it did bring the heifers near. But we wouldn't get those animals back inside the fence for nearly three weeks. When we finally coaxed them in through the gate with some fresh hay, they were so wild I didn't think they would ever be much good. But by the end of the spring they were behaving almost as well as the other cattle.

Al came down with his cattle truck and hauled them to Quesnel himself. He told me one went loco a few weeks later when he drove her into the squeeze in his corral to give her a shot of penicillin. She did not like being hemmed in and climbed right up and over the six-foot pole fence, an amazing feat of athletics. I'd like to have seen Al's face when that happened.

Tom left us — with $999.89, the usual amount paid by the Workman's Compensation Board for accidents on the job such as his mangled finger.

THE FINAL PHASE of the battle against the tansy ragwort began with a phone call from John Zacharias, the district agriculturalist. He said he was going to get spraying started along the highways. He was pleased with the work of the cinnabar moth, but added, "We want to try another insect. With your permission, Joe. The moth does a great job on the flowers of the plant but there are still too many seeds left to germinate. We've now got this fly that ..."

"You've got what?" I asked.

"A fly, Joe. *Mylemya seneciella*. It survives only on the tansy ragwort seeds."

"Then conveniently dies when their food supply is gone?" I asked.

"That's right. That's what's supposed to happen."

"Well, I trust you scientists know what you're doing. Let me know what I can do to help."

"You can set aside five acres where we'll release this fly and watch its progress."

Our annual field day was held in June. Most of the farmers in the area who were concerned about the weed problem had come to the ranch to share experiences. The CBC sent out a reporter and a camerawoman, Alf and Aggie Flett, to cover the story. They interviewed Fred Wilkinson, entomologist with the Canada Department of Agriculture at U.B.C. Wren Green was there, still working on his doctoral thesis. Our report told them that spraying with 2,4-D had been done, but within two years we discovered the plant was growing twice as tall and had at least double the number of seeds. We then tried adding diesel oil to a mixture of 2,4-D and 2,4,5-T, a very potent weed killer and brush spray. It was far more effective. We tried burning with propane torches donated by the local distributor, Dick Bond, but the fuel proved too expensive. Ed Torkko reported he had spent a small fortune and a lot of valuable time mowing, spraying and burning the weed, but had fought a losing battle.

Looking back, there is no doubt the cinnabar moth and the seed eating fly were our salvation. The message the Fletts conveyed to their television viewers was that we had waged a long war with the tansy ragwort, and we were winning. Thirty years later there are few, if any, ragwort plants visible in the fields around my house. I yank out any I see, but they are coming back along the roads and in other fields not far away.

IN 1971, I asked Michael Gergely to do a large landscape painting of the ranch and valley. He had studied under Picasso.

One day two years later as we were driving out for a morning's fishing on the Koksilah River, Picasso's death was broadcast over the car radio. Michael asked me to stop. He got out and stood silently in respect. I got out and stood beside him. As we stood there looking skyward, a comet came from the west and travelled directly over our heads to vanish from sight in the east. What did this phenomenon mean?

Minutes later we scrambled down the steep trail to the river without a word being spoken by either of us. By ten o'clock we had landed several good-sized steelhead so we headed for home. Neither of us ever mentioned the strange appearance of the comet.

The timing of the painting was certainly appropriate because later the valley would look quite different. Nanaimo was growing rapidly and there was a strong demand for building lots. The second subdivision was near completion when the New Democratic Party, the first socialist government ever elected in B.C., brought in its highly controversial Agricultural Land Reserve legislation. All land that was classified as agricultural was frozen, at least for the present.

Ted Barsby, a prominent Nanaimoite, was appointed chairman of the local land commission that could make decisions on doubtful lands that should or should not be included in the freeze. I'd known Ted for years — he was a dedicated outdoorsman — so before things got too complicated I invited him out for an informal meeting. We were sitting on the front porch looking out over China Lake.

I said, "Ted, I don't think much of this government. It appears they have classified that lake as farm land, given it a lot number, and put it in the land reserve."

Ted looked confused, saying, "Are you telling me the lake was surveyed with the surrounding land?"

"That's right. They surveyed this place when the lake was frozen and there were about six inches of snow on the ground. They ended up driving some of their survey pins into the ice. They're now somewhere out there in the mud."

"I'll be damned! And the government approved your subdivision plan?"

"It's been through every office as a surveyed lot. So I'd like to suggest, Ted, that the block which contains the lake be taken out of the land freeze. It will also save the government some embarrassment. If that doesn't happen, I'll probably see you in court. The best legal opinion I get so far is that you'll lose!"

"Joe, you have a point there all right." Ted agreed.

I handed him another beer and we chatted about other things as we watched the sun go down. Three days later, I received a letter which informed me that the lake and two adjacent acres of land were no longer in the freeze. The result was my plans for a trout farm and the possibility of getting into the topsoil business were no longer in jeopardy. I had long thought about the trout farm idea, and had looked at operations in Washington and California as well as in B.C. Our lake appeared to be ideal. A spring-fed creek ran down the hillside at the southwest corner of the ranch and emptied into China Lake after first filling a small pond nearby.

As a result of centuries of growth and decay, lowland lakes slowly become marshes and eventually dry land. The banks of China Lake were at the stage where they floated as a rich mix of vegetation that was slowly being converted to peat at deeper levels. Dig a hole a fair distance from the lake and it would immediately fill with water. If we dug a few more ponds we could use this source of water.

Fishing is both an exciting and relaxing activity for people of all ages and I recall Gerry once saying, "Dad, I'm going to bring up seven buddies from Victoria, school friends. We'll camp here next weekend. That okay?" It was more a demand than a request.

"Sure," I said. "Where are they all going to sleep?"

"We'll pitch tents up on the ridge and we can do some hiking and trout fishing."

"That's a good idea, Gerry. There seem to be lots of trout both in the creek and the lake this year."

They were a great bunch of youngsters and some of those teenagers caught their very first trout that weekend. I thought of a setup where old-timers or handicapped people could easily get down to the lake and cast a line, even from a wheelchair.

In California looking at state and private trout farms I learned a great deal. The need for water quality, aeration and temperature control for raising healthy trout was a must.

But, things happened, and for a couple of years I put the trout farm on hold again. We were fully involved with the subdivisions and selling lots and I even decided to build a few houses myself. I contacted my old partner Shorty Berkey, "It would be great to have you supervising construction again, Shorty. He showed some early interest but then declined, saying,

"Thanks, Joe, but my wife has not been feeling well lately.

Remember, I'm officially retired. Isn't it about time you retired yourself?"

"Don't think so, Shorty. Tried it once and didn't like it."

Ed and Gerry moved back to the ranch early in '73 to work with me on the subdivisions, helping to install the 10-inch water pipeline from the Extension district to Cinnabar Drive. They both worked as flagmen controlling traffic on Extension Road, supervised by John Harness who lived at the end of Extension. He was 80 and took no guff. Anyone who didn't come to a full stop when he waved his red flag got a blast: "Don't forget you s.o.b. that I lived here long before you were born, so you had better pay attention or you won't get through to your home this way." The boys named him "Mr. Stop and Go" and sent any irate commuters they couldn't handle to him to be straightened out. While installing this pipeline I twice fell into the ditch, which didn't do much to help my loosening hip or my outlook on life.

THAT AUTUMN Ed decided he wanted to finish his education at U.B.C. I was extremely proud of him three years later at the

First university graduate in the Garner family, Ed flanked on left and right by Tom and Gerry with sister Joanne.

spring convocation in 1976 when he made the Dean's Honour List and graduated with a Bachelor of Arts degree, majoring in commerce and economics.

My children were all making decisions that would lead to independent careers, so I decided to do a third and final subdivision. The ranch house and lake would be left in a 20 acre package which would allow for the development of the trout farm. I divided the remaining land up in parcels of equal value and gave one to each of my five children, but kept six acres on the bottom of the ridge for myself. I took this step after a meeting with Laurie Burt, our chartered accountant.

"The tax man will take a mighty big bite out of any profit you show from land sales, Joe," Laurie said. "Moreover, your children will benefit significantly from land possession now, rather than having to wait until you're gone. Your death duties could be as high as $600,000, so this way just makes good sense."

The ranch house package I decided to sell outright and even carry the mortgage if the right buyer came along. Then John and Sherry Heisterman dropped in to tell me that they had recently sold their home in Victoria. John was quitting his government job at the Water Rights Branch and was looking for a place to go into business for himself. I was immediately interested. Here was a good prospect. I'd known John since he was a lad in Victoria. His mother Peggy had got my kids started in Boy Scouts. In fact, I knew him very well and he wanted land. Could we do business?

"Maybe you've come to the right place at the right time, John. How would you like to buy this place?" I asked him.

"I don't have that kind of money, Joe!"

I named a price. "How much could you handle as a down payment? I'll carry the rest as a low interest mortgage," I told him.

"Gee, I don't know, maybe fifteen percent."

"That could be enough."

"But we don't know much about cattle, soil or trout," he added. "In fact, I guess we know nothing about farming."

"No problem. You can learn, I'll work with you for a while. As for the cattle, I'll sell off most of them but leave you with a few, so you can retain your farm status for income tax purposes."

"I don't know what to say."

"Go away, think about it for a couple of days. If you like the deal, give me a call. I can get the papers drawn up, and you could start moving in here the end of May."

"Here? In this big house?"

"Yes. Marjorie and I should be out of here by then. We've been building a smaller house over there at the bottom of the ridge. It should be ready by then." The Heistermans liked my proposal and moved into the big house right away, renaming it Cinnabar Valley Farms.

John and I had some interesting times together during the first couple of years. John also was interested in trout ponds. This meant digging about 6,500 cubic yards of soil from a site near the lake. I was showing John how to use the big backhoe when it threw one of its tracks and the engine stalled. We bailed out as it started sliding slowly into the deep hole we had just dug.

With a trace of panic in his voice, John shouted, "We're going to lose her, Joe!"

"Not if I can help it," I yelled and headed for my truck. "Try to get a heavy cable on the main axle. I'm going for the cat!"

I don't know if anyone has ever checked just how fast a big cat can travel downhill. Whatever the top speed is I surpassed it on the TD14. Once I got the machine rolling I kicked it out of gear and let it free-wheel down the steep hill. I'm sure it was going 40 miles an hour. John must have thought it was out of control but he had the cable ready to hook on when I got there. The drum line tightened and the shovel was soon pulled out of danger. Without a doubt, minutes later that machine would have disappeared in some 20 feet of soft mud and water.

One morning John called me. He'd broken the main belt on the big shredder that made soil out of the peat and he didn't know how to lace the belt. I drove down to give him a hand. When the job was finished John and Sherry walked with me to my pickup. We didn't know their young son Tyler had been playing in the driveway and had crawled under the front end.

As I started to drive slowly forward I thought I felt an obstruction, then Sherry screamed, "Tyler's under the front wheel."

Instantly I felt nauseous.

Fortunately, the slow-moving wheel had pushed him forward instead of rolling over him. Tyler's hip was broken, but after a few weeks in a cast he was walking again, in fact Tyler would become one of the fastest middle-distance runners in B.C. in his mid-teens.

THE SMALLER HOUSE was a letdown for both Marge and me. There wasn't as much space as we had been accustomed to the past few years. We had actually started planning the previous fall. Marge had wanted some special features in the house. She worked in real estate, so I went along. A sunken living room worked. Having only one bedroom didn't. I had always had family and friends visiting and that wasn't about to change. So I built a guest house nearby.

When we first started living together, Marge had recently been widowed, and I was in the process of getting divorced. We each lived our own lives day-to-day. Marge sold real estate and I looked after the valley. We always had a housekeeper and we enjoyed entertaining. My children liked her down-to-earth ways. But there had been little talk of marriage. Then Marge told me she wanted to move nearer her son and grandchildren in the Fraser valley. I'm sure she knew her health was failing. We loaded her belongings into the farm truck and moved her into an apartment in Abbotsford. I was now 65 and although I have had a number of short term relationships since, no woman has shared my mailing address since Marge and I split.

I HAVE NEVER liked travelling alone. In Vange Brossard I found a willing companion who always made trips eventful. Vange's father and I were both past chiefs of the Pacific Indians and it was at one of these shoots that I met her. I learned early that Vange didn't always accept advice graciously, but then I'm afraid I've always given it too freely. She was clever, artistic, and independent, always interesting to be with, but certainly had a mind of her own.

Hiking the rugged highlands in Scotland near Inverness was hardly a wise pastime for an old guy with an artificial hip, but I decided I would like to return for one more bird shooting trip there. Would she like to come along?

"Maybe you'd enjoy organizing a dinner for the gang who will be shooting with us," I asked cautiously.

"I can handle that. How much money can I spend?" she asked.

"Not too much."

"Give me a figure. If you want it done right, Joe, you've got to pay the price," and I remembered Vange's father had been quite wealthy so she was never prepared to cut corners. She came and the dinner was a huge success. We supplied the pheasant and the hotel did the catering for twelve. It cost me $600, but it was worth every penny. Captain Robertson's wife was still talking about it a week later when we went to their home for afternoon tea. Robertson was in the Royal Navy and had commanded a destroyer.

The long driveway leading up to the Robertson's beautiful old house was edged on both sides with curling stones placed about three feet apart. Some of those granite stones were more than 300 years old and not all were as polished as the stones used today. You could still see the chisel marks on the edges of some of the older ones.

That afternoon the main topic of conversation was about Canada not allowing the huge Concorde jet aircraft to land at Vancouver Airport because it might break the sound barrier during its descent!!

One of our gang was a medical doctor who had put himself through university by poaching game in Scotland. He was a good guy to have around, as he knew the game habits and the best places to be. He told us he spent many nights in the hills, hiding out from the gamekeepers who suspected him.

The following year Vange went with me to Hawaii, but unfortunately, things didn't go as well there. Vange was moody, constantly complaining and when we got home I said, "Never again!" That remark effectively ended our closeness.

However, we did get back together many times and still see each other occasionally. We've argued over lunch whether the sun at that time is on its way up or going down. Never a dull moment with Vange.

THE CHILDREN handled my gifts of Cinnabar Valley land in different ways. Dana sold her lots and used the money to open an antique store in Nanaimo. This venture was a complete disaster because of numerous robberies.

Joanne was given the old farm house, the farm buildings, and adjoining pasture land. She and Grieg raised cattle there for several years and then sold out to the Heistermans who needed more land. They used the cash to improve the dairy farm she and Grieg owned at Yellow Point, a few miles to the east.

Tom got the land on top of the east ridge with the under-standing that I could build a house on it and live there for as long as I was able. Tom has recently developed and sold most of that land.

After Ed graduated, he and Gerry wanted to go into business together. They were close and saw things much the same way. I suggested they take over G. B. Western Pulp Ltd. — a company that had specialized in salvage logging and was now a company in name only. They opened an office in Nanaimo right above the new squash courts at the corner of Wallace and Fraser Streets. Through the company they started developing the land they had been given, but unfortunately on the days it rained they spent more time playing squash than operating their equipment.

John Heisterman, after digging more trout ponds and deepening the creek bed to join the two lakes, was making a good living selling top soil. He sold some pan-sized trout to restaurants and immature fish to those who wanted to stock their own ponds, but John never got my idea of a Pay-n-Fish operation underway.

"It's just too hard to control," he told me. "You need somebody around twenty-four hours a day or people will steal your fish." It was a problem I had never really considered.

Ed and Gerry also had topsoil on their land around the south end of the lake. They worked on their own for a while, but as Heisterman had the all-important soil shredder and swamp mats, they decided to try working jointly with him. This arrangement proved unsatisfactory. They didn't believe in working the long hours that John thought necessary, so they decided to get out of that business and stick to house building which they did well. They didn't discuss their decision with me and their 30 acres, including the topsoil, was snapped up by John for $110,000. He began mixing the soil with sand and fertilizers and bagging it as potting soil. The Heistermans would market over a million dollars worth of topsoil in the next 18 years.

After I'd been away, I was anxious to see what the children had been doing, even though there were times I'm sure they were not keen on receiving my fatherly advice, particularly if things were not going well. When Ed and Gerry were building houses, especially when they were trying to put on a cottage-style roof, Gerry would say, "If anything can go wrong, it will — just the minute Dad arrives."

It's easy to say, "Too much, too soon." Hindsight provides one with 20/20 vision. Be that as it may, both Ed and Gerry have done well in a number of business ventures and are now real estate salesmen. Ed also has a night club in downtown Nanaimo.

Having got rid of my real estate I now had only a small herd of cattle. Retirement seemed again to be a possibility. I wanted to build one more house, my design, my material, truly a British Columbia house. I chose a site where I was grazing my cattle on the west side at the top of the ridge I'd given to Tom. It overlooked the lake and valley and the 60-mile view to the east.

THIS HOME would be built entirely from logs. I finally found what I was looking for at 100 Mile House, in the Cariboo. The Donovan family for five generations had built log homes throughout the province. With their experienced log house designer we planned a large cabin with no steps, as I expected to have trouble walking in the years to come, and with a covered walkway all around. The cantilevered overhang of five feet would be a major factor in supporting the flat roof. The overall external measurement ended up being 68 x 36 feet, nearly 2,500 square feet — certainly quite a bit bigger than the log shed I was born in. The house was built at 100 Mile House, then dismantled and delivered to the building site on Cinnabar Ridge.

In the meantime, there were many preparations to be done. The first project was to get power to the site. They used the same rock to support the hydro pole that the Richardsons are said to have used long ago for their meeting place on Christmas day when they exchanged gifts. In late November, we poured the concrete for the house foundation, the floor and the huge nine-foot wide fireplace in the center of the living area. There would be two separate flues in the chimney, one for the open fireplace and one for a wood-burning stove in the kitchen.

A big cat would be needed to help the two trucks get up the steep hill to the building site. I thought if the school children in the area could come and actually watch the cabin being assembled it would be an enjoyable learning experience for them.

We had a large tent erected the day before the trucks were to arrive. The Baker family all pitched in setting tables up and collecting dishes. I had asked Mrs. White of the local Nanaimo Indian Band if she would prepare sea food for 120 guests. She was teaching Indian history and folklore at several of the schools in the Ladysmith, Nanaimo and Cedar districts.

February 8, 1977: for me a truly gala occasion. The two logging trucks had taken the first ferry from Horseshoe Bay to Nanaimo. At the bottom of the hill we used a stout cable to join the two loads together. I hooked the D7 onto the leading truck, yet with those three powerful engines going full out we barely made it up the steep muddy incline. What would have happened to our party if they had failed? Even now I don't want to think about it!

By the time the school children arrived both trucks were in place. The crane began unloading. Two of their men set the tongs and then rode the logs up and onto the walls, where they carefully put each numbered log in place. Then they rode the empty tongs back and hooked up the next log. This seemed to mesmerize the children. The younger ones must have thought they were watching a circus. I was certainly pleased that there were no Workmen's Compensation men around at this stage of the game. These men didn't even wear hard hats.

The first log taken off was the last log put on at 100 Mile House. Each log had been carefully numbered when they were originally assembled. The Donovans had perfected their system and it was impossible to foul up. Before the end of the day, everything was in place. It had taken weeks to assemble, yet it was reassembled in less than a single day. Amazing.

Aggie Flett, of CBC television — our cinnabar moth friend — covered this event. Carrying her heavy camera and wearing her high gum boots, this lively woman hiked up that chewed-up muddy road with her unfailing good humour.

The crab, salmon and clams, prepared under Mrs. White's supervision by 20 of her young native students, were superb. I had also asked her if she could serve some smoked cougar meat. My longtime friend Freddy Holman from Westholme, a cougar hunter, had given me some as a novelty, but not everybody enjoyed the unusual sweet, wild taste.

In a separate tent, near the mossy knoll where Mr. and Mrs. Richardson met on Christmas Day, Jack Baker served the adults beer and wine. Near the cooking fire, soft drinks were guzzled by the school children.

After the crowd had left, I stood inside the four log walls. This was my new home. Reflecting on the day's events I spoke aloud, just to myself, "Yes, this has been a good day, one I'll never forget."

That night it poured, so we weren't able to get the tar and gravel roof underway for a couple of days. Two inches of insulation had to be laid over the wooden decking before the tar and gravel could be applied.

On February 11th, my birthday, the film taken by Mrs. Flett was shown coast to coast on CBC television — there couldn't have been a nicer gift.

Exactly three months later, on May 12, 1977, I spent the first night in my new home. It was the first day of the rest of

Joe's log house being erected on wooded Cinnabar Ridge.

my life and I would do things I had never dreamed of.

Now that I was on my own again, with more spare time, I shopped around for a power boat. I found her at Canoe Cove — a 40-foot beauty with twin diesels. The soft rumble of the engines was like music. I had a boat house built and moored her in Ladysmith Harbour, less than half an hour from home. I enjoyed many trips in the Hai II with family and friends, around the beautiful Gulf Islands and as far north as Port Hardy. Little did I know I would one day be using it for business. Business? Hadn't I stamped on that bug forever.

IN NOVEMBER, I was in St. Joseph's Hospital in Victoria going through another hip operation. The pain had become unbearable again. Convalescing has always been stressful for me. But on that occasion, with plenty of time to think, I made a very important decision, one so alien to my nature that it literally blew everyone away.

A few months earlier I had a visit from Gloria Hobson whom I'd known for many years. We talked about her late husband, Rich, and about his classic book which had been a top seller, *Grass Beyond The Mountain* — a story of twentieth century pioneer ranching in the Chilcotin country. I read the book again, and was impressed with Rich's clean expressive writing of one hell of a good story. If he could do it, why couldn't I?

By Christmas my mind was made up. I went to Galiano Island to brother Ollie's with three of my sisters. We were bringing in the New Year together. In the living room, sipping Crown Royal, I tossed my grenade, if it was to be that, into the conversation.

"I'm going to write a book about our family."

It was greeted with smiles, a few comments from those who would be in the book, but nobody seemed excited. They'd watched me in action for years.

However, my children were more to the point, as kids usually are.

"Dad, why would you want to write a book?" Ed asked.

"Because there is a story to tell."

PART VII

THE WRITER

ON THE MOUNTAIN I was reliving these incidents in clear detail. I was completely numb. The only feeling was the steady pain in my hips. In my semi-conscious and muddled state I clearly heard Virginia's voice saying the words she had said so many years ago. "I'm going back now. Good-bye Dad."

I didn't realize I had actually staggered past the shack which could be my salvation, until I saw the fork where the two roads met. I turned my eyes skyward and Virginia was no longer there.

On flat ground now I could walk more safely until I dimly made out the outline of the old building. Only then did I believe there was some hope of remaining alive. Shelter. I felt cautiously along the walls until I found the opening where the door had been. I sat on the wet floor and by using my arms I was able to somehow slide backwards until my feet were under the roof. I was out of the bone-chilling rain. My lightweight pants, socks and shoes, everything was soaked through.

It was then I lost consciousness again.

WRITER IN RESIDENCE

FOR CENTURIES others knew it. I didn't, but soon would. Writing is a lonely pursuit. It would not be easy. I wasn't even sure I could write.

"Joe, how did you do it?" people would ask later.

"Well, I guess I was stupid enough to start, and too damn stubborn to quit."

My schooling ended at Grade X, but as a youngster I read every book I could lay my hands on. *Burning Daylight* by Jack London, a story of life and survival in the north, was one of my favourites. I read it from cover to cover at least a dozen times. I could recite it almost word for word. "Never waste one minute of daylight," was London's message to the men. "Once lost it is gone forever." The story had an everlasting effect on my life. Even as a child, rising at dawn to do the daily chores before breakfast seemed the only right way to start the day.

The daily diaries I kept for years and the log books from my aircraft and crew boats were most helpful with the research. The short, choppy sentences I had written years earlier stimulated my memory. I would recall things I had almost totally forgotten. But there were times when it was tempting to just forget it all, this crazy idea, let it all go, as most people my age often do, unfortunately. They don't know what they are missing. It is like starting a new life.

I was enjoying the comfort of my log home and the huge fireplace in the living room which I often lit when the wind howled and the winter snows covered everything so beautifully outside. There is something very friendly and basic about heating and cooking with wood. During the colder weather the wood cook stove was always kept burning. My longtime house-

Massive fireplace of native stone and large enough to roast a pig, dominates living room of Joe's unique log home.

keeper Joyce Baker loved this old-fashioned stove, and cooked many a tasty meal on it. She had learned the old-fashioned ways of preparing and cooking game from her mother. When I cooked for myself, I usually put on a big venison or beef stew, enough to share with friends who would drop in and frequently stay for supper. They seemed to like the quietness and isolation of the cabin and its surrounding woods.

As an adult, I've always enjoyed splitting and piling firewood. In younger days I was sure that swinging an axe somehow improved my baseball batting average. I now discovered that splitting firewood provided a great outlet for the frustrations of trying to write. Yes, I had gone at it with no idea where I was going — a method not uncommon to many writers.

The dining area was to be the writing center. I did try for a while to work there, but ended up at the kitchen table. That's where I would, over the next 17 years, produce five books.

My sister Edie, who lived in Vancouver, suggested, "Why don't you ask Gloria Hobson over for a visit? She's living just a few blocks from me here on Main Street. She spends her winters in Vancouver now. You liked Rich Hobson's writing. I'll tell you something. Gloria had a great deal to do with the writing of his books."

Jack Baker, Joe's handyman and cattleman, and his wife Joyce beneath Gergely's painting of the Cinnabar Valley which hangs over the huge fireplace in Joe's living room. (Christmas, 1978)

"Sounds good," I replied. "I'd like to see her again anyway."

So she came over, and our friendship and mutual respect grew until she died in 1986. She had strong opinions and she didn't hesitate to express them.

"Writing a book is tough to do, Joe," she kept repeating. "Particularly the first one. I remember how Rich and I would sit on opposite sides of the fireplace during those long, cold winter evenings. We'd throw crumpled sheets of paper into the fire. No good. Try again. Finally Rich would scratch out a bit of a story we could agree was worth keeping. Then I'd shift the coal oil lamp to my desk and with two fingers I'd type out on my old machine everything we had thought worthwhile."

"Must have been exciting for both of you when the book was finally published. Getting all those great reviews. Giving

Joe working on this book at his kitchen table, in the Fall of 1994.

city people an idea of what living in the wilderness of the north country was really like."

"It was," Gloria said, smiling at the memory of the petty arguments that would develop during the writing, which would sometimes result in them not talking to each other for days on end.

"But I don't want to be that involved again, Joe. I'll read your stuff. I'll be an honest critic, but beyond that I don't know how much help I can be. My daughter Cathy might be interested. She's been studying literature at U.B.C. and she's an excellent researcher. She also types well. Publishers don't take hand written manuscripts, ever," she told me.

Cathy was surprised when I called her a couple of months later, "I'm going to write a book. Would you be interested in working with me for awhile?"

She hesitated, and then replied, "I don't know, Mr. Garner. What do you have in mind?"

"Well, let's talk about it, Cathy. Why don't you just jump on a bus for Williams Lake later this week? I'll be there, for the annual bull sale. I'll contact your mother, and get her down from Vanderhoof and the three of us can talk about the project."

It was the last cattle sale I would attend. I was ready to get

269

out of ranching. The procedure was to judge the cattle before they went into the ring for auction. I was surprised when my best bull, one I'd bought as a calf from Tommy Hopkins in the Fraser Valley, stood last in a group of ten. When the bidding started it was evident the cattlemen had opinions very different from those of the judge. They recognized a top-notch bull, and mine ended up fetching the highest price at that auction. Dan Lee, of the well known Chilcotin family, made an opening bid slightly over a $1,000, and it went up and up from there.

Gloria, Cathy, and I put our heads together.

"I've got some bits and pieces of stories," I told them. "Why don't the two of you come over to the island for awhile. I've asked my brothers and sisters to write down some of the things they remember about our childhood days on Saltspring. Just to get some different slants and memories. I'm also thinking about going down next month to that county in South Carolina from which my parents fled to Canada."

"Where will we work, Joe? Where will we stay?" Gloria asked.

"Easy. I'll move a trailer up beside my house. Should be comfortable enough for both of you. You can work there or in the house, wherever you like." I tossed out an offer of money to make it worth their while. I must have been close. Gloria said the deal was fine with her.

"Sounds okay to me." said Cathy. "It'll take me a couple of weeks to clear off things in Vancouver. Then I'll be over."

I bought a good tape recorder, and gave a lot more thought to getting some words down on paper. I'd been rereading John Steinbeck's *Grapes of Wrath*, and perusing Alex Haley's work on African Americans, *Roots*, but I was an amateur starting from scratch.

The Hobsons moved in, first into the guest house down in the valley and then into the trailer once it was in place up on the hill. We settled into a working routine, which suited all three of us although I kept being pulled away by subdivision problems.

I decided it would be best to take Gloria and Cathy with me if I was going to do research in South Carolina. The Hobsons were thrilled. Rich Hobson had originally come to northern B.C. from the southern U.S. during the Great Depression looking for ranchland in the wilderness.

WE FLEW to California where I talked to sister Dorothy and brother Lloyd and then went on to Spartanburg in South Carolina where we picked up a car so we could tour the Blue Ridge Mountain area. I was fortunate to meet some old-timers there who actually remembered my grandfather, George Washington Garner.

"I remember Wash and the "Georgia Buggie", the two-wheeled cart, he pushed," one man told me. "I was just a boy at the time, but everyone in town was curious about Wash's comings and goings. He'd walk away for months on end, often telling no one where he was going. People would just forget about him. Then a year or so later he'd be back in town to rest at his sister's for a brief period before he loaded his cart and wandered off again."

I met my grandfather for the first time when I was nine years old. He was a dishevelled old man, tough as leather, but he had twinkling eyes, and a smile spread across his bearded face when he gently squeezed my shoulder.

"Just be here for a short visit, Oland," he said to my Dad, "and then I'll be on my way." That old man had walked clear across the continent all the way from Spartenburg to Vancouver, or so he said, and, since he was a wanderer, it could have been true.

We next flew to New Mexico to visit sister Pearl who lived near Farmington on the San Juan River. She was obviously pleased to see us, but said, "I haven't written anything yet, Joe. But I will."

THE TRIP produced a few facts and stories but I knew this was going to be a long haul. Cathy stayed in the trailer when we got back to the island.

Gloria returned to the mainland but would come over occasionally to read and help with my early chapters. She also accompanied me on a short family hunting trip to the Moverhill Ranch in the Chilcotin, not too far from where she and her husband Rich had grazed their cattle and developed their ranch with his partner Pan Philips. Pan also became a legend in that rough country, although nobody knew of them until Rich's book was published.

The Moverhills supplied the bucking horses for the Williams Lake and Anahim stampedes, both famous for the quality and rangytangness of the horses, bulls, cowboys and the hard-drinking spectators. Randy Moverhill who had known Rich and Pan from the "good old days" approached my truck with a big grin, saw who was with me, and chuckled, "So you brought my girlfriend along with you, Joe."

"Gloria, I chased you for over seven years, sweetheart. See what you lost," he said, as he swept his arm towards the nearby swamp. "I would have made you Queen of the Buckbrush, queen of this whole area."

"And what good do you suppose that would do me now?" Gloria said with a sparkle in her eye. "You old goat. I was queen of this land when it was just that — buckbrush."

We walked over to join brothers Al and Ollie and their wives, Barb and Ruby, at the camp fire. Ollie said some mallards and Canada geese had been slowly cooking all day, enclosed in clay and buried under the glowing embers. When they were dug out we saw half a dozen jet black chunks of charcoal. But we were starving, so, undaunted, we broke off the wings and legs and carefully peeled off the outer layers, then ate what we could. Something had gone wrong. Only the breasts were edible. The fire had been kept too hot during the day by Ruby. She was on her first hunting trip with her new husband, Ollie. It takes a while to get the hang of cooking in a fire pit.

Gloria and I stayed on for a couple of days. We didn't have a tent with us so we just slept in the back of the pickup. I didn't do any hunting and spent most of my time fishing in a nearby creek.

When I got back home Cathy returned to Vancouver. As she prepared to leave she assessed our progress and gave me some worthwhile advice:

"We've got the first three chapters pretty well organized. You know what you've got to do. Just keep your pencil sharp, and get the words down on paper, nothing fancy, just the way you talk. Keep writing. Don't worry what it looks like. Just keep going. It will sort itself out."

MY WRITING varied from day to day. Sometimes I'd work from daybreak into the late evening. Sometimes I'd get up early with good intentions and give up within a couple of hours, knowing I'd get nothing done that day. At times it seemed I spent more time sharpening my pencil than writing. But how does any other writer start? Nevertheless, that first year the manuscript grew and went through one rewrite after another. I continued to do research and one fact would lead to another.

One day, looking for inspiration, I took a trip to Saltspring Island and hiked up to the place where I was born, half a mile from the top of Maxwell's Peak on a quarter section of wooded plateau. I wondered aloud, "Why would anyone choose to live up here, when there was good land everywhere at that time?" The choice had been my father's, and he rarely gave reasons for anything he did.

Gloria visited periodically and she would be merciless with her editing pencil.

"Joe, you can't say this for goodness sakes," she'd say in exasperation. "And this doesn't fit! Not here! We'll have to take it out. Maybe we can use it later."

This went on for over a year. Gloria remained an honest and helpful critic and a very patient one, I have to say. On one visit she handed me a little book, saying, "Read this, Joe. Keep it near. It will keep you out of a lot of trouble." It was Strunk & White's *Elements of Style*. Its message: keep it simple. Its pages became frayed from constant use — "Keep It Simple" was etched into my brain. Keep the damn thing simple.

Joe, a writer in his 70's with advisor Gloria Hobson, a Chilcotin friend, during writing of his first and biggest best seller 'Never Fly Over an Eagle's Nest.'

Often my frustration would boil over, and I'd start shouting at Joyce, my housekeeper, or her daughter Debbie whom I had hired to type for me.

"Am I ever going to finish this thing, Debbie?" I'd ask.

"Sure you are, Mr. Garner," she'd reply. "You always finish what you start." These wise and true words from this girl would usually bring my temperature down.

"Sorry I shouted, Debbie. Have a cup of tea while we listen to this tape again. Maybe there's some better way I can write this incident. Let's try."

More than once, Joyce pulled the manuscript out of the unlit wood stove, where I'd thrown it after a couple of hours of useless scribbling.

"You're in too big a hurry. You don't have to get everything done right here and now, Joe. I'll finish vacuuming in the living room. Then you and me, why don't we take your 4 x 4 up towards Green Mountain. Look for a deer or some grouse. That always seems to relax you." She was right.

I read fiction and nonfiction, trying to figure out what made some books and writers so popular. I hadn't thought much about the mechanics of writing since I left school, but now I became extremely conscious of these things. Every writer has his or her own style.

I celebrated my 70th birthday in Hawaii in February of 1979. Gloria Hobson came as my guest that year. She had come to know many writers and publishing folk over the years, and she introduced me to a few.

The next year progress on my book slowed, in part because of unexpected complications. Jack Baker, my only regular employee and a valued friend, had a serious heart attack. His health deteriorated and he died within a year. So I ended up back on my D7 cat, building roads in the subdivision. It sure felt good to ease into my new heated waterbed on those evenings when my hip was painful. I wrote in my diary after a long day of bulldozing, "Getting too damned old to be working on roads!"

THEN I BECAME ILL. I'd been having bouts of nausea and dizziness, just feeling physically weak far too often. I had returned from a short hunting trip in the Chilcotin where I lived almost entirely on beer and sandwiches soaked with sweetened condensed milk.

"Don't you think you should call a doctor, Joe?" Joyce asked as she cleared away the untouched meal.

"No! I'll be fine. Just a flu bug," I replied. How wrong I was.

"I'm going to bed for awhile. Get yourself a cold beer and sit down when you finish what you're doing," I said as I staggered to the bedroom.

Joyce phoned my daughter Joanne. In the short time it took her to drive over I had become very ill. I was delirious, hearing loud music and climbing the walls.

The always alert Joanne immediately called an ambulance and I was rushed to the Nanaimo hospital. The emergency medical staff skillfully diagnosed a diabetic coma. My blood sugar level was high enough to kill the average person.

On October 29, 1979, I awoke with an intravenous tube stuck in my arm. Dr. Larry Giovando came over to my bedside. "We've got you on insulin, Joe. But tests show your heart is strong. Besides the diabetes, you have an infected bladder, some gall stones, and a streptococcal infection in your throat. You'll be here for a while, and you'll need someone to stay with you at home. You're in bad shape and you'll be in no condition to look after yourself."

Ten days later I was hungry for the first time. I'd lost 30 pounds. My long-ago wife Pat paid me a visit.

"Would you like to stay with me for a spell when I go home?" I asked. "Got to have somebody to cook and keep me on my diet. See that I have my insulin shots. I'm not doing so good right now."

"You offering me a job? If you are, okay. I'll present you with a bill when I leave. Nothing for free in this world anymore, including me," she said.

"Okay by me," I replied, with a laugh, my first since I'd got into this unholy mess.

I got lots of advice on how to deal with diabetes, a bunch of don'ts, including: "No booze, and be careful what you eat." And, "You'll get used to it all."

Gradually I started feeling better. But that manuscript was still waiting. I felt I needed some fresh air and scenery, so for a break, and to bring in the New Year, I took the cruiser to Galiano Island and returned home ready to tackle the writing again.

In January my doctor took me off the needle and put me on pills and I thought, "Thank God, no needle every morning and every night. Maybe I'm getting lucky."

Joanne and Grieg planned a trip to Disneyland with their two girls and Dana's two children.

"Want to join us, Pop?" asked Joanne. "We're inviting Momsy."

Joe, with his first wife Pat surrounded by most of his grandchildren at a family get-together, Christmas 1983.

Recalling our rather ill-fated excursion 20 years earlier I hesitated, but finally Pat and I agreed to come along. Spoiling four granddaughters certainly beats disciplining your own kids. We had a wonderful trip.

THAT SPRING, with my new rule "Keep It Simple" in mind, I was making steady progress towards the final chapters. The end was in sight. Some chapters almost wrote themselves but in truth, I continued doing rewrites almost to the day it went off to the printer.

I could never, and I mean never, have anticipated some of the problems entailed with preparing a manuscript for publication. I knew I would need professional help. I turned to a new local company, Oolichan Press of Lantzville, north of Nanaimo. The publisher, as most publishers do, said it "had merit" but would need a great deal of "tightening up". I was to learn there is much more to publishing a book than just writing a manuscript.

"So what's the deal?" I asked. "Who pays for what? Where do we go from here?"

Publisher Ron Smith grandly informed me "Well, usually, when a publisher assumes all costs of production, the editing, graphic work, layout, printing, and promotion, the author receives ten percent royalties on book sales. We're talking the retail price, the store price. There is a big financial risk involved for us. There are no guarantees a book will sell, you know."

"This book will sell," I replied, emphatically. I knew I had a good story. "Doesn't seem that a writer receives much for his efforts under the arrangement you've described. What if an author invests in the production of his book?"

"Then he stands to make more money if the book sells well."

"Hmmm. How be I pay half the cost of producing the book, and take half the profits?" I suggested.

"Put that in writing and we've got a deal," said Smith.

I did, and I spent many hours working with their people over the next few months. Steve Guppie was assigned to do the editing. He had recently graduated from the University of Victoria and was eager to do a good job.

"You're not going to want to make some of the changes I suggest," Steve told me. "But I really believe they'll make those great stories of yours more readable."

Steve was right. I objected to many of his proposals, but

went along with others. In years of attending authors' conventions since then, I've learned authors rarely win arguments.

We decided on a title and an illustrator to do the cover. Pat Wright of Saltspring Island agreed to do the job.

I had long admired author Paul St. Pierre and he agreed to write the foreward. Paul and I had kept in touch over the years since that time he featured me in a front page article on gyppo loggers for the *Vancouver Sun*. His endorsement would be a real boost.

But things happen.

In August I had another operation on my hip to remove broken wires which were causing me considerable discomfort. The doctor allowed me to recuperate at home but someone would have to be available to assist me, to keep me off my feet. Ruby King, a tiny and vivacious woman I'd met earlier in Parksville, agreed to nurse me for a few weeks. Ruby had no intention of extending her working relationship with me but during the next few years she would twice join me on book promotion tours across the continent.

By October I was again mobile and concerned we might not have my book on store shelves in time for Christmas. My exasperation increased when I learned that what was supposed to be the final draft, set as it was on Oolichan Press's outdated Copygraphic typesetter, might not have print sharp enough to be produced at Morriss Printers in Victoria. Dick Morriss, a soft-spoken and highly competent craftsman, well respected in his trade, fortunately was able to make the necessary adjustments. He had the first run of *Never Fly Over an Eagle's Nest* — 300 hard cover and 1,500 soft cover — ready for us by the first of December.

When I finally held the finished product in my hands I knew the thrill any first time author must experience. Against all odds, sometimes, so I thought, against common sense, I had done it. I remembered Debbie saying, "You always finish what you start, Mr. Garner." In a way it had been that way all my life. If there was a job to be done, I did it.

That December turned out to be one of the busiest, and most rewarding of my life. As well as the usual Christmas festivities I began the promotion circuit on Vancouver Island. We gave it our best shot and went to the towns where I was already well known. But still, it was like entering a whole new world!

We did radio talk shows and television interviews all of which I thoroughly enjoyed.

We did book signings. Just seeing "author" before my name gave me a strange feeling. When I mentioned that to Barry Broadfoot who had moved to Nanaimo, he laughed and said, "You'll get used to it soon enough, Joe. I have. Soon you won't even have to think about what you're saying. It's a snap."

One of the greatest pleasures was visiting Miss Mercer who had been my Grade III teacher at the Divide School on Saltspring Island. Miss Mercer, then 83, was confined to the Lady Minto Hospital in Ganges. I visited her after our first autographing session, which was held at Mouat's store in Ganges. I gave her an autographed copy, then read her some excerpts.

When I had finished, she smiled and told me: "Joe Garner, as I recall, you were always quite a story teller when you were a little boy, but I would never have guessed you'd grow up to be a writer. I'm very proud of you. Wish I had a gold star to put on your work. Now I can go to sleep. I've been waiting all day long for your visit."

There were tears in her eyes.

BUILDING OF CINNABAR PRESS

NEVER FLY OVER AN EAGLE'S NEST sold beyond my wildest dreams and its Christmas popularity continued far into the new year. More than 5,000 copies had been purchased within a few months, making it a Canadian best seller.

I hired a part-time public relations agent and continued to promote my book through newspaper reviews and radio and television talk shows. Only one of those events turned out to be an unpleasant encounter. There was an arrogant Toronto interviewer who hadn't read the book. I was to learn later that, due to extreme work pressure, many interviewers find it impossible to read the flood of new Christmas books.

I had sold a variety of things during my lifetime, from logs and building supplies to land and cattle. It seemed to me, at first, that a book was just another commodity. However, it soon became something far more important to me than anything else I had ever done. I soon realized you do not write for yourself but for the pleasure of the reader. I also realized I had an awful lot to learn about the publishing business.

Now, the biggest challenge became getting more books into the stores. The first major marketing trip Ruby King and I made was into the B.C. interior. I packed 200 books into the station wagon and headed north. The reception we received was, in some places, overwhelming. The bald eagle on the cover may have been part of the reason for its popularity.

Phoning ahead to radio and television stations, we were usually enthusiastically welcomed. Bob Harkins, who was then known as "The Voice of the North", working out of a radio station in prosperous Prince George, was a great help in lining us up with most of the news media up there.

I'd locate the local book stores in the Yellow Pages, so when phone-in listeners asked, "Where can I buy your book?" I could direct them instantly to the stores in town. The bookstore owners appreciated this.

I visited Rotary clubs to keep up my weekly attendance and often the club president would fit me into their program. It always surprised me to find my book so well received everywhere.

When spring arrived I decided to try some new outlets. It became evident as I toured the province that many of the smaller stores might be able to sell the books. This was something the major distributors and publishers had not tried. The West Coast of Vancouver Island didn't have a single copy for sale anywhere when we first went out to Tofino, simply because these fishing, logging and tourist villages were not considered book markets. But when I made my book available it sold well.

When I went cruising around the Gulf Islands, I would occasionally pull into a marina and often swap a book for a moorage spot.

"Would you like to try selling these?" I'd usually suggest to the owner.

"Dunno 'bout that. Not much of a market for books at this little store. Fuel, groceries, fishing tackle, fishing bait, that's about it."

"Well, I bet there is," I'd reply. "Look at all those boats down there in the harbour. Canadians and Americans. They've all got money. They read. Every one of them likely has somebody aboard who would be glad to get a good book, especially when it's about this area. This book is history."

"You think so?"

"Absolutely. Try a dozen, there's no middleman. Just you and me. I'll give you a nice little stand made from local cedar by the handicapped children in Nanaimo."

"You want cash? What if the books don't sell?" he'd ask.

"You're getting a forty percent discount. They'll sell, and if they don't, they're returnable. So you can't lose. Or I can leave them on consignment and you can pay for them after they've sold," I'd say, and that was the clincher.

"Sounds like a fair offer," they'd usually reply. How could it fail?

By the end of the summer the book was already into its fifth printing. They were small printings, but I learned later that most books never make it to a second printing.

RUBY KING was a big help, a sharp businesslike widow who was retired and living at Nanoose Bay, north of Nanaimo. She had studied children's literature at U.C.L.A. and had a genuine interest in books, and she loved to go cruising and to travel.

We took several sales trips with the station wagon but we needed a bigger vehicle. I bought a Dodge Ram motor home and had an enlarged picture of the book cover painted on it. I found it was heavy on gas after our first trip so I had the fuel system removed and replaced with a propane system. There was also an auxiliary propane tank that operated a refrigerator, heater and oven. We could camp out in the backwoods, free and independent. This small tank could be switched over to supply the motor if our big tanks ran out, giving us another 60 miles. Apart from being cheaper than gas, propane burns hot and clean and is non-polluting. A lot of smooth and not-so-smooth miles would be rolling under our tires.

I was pioneering a unique way of selling books on the highways and byways, not unlike an old time peddler, and it was a lot of fun. I would drive just over 450,000 miles in that Dodge during the next 10 years.

I started chelation treatments early in 1981. Gloria Hobson had suggested it after learning that I was back on insulin to control my diabetes and related blood problems.

"Chelation therapy has kept me going, Joe," she told me.

By summer I was again off insulin shots, this time for keeps, and I was feeling so good that I was planning to take *Never Fly Over an Eagle's Nest* across Canada. I knew the major book distributors would not allow their retail outlets to purchase books that were not on a "selected list." I would be wise to meet with those who rule this autocratic roost and naturally the head offices were in and around Toronto.

It was a strange way of doing business, but I was learning almost daily that the publishing, distribution and sales system for books differed greatly from anything I had ever experienced.

Bill Gilmour, one of my fishing buddies, managed all the Eaton's stores from Winnipeg to the West Coast. He gave me letters of introduction.

"These should open a few doors on your way across Canada, Joe," he explained. "I've also informed Jean Sawicki, who is our chief book buyer in Toronto, that you'll be dropping in to see her."

To further understand the complexities of this business Ruby and I attended the Canadian Book Sellers convention at the Hotel Vancouver that July and a major book fair at Robson Square in August. I certainly learned a lot.

Smith, my small town Lantzville publisher was not as confident as I was that the venture would be successful, mainly because Oolichan Books was small and his main work was teaching literature at Malaspina College in Nanaimo. Publishing was really a hobby financed by Canada Council grants, which he was an expert in obtaining.

"A local non-fiction book with a B.C. setting will not sell on the other side of the Rockies," he informed me, and he could have been right, but I wasn't convinced.

"I'm going to put 1,500 books in that van of mine, and we'll see!" I paid for the books by cheque, saying, "When we run out I'll phone you for more."

I phoned to make sure Ruby would be ready the next day and all she asked was, "Which ferry?"

"The first, the seven. I'll pick you up at six."

"That figures," she said. "Never known you to catch a later one."

We did some selling in Vancouver and spent the first night at a government campground east of Chilliwack in the outfitted van. I traded a book for a camp site and sold three to neighbouring campers before breakfast next morning.

"A good way to start the trip east", I said to Ruby. I did a radio talk show in Kelowna that day and later had an autographing at Woodwards' bookstore where we sold over a hundred books. Any author will tell you that is outstanding.

The following evening we were at Blue River on the North Thompson River. Next morning we were up early and drove on through the Rockies towards Edmonton.

For an unknown writer sales were very brisk on that first trip through Alberta. In one small town I chatted with a druggist who probably had never seen an author selling books, much less a salesman from a publishing house, as they only hit the bookstores in bigger cities. I said, "Looks to me like you could sell some books in here if you had them."

"No," he replied. "Not many people come in here for that sort of thing. Drugstores sell magazines and Harlequin paperbacks but no books like yours."

"I tell you what I'm going to do. I'll trade you a book for a small tin of Zam-Buk. Looks like your store has been here long enough to have stocked that good old green ointment," I said, determined I wasn't leaving without making some sort of deal.

"Zam-Buk! I'm going to call you on that one. I think we

283

still have some of that in the back room," and the deal was done. I was autographing his book, when the druggist said, "You're from Vancouver Island, aren't you?"

"Yes, I am."

"Ever run into a ball player name of Pete Hawryluk."

"As a matter of fact I have. Played with Pete for about four years back in the forties.

"I'll be damned. Pete was the best ball player this town ever had before he left for the coast. By the way, why don't you leave me a half dozen of those books. I think I can sell them for you."

"Okay," I said with a smile; and that wasn't an unusual occurrence.

OUR ITINERARY was to travel the northern route through Edmonton and Saskatoon and return the southern route across the prairies, visiting bookstores in Calgary and Regina and all the smaller cities. I did practically all of the driving. Ruby did the cooking and other chores, offering support and advice. Each evening at a campsite we'd plan our next day. We'd held to our decision to go on to Winnipeg and hit Toronto even though we knew the Eastern Canadians would say, "What good is a western book? They don't sell."

At a beach store in Thunder Bay, I walked in with several books, and returned, feeling dejected. I had hit the resistance firmly and quickly.

"Here, Ruby," I said, handing her a little jewelry box. "They're not interested in carrying the book, but this pretty amethyst ring caught my eye and I was able to make a trade. He said he would size it for you if it didn't fit." Was this going to be a bartering trip? Would I return with a load of stuff I didn't want? Didn't Ontarians care about the rest of Canada?

Sudbury had several bookstores but sales were not good, undoubtedly due to the closure of two of the bigger mines. As I lay in bed that night feeling low, little did I realize that within the next 15 years my book would sell very close to 100,000 copies.

In Toronto I put on my last clean shirt and silver bola tie for a TV interview. It went well. Then we visited Eaton's, Coles and W.H. Smith, the major book stores. They seemed happy to stock the *Eagle's Nest*, but again, perhaps they were amazed I would spend so much time and money flogging a western book. But we were having a lot of fun and seeing a lot of Canada.

Next morning, Ruby found a laundromat, and I went on a coast-to-coast radio show. The last quarter hour was opened up and I was delighted with the number of calls. And I was pleased to be able to say our books were in the stores.

In Quebec, sales were very slow which did not surprise me. In some parts of the Maritimes the book sold well. Perhaps they felt a closeness to the western "outsiders", as we did to them. Ocean to ocean friendship.

When the ferry docked at Prince Edward Island, all the campgrounds were closed for the night. Ruby asked, "Where are we going to camp? I'm exhausted."

"You tell me and we'll both know," I replied disgustedly, feeling there must be a better way to run a tourist system. Up ahead we saw the lights of a gas station and drove in. The attendant was locking up. We asked him if he knew where we might camp.

"Half a mile up, turn right and follow the road until you come to a big potato patch, then follow the signs."

We found the potato patch and an arrow on a sign nailed to a tree which said to pay at the farm house in the morning.

A red and white vehicle, almost identical to ours, was parked some 50 feet away. They were Bert and Ruth Ford from Vancouver. Their vehicle was also powered by propane — another traveller smart enough to convert. We talked for some time, and next morning Bert asked for an autographed copy of the book for his mother and another for himself.

When we drove up to the house to pay, we asked the farmer if we could buy some of his good potatoes. He noticed the Eagle picture on the van and asked, "You the author?"

"Yes," I said and I showed him the book.

"I'd like to have a couple if you'd autograph them for me."

"That should square us for the potatoes and the campsite," I suggested.

"I'll settle for that," he said, looking pleased with the deal.

In Charlottetown, I walked into a radio station and asked to see the manager. He was not that busy and invited me in. We chatted about the book and why I was there and he suggested I come back after lunch for a live interview. I was getting the hang of hitting a town "cold". We visited a bookstore in the nearby shopping mall and told them I was going on "open mike" that afternoon. We agreed that I would do an autographing immediately after the interview so we set up our card table and chair in a convenient spot. We covered it with a bright red table cloth and put our autographing sign on top of a box of books.

As we walked back to the bookstore after the interview we could see a line-up. So much for the theory that a B.C. book wouldn't sell east of the Rockies. This gave us confidence as the selling tour had not gone all that well, probably because what we were doing just wasn't done.

The following day in Halifax I did an interview with the *Herald News*. Because of that interview we were able to place four dozen copies with the book stores and other outlets.

That night we took inventory and estimated we would be out of books by the time we reached the Alberta border on our return trip. So it was going better than we thought!

I phoned Oolichan Press and asked them to ship 500 books to Calgary and I'd pay the freight on arrival. I also asked them to order a new printing.

I was disappointed and upset when we got to Calgary and found there were no books waiting for us. We had sold out. All we could do now was head on home, and miss out on the active southern B.C. market.

WHEN WE RETURNED, feeling good about sales and peeved about my publisher's failure to follow through, the word was getting around. Phone calls, people stopping me on the street, asking, "Where can we get a book, Joe?"

My "home" sales got a big boost when a young newspaperman named Gordon Hamilton came for an interview for *The Cowichan News* at Duncan, my old stamping ground. It was my first major newspaper exposure and I must admit it gave me a "rush". If I wasn't hooked on writing before, this story might have done the trick. Here it is:

Island author Joe Garner has proven the experts wrong.

You can't turn a family history into a best seller, especially in Canada, Garner was told when he wanted to take a cross-country tour to promote his book Never Fly Over an Eagle's Nest.

Today, his story of pioneer life in the Cowichan Valley and on Saltspring Island can be termed a best seller. With 10,000 copies in print and another 2,000 at the printers right now, Garner has taken what publishers refer to as a parochial book, of interest only to the people living in the area concerned, and turned it into a national book.

Never Fly Over An Eagle's Nest is into its sixth printing and has received critical praise from some of Canada's literary giants. "Take my word for it ... the book is blue chip," says Barry Broadfoot. "Written in such a lively style that I could not put it down until I had read the last page," commented Bruce Hutchison. "Joe has written his story plainly and the ring of simple truth is in it," is Paul St. Pierre's opinion of Garner's story.

Garner has proven his book is not about a place, but about people — Canadian people — and that, he says, is what is making it so popular.

Since the first modest printing of 1,800 copies in December, 1980, Garner has travelled around the province and across the country promoting Never Fly Over an Eagle's Nest.

He just returned from his cross-Canada odyssey after personally selling 1,500 copies.

"My publisher said it wouldn't sell east of the Rockies, but I proved him wrong," Garner said.

Garner sold his book in small towns and cities across the country. Although one nation-wide chain is considering distributing the book, Garner has concentrated on the small, independent book sellers.

"The small independents are the lifeblood of small publishers and budding authors," he said.

Naturally the publisher, Oolichan Books of Lantzville, is delighted to be proven so wrong, Garner said, "He is elated. This is the first big seller he has ever produced."

And Garner is deeply satisfied himself to have his first book received so well.

"It makes me feel good as a Canadian. The book helps the Cowichan Valley, it helps British Columbia and it helps Canada. People are getting pleasure from it."

Garner describes his book as a true story of Canadian pioneering, taking it beyond the confines of the definition "family history." He admits, however, that is how the book originally started out.

"It was initially started for the family. I had kept a diary for 40 years and I have written a few short stories so I started it as a family history."

He originally intended to call it From Ox Cart to Aircraft, in reference to the method Garner's family first arrived in the Cowichan Valley and how, in later years, they operated B.C.'s only float plane instructional school out of Quamichan Lake. He agrees the title finally chosen is appropriate, although he confesses, it sounds a bit like a book about birds.

Never Fly Over An Eagle's Nest was three and a half years in the writing and, Garner says, now that the book is selling so well, it was all worth it. "Writing is a lonely pursuit."

Garner says one of the deepest satisfactions he has gained from the book is that it has kept those pioneer days alive. "It brings people back to life who were active in the community and it will keep them alive as long as people read the book."

The 72-year-old author won't be quitting with one success under his belt. Already, he says, a sequel is in the works, bringing the family history up to date.

And, he says, he is not about to stop promoting Never Fly Over An eagle's Nest. "We have had an offer to have it translated into French, but that's not really my decision. That's up to the publisher. And I would really like to take it over to England with me. I think there may be a big market there for a book like this. After all, most of the people living in the Valley originally came from England."

Garner admits he is doing work that, rightfully, the publisher should be doing. But, considering the book was published by a small outfit and the fact Garner enjoys travelling, he is more than willing to do it himself.

His first tour, from Vancouver Island to Prince Rupert, Prince George and back to Vancouver, got him hooked on taking his book to the people. "We took 600 copies with us and we ran out at 100-Mile House. Prince George alone took 200 copies." And, he says, the people he meets along the way make it all worth while.

In crossing the country, he went all the way to Halifax. The people in the Maritimes, especially, took to the book.

"It was a wonderful trip back and forth. The people we met were all so courteous and friendly.

A year had passed since the first printing of *Eagle's Nest*. My publisher believed that the market was already completely saturated, so he refused to print any more books. His attitude alarmed me.

I went to see Dave Williams who had been the senior lawyer for our businesses and was himself an author. He had been the Writer in Residence at the University of Victoria. I asked him to terminate our contract with Oolichan Press because the situation was impossible.

We put together a good financial offer and presented it to Oolichan's Ron Smith, expecting he would surrender the original contract. After all, it was win-win for him from the start as I had done all the vital promotion and sales work. One day in downtown Nanaimo, after months of haggling we happened to meet in The Bookstore on Bastion Street. He stuck out his hand, saying, "Joe, there's no use both of us being so damn stubborn." There and then we agreed to settle and go our separate ways. I had not been the one who was stubborn. My offer was more than generous.

During this haggling the book had been legally out of print for the best part of a year.

NOW I could do it my way. I formed a company — Cinnabar Press. I've always liked to be in complete control, and now I was. I immediately ordered Morriss Printing to print 5,000 copies of the revised edition. Since then, through stores, personal selling and the all-important word of mouth, this book has gone through 18 additional printings — approaching 100,000 copies.

I published the second book *Never a Time to Trust* in the fall of 1984. It also became a best seller, partly based on my reputation from Eagle's Nest.

I'VE HAD MANY interesting and pleasant experiences travelling with my books. They provide an opportunity to meet new people wherever we go. Getting out and meeting the readers continues to be one of the greatest pleasures of writing.

While on vacation, I attended a large Rotary meeting in Hawaii where over one-third of the people were vacationing Canadians. I was approached by many who wanted autographed copies of my books. I always lugged along a few books, even on the airlines to be able to supply a copy, or many copies, on request. It was one of the advantages of being your own publisher, and it was a pleasant way to do business and make friends.

In South Carolina, however, I had the kind of attention I could certainly have done without. I was in Dallas for a world Annual International Rotary Conference. I was curious also to see the building from which President John F. Kennedy had been assassinated. It was an ordinary building, as I suspected it would be, although it is as famous as the Parthenon in Athens.

From Dallas we drove to Pacolet Mills in South Carolina, where I visited my niece, Sally. We stayed with my mother's cousin, Albert Edwards, who was an active member of the Ku Klux Klan in Spartanburg. We made arrangements to go on local television and talk about the books. It was a good interview with lots of public response. However, most callers wanted to know about the *Eagle's Nest* and my father's escape to Canada from the Ku Klux Klan.

After signing off I was told my cousin wanted me to phone him right away.

"What's up?" I asked when he answered his phone.

"Joe, I don't want to alarm you, but I've been told that there are some Klan members who are upset over what you said on the program. They're going to keep an eye on you."

"Should I be worried?"

On the road in 1984, selling *Never Fly Over an Eagle's Nest*, and his first self-published book *Never a Time to Trust*.

"Don't think so at the moment. Just be a little careful who you talk to, and what you say."

In the station's parking lot I noticed two men in a pickup truck. When I drove my van out, the truck pulled in behind and followed until we got to Albert's house. I didn't see that vehicle again but there were others. The Klan — a once powerful and feared anti-coloured and anti-Semitic secret "sect" — maintained their escort service until we left the area three days later.

I have spent a great deal of time on the road since I started writing, across the United States and three times across Canada as well as numerous trips up north into the Yukon, Northwest Territories and Alaska. There is not a major road in B.C. where my van hasn't left tracks in the rain or snow. When I've not been writing I've been on the road, either doing research or selling. Mishaps are bound to happen.

My travelling companions and I have had speeding tickets and fender benders. We've been lost on back roads and stranded at ferry terminals. We've gone miles beyond a missed turnoff, and run out of fuel on the 401 in Toronto at rush hour. Now, that was an experience! Surely the busiest highway in all Canada — and I ran out of fuel.

I needed more and more help in my office on Cinnabar Ridge. My assistant would have to handle the word processing, the accounting, and put up with an old writer who has been known to get cranky when things went wrong. Moreover, she would be expected to help market the books, joining me as a travelling saleslady.

JOAN DAVIS of nearby Ladysmith had done some word processing for me in the fall of 1987 and the following spring I asked her if she would continue working with me. She is still my indispensable assistant, officially now the vice-president of Cinnabar Press Ltd. Without her, the train wouldn't leave the station.

Joan's husband Bill, a retired professor from both the University of Manitoba and the University of Winnipeg was very helpful with my third and fourth books, proofreading drafts and offering constructive criticisms.

He also saw what an untypical sales trip was like on a memorable drive into the Bella Coola Valley, down into a steep canyon on a road that government engineers declared could never be built. The loggers of Bella Coola and the Chilcotin country picked a route and by incorporating several switch-

Joan Davis, Girl Friday, road companion and business partner.

backs proved nothing is impossible for a bunch of determined "frontiersmen" when it comes to road building. This road has to be driven to be believed, and I think we were the first book salesmen — and probably the last — to visit that town.

Joan says her first selling trip in November of 1988, when *Never Chop Your Rope* was published, was almost her last. It was hectic but good for a few laughs. One morning we were waiting in a Vancouver parking lot for our distributor's promotion rep to drive us to radio and television stations. A small car drove up beside us. I rolled my window down.

"I don't think that's our guide," Joan warned me in a quiet voice, as an attractive woman stepped out and smiled at me.

"Are we going in your car or mine?" I asked.

"I don't think we are going in the same direction, sir," she said as she turned on her heel and walked away.

"Joe, is that the way you usually greet good-looking young ladies you don't know?" Joan asked, laughing, but somewhat amazed.

Never Chop Your Rope, my third book, made it to the top of the *Vancouver Sun's* best seller list by February, 1989. This was very unusual, as self-published books are often ignored by book people on the theory that a self-published book is done because no other publishing house would do it. I was self-published because I now knew something about publishing. That book stayed among the top ten best sellers for weeks and I won second place in the annual Duthie Book Awards. This led to me speaking at the seventh annual Festival of the Written Arts in Sechelt, one of the most remarkable, but largely unknown, festivals in Canada.

BY THE SPRING of '92, our fourth book *Never Under the Table* had been printed, about forest management and graft and chicanery under the Social Credit government's long regime in power. Joan was spending as much time behind the wheel as I was. We had just come through Falkland, southeast of Kamloops. Our destination was Chunky Woodward's ranch. I had met him on Galiano Island at sister Margaret's log cabin years earlier, while he was chief of Woodward's Stores.

The road to his ranch was well off the beaten track, and covered in freshly-crushed rock. We were enjoying the scenery when the right back tire went flat.

"So what do we do now?" Joan asked.

Ten years of travel and selling wore out Joe's first van and this second hand propane Dodge Ram, bought in 1991, still travels the highways and byways, a mobile book store.

"We change the tire," I snapped. It is worthy of note that by this time I had two replaced hips. Moreover, Joan had never changed a tire in her life.

"Where's the spare?" she asked, ready to follow my directions, and get on with the job.

"Tied on the roof of the van. You'll have to climb up the ladder on the back, untie the rope that's holding the tire down and push it off."

Joan made it up onto the roof, but soon found her hands weren't strong enough to untie the knots. So back down she came, using some unaccustomed language.

"Well, I had some help when I put that tire up there, but now I'll obviously have to get it down on my own."

By pulling myself up with my hands, I finally made it to the top of the ladder, bad hips and all.

"Look out below!" I shouted as I pushed the tire over the edge. Unfortunately, it flipped, landed on its tread, and went bounding off down the road and into a gully 150 feet away.

"You'll have to go and get it, Joan," I said. "If I get down in that gully, I know I won't be able to make it back up."

I got the jack and tire wrench out of the vehicle. By the time she returned, a bit dishevelled and out of breath but still managing to smile, I thought we had things pretty well under control. But the wheel nuts had rusted so badly neither of us could budge them.

"Look," I suggested, "you jump on the wrench handle as I hold you up." Joan weighed about 125 pounds, but even when she bounced up and down, the nuts wouldn't give.

Eventually we both stood on the wrench, and leaning against the van, while hanging on to each other for balance, did the comic dance needed to loosen each and every wheel nut. I'd love to have a video tape of that crazy performance.

Just as we had the spare tire loosely bolted on, a young couple drove up in a 4 x 4. The driver put his head out the window and shouted, "Looks like you could use some help."

Joan and I just started laughing. He not only tightened the bolts but put the shredded tire back up on the roof and tied it down for us. We now had no spare and a fairly heavy load.

"I would like to give you something for your help," I said to the young man, handing him a copy of *Never Under the Table.*

"Not necessary to give me anything, Mr. Garner," he replied, "but I do appreciate your offer. I've read your first three books and enjoyed them. It's been a pleasure to meet you."

"Then you must certainly accept that book for your much

appreciated help," I told him. "Now you have the complete set."

There was the time at the K.O.A. campsite west of Prince George, when we set the alarm to get an early start for Fort St. James. After a quick breakfast we were on the road bright and early. Fifteen miles later, a large marmalade-coloured cat looked mournfully up at us. Some camper's cat, for God's sake!

"How the hell did that get in here? Nothing to do now, but turn around and head back to the camp site," I said.

"So much for our early start," Joan lamented, as I wheeled around and headed back to Prince George, not just a little annoyed. We left the cat with the campground owner hoping it would find its "family" again.

I remember one cool, clear evening arriving late at the Bowron Lake Provincial Park, east of Quesnel and beyond the restored ghost town of Barkerville. We made the mistake of lighting a campfire and sitting and watching it for a while when Joan wanted a drink. I've always carried a bottle of Crown Royal in the camper, as I believe that anyone who has spent a day travelling with me needs a good drink at the end of it.

After some 20 minutes, stiff and tired, I headed for the washrooms. I'd just got nicely settled when all the lights went out. I now knew the meaning of the words "pitch black", but I didn't know Joan had heard the generator die. Much to my relief I heard a laugh, then, "Thought you might need this, Joe," as a flashlight was passed under the door.

MANY ADVENTURES, MUCH FUN. But why did I write these books?

Never a Time to Trust was written to show the number of cougars there were in the 1920s and '30s as compared to the cougar population now. To record the human attacks, the amount of game and farm animals killed. To compare the game laws then and now. You didn't have to get a permit to shoot a cougar. You didn't have to identify males from females to shoot them. Now you are not allowed to shoot a female cougar and the game laws seem to be very awkward. In the old days, to keep wolves, cougars and bears under control a bounty was paid for each dead animal. Now you need to buy tags and permits.

Never Chop Your Rope was written to record for history the progress of logging from oxen and horses to spar trees and high riggers and on to helicopter logging. To record the struggles, the ups and downs of the typical gyppo, the small to medium-size logging company. People who could be trusted to do business on a handshake.

I had to write *Never Under the Table* to point out what was going on in government circles and how management licences were handed out. We weren't the only ones offered a management licence in return for a bribe. What's the difference between a bribe and what they call today an election campaign fund? There were plenty of mistakes made in the forests. I don't believe in good usable timber being left to rot on the ground.

The people I interviewed for my books were mostly people that I knew. Some of them I had worked with for maybe 20 years or more.

Why did I spend so much effort, so much time? I did it to tell my story, to give people the facts and, I hope, pleasure. It has been a gratifying thing for me, and it has given me a great deal of pleasure — something to live for. Hell, maybe writing has even kept me alive.

BUT I TRULY BELIEVE that if it wasn't for the chelation treatment I started back in 1981 I would never have been able to accomplish what I did. It is now 14 years ago since Gloria Hobson suggested I take a trip to California and visit Dr. Saccoman's clinic at El Cajon, saying, "Talk to them. They're the experts."

"Doesn't anyone give this treatment of yours in B.C.?"

"Yes, but only for specific purposes and you wouldn't qualify."

"Will our B.C. Medical Plan pay for it?"

"They may cover your travel costs, but not the treatment."

"Well," I thought, "Why not try it?"

I drove down after phoning ahead, and Dr. William Saccoman met me in the lobby of his clinic. I told him I was checking out a friend's recommendation.

"You're probably a bit skeptical, Mr. Garner. That's natural. Let me tell you about the process as I show you around our clinic. Chelation therapy was developed in Europe. In truth, it is a fairly simple procedure — a series of slow intravenous drips of ethylenediaminetetraacetic acid, commonly called EDTA. It's a synthetic amino acid, which has the ability to alleviate heavy metal poisoning by removing lead, cadmium, aluminium and mercury from one's system."

"Why do you suppose they don't allow this treatment in Canada?"

"I'm sure they do, for removing heavy metal from the blood," he replied diplomatically.

"Do you get hassled by the medical profession in California? That seems to happen to most practitioners in Canada," I informed him.

"No, but once in a while the medical profession will make a statement. They'll say there is no substantial scientific proof that chelation is beneficial. They stop there. They know if they ever tried to shut down my clinic they'd be faced with hundreds of my former and present patients. They'd show up with affidavits affirming the benefits they've experienced and that would include my own father."

"Your father?"

"Yes. My father was an old man when he started chelation therapy thirty years ago. Now he's in his nineties and is a very active man. You can see him working with his horse almost every day out at our ranch. He loves to ride."

After a thorough medical examination I started my first series of 20 chelation treatments. I even sold a few books to fellow patients, including one couple from Vanderhoof, where Gloria had lived. I'd taken a batch down. Who knows?

I was feeling better than I had for years when I left for home. I was determined to follow the assigned diet and I made arrangements to return for booster treatments. Within a month of returning home I was taken off insulin again, this time for good. One Diabeta pill a day is all I ever take now.

The therapeutic use of chelation did not cross the ocean from Europe until the early 1950s when workers suffering lead poisoning in a battery factory in Michigan were successfully detoxified. The chelating agent used was EDTA.

The first indication of EDTA chelation therapy's potential for conditions other than lead poisoning came when chelated persons reported surprising post-chelation health improvements — better memory, better vision, better hearing, clearer thinking — all seemingly unrelated to lead removal.

Patients suffering from atherosclerosis reported being able to walk farther with less chest or leg pain. Those with angina were able to exert themselves without discomfort, tiring less easily and with improved physical endurance. Patients with pasty complexions developed a healthy glow. Cold limbs regained warmth. Icy toes and fingers warmed up.

Such dramatic benefits, chelating physicians theorized, could not possibly be explained simply by the removal of lead in the blood. They had to be related in some way to increased blood flow through or around partially blocked arteries. I've known people who had one heart bypass and needed another within a few years. I decided I would find out how much interest there was in getting a clinic started closer to home.

Two years later found me in the new Victoria General Hospital having my left hip replaced again. The shaft that goes into the leg bone had broken.

"I'm Joe Garner," I said to my room mate. "Hope you don't mind my saying so, but you look terribly distressed."

"Archie McCulloch," he replied. "And yes, I am upset. Just had some more tests done. My doctor is making arrangements for me to have triple bypass surgery right away. They tell me my heart's in very bad shape. I'm very much afraid I won't make it off the operating table.

"I've already had one bypass and I certainly don't want another," Archie said. "In less than five years, the first one has already started plugging up again. They were examining me today and could find no pulse in one of my feet.

"I also have a blockage very close to my brain. Don't think that isn't causing me concern. It explains why I'm having quite a bit of trouble with my right eye. At times I have very limited vision, able to see someone only from the knees to their shoulders. Sometimes nothing at all. They told me I'd had a stroke. I'm only 61 and I'd like to see a few more years," he concluded.

"Archie, before I went down to California and had chelation treatments I couldn't read the phone book," I told him. "When I came home, I found I could read it with ease."

He was the professional at the Ardmore Golf Club in Saanich and he was worried about being unable to continue giving lessons if he did survive the heart surgery.

"Archie," I said boldly, "I'd like to offer you some advice. Sign yourself out of this place and visit a chelation clinic in California for a second opinion on that heart condition of yours."

"Just like that?"

"Right! Just put on your clothes. Get out of this hospital. Go! First, buy a book called *Bypassing Bypass* and read it."

A couple of months later I dropped in at the golf course to see how he was doing. I shouted to a man nearby, "Have you seen Archie McCulloch?"

"You're looking at him, Joe."

"Well I'll be damned. I didn't even recognize you, Archie. You look ten years younger."

"Well, Joe, the day after I checked out I phoned my specialist and told him I was going to take chelation therapy treatments."

"'You'll be wasting your time and your money if you go through with it,' he informed me.

"Well," I said, "it's my time, my money and my choice, and I intend to make up my own mind."

"I phoned San Diego and went down there immediately. Dr. Saccoman was booked solid so I saw a Dr. Dosuma Johnson from Africa. Black as the ace of spades, with a big smile and a great sense of humour, just a great guy. I took five treatments a week, twenty in all.

"When I came back I went to see my doctor. One of the first things he did was check the pulse in my foot.

"You've got a pulse," he said, showing surprise.

"Yeah, I took chelation. I can now play eighteen holes of golf again," I told him.

"Joe, before I went down I not only had no pulse in my right foot but I couldn't even walk across the fairway. I feel years younger. What's more, my eye problem has completely cleared up."

I eventually met two men who were as enthusiastic about the idea of opening up a chelation clinic on Vancouver Island as I was, but that was five years later. I was tired of having to travel to California or Washington State to have my treatments.

Dr. Alan Matthews of Victoria was aware of the value of chelation and that in Germany and New Zealand state medical plans support the therapy and pay for it. He told Bud Bell, a semi-retired Victoria businessman, and me that if there were enough patients he would hire nurses and provide the service.

Bud and I set up the Vancouver Island Chelation Therapy Research Society. It was easy raising the funds to furnish the clinic. I covered the area north of the Malahat to Campbell River and Bud worked the Greater Victoria area signing up members. The equipment included a Doppler research machine to provide comprehensive blood flow data and analysis. The Prince George Chelation Group also sent funds to help pay for this $20,000 piece of equipment, with the understanding that their members could have the use of it.

Bud Bell had been very interested in chelation therapy since the early sixties. And for good reason. He had had two serious heart attacks by age 55. His doctors now recommended heart surgery and, because of poor circulation, one leg should be amputated below the knee. Bud is now 71 and playing golf on that same leg, thanks to chelation and a proper diet.

"Too many doctors turn to surgery when there could be better ways available," he said.

Dr. Matthews opened his clinic on Goldstream Avenue in Langford, just north of Victoria. We soon heard that critics were declaring EDTA an illegal chemical substance in Canada. Bud had to satisfy his curiosity. He visited a medical supply house in Bellingham, just south of Vancouver in Washington and purchased enough ethylenediaminetetraacetic acid for one chelation treatment. Then he crossed back through Canadian Customs. He told the customs officer exactly what he had, and asked, "Is there any problem with this?'"

The officer checked his regulatory documents, then said, "No." There was no reason why this chemical couldn't be brought into Canada.

In the late eighties, after only three years, Dr. Matthews was forced to close his Langford clinic by the Physicians and Surgeons Medical Association. They told him his hospital privileges would be cancelled if he continued. They said there wasn't enough scientific proof that it did any good. The clinic had provided chelation treatments to some 360 patients. Some had been sent home by their doctors to die and were again leading active lives. Why would they close it down? What were the doctors afraid of?

I visited Archie recently, 11 years later, to find out how he was feeling: "I'm 72 now and not walking 18 holes anymore, but I am walking nine and enjoying it. When people ask me how I keep so well, I tell them chelation therapy. Then they say, 'I'll ask my doctor about it.' I tell them, 'Don't waste your time. They'll just tell you it's no good.' When they find they have to pay for it themselves they don't want to put out the money. My response to that is, 'You can't take it with you.' Three of the fellows I urged to take chelation chose bypass surgery. They're now pushing up the daisies.

"The provincial medical insurance plan is in trouble, yet the surgeons won't try chelation which would save the tax payers millions of dollars a year," Archie concluded.

It may not be for everyone but when I go without chelation therapy for an extended period I suffer the consequences. I've taken 198 chelation treatments over the past 14 years. It's not just the number of extra years it has given me, but, more importantly, the quality of life it has enabled me to enjoy.

BUT THEN AGAIN, if it wasn't for chelation I probably wouldn't even be alive, and I wouldn't now be struggling to stay alive.

PART VIII

NOT THE END - BUT DAMN NEAR

A T THE BOTTOM OF THE MOUNTAIN I was awakened by what sounded like a logging crew bus going up the river road. Thank God, people, whoever they were. I knew they would have to come back out this way. But soon? Or hours later? I did not know how long I could hang on. Who are they? Then I remembered. Logging had shut down for the winter. Maybe I just imagined hearing an engine. I had seen no head or tail lights.

I clearly heard the sounds of an airplane — of a Cessna 180 — in the distance. It was such a familiar sound I felt sure it was my long-dead brother Tom coming to pick me up and fly me out to food and safety. Then the sound was gone.

I still couldn't make out my surroundings though there was now definitely some sign of daylight to the east.

But I was still alive.

I felt in my pocket and found my last Rolaid. Carefully unwrapping it, I put it in my mouth, hoping it would provide enough sugar to prevent another diabetic coma. My brain slipped back into gear. I had work to do if I was to improve my chances of being found. No time to rest. I might pass out again at any minute. I manoeuvered forwards until my feet were beyond the door opening. Now, I could pull myself slowly up into a sitting position by using both hands on the old door frame. I then slowly lowered my feet to the ground. Using the cane, I managed to push myself up onto my feet. I still don't know how I did it. I just stood there until I felt reasonably steady on my feet. Then I made my way to the road that led up to Green Mountain.

In the growing light I was able to find some old pieces of plywood laying in the ditch. Somehow, don't ask me how, I tugged and wrestled them over to form a barricade across the road, leaning them on edge against each other so they stood up. I found a dirty red cloth and hung it on a stick near the center of the barricade. Any driver would see it and stop, and they'd check around. Men who work in the woods have a sixth sense of danger and trouble. Then I hobbled back to the shack.

The logging company dispatch shack, long abandoned. Joe's first hope that if he could survive till daylight he might make it. In all, Joe had travelled twelve kilometers down the logging road.

It was now light enough to see the inside of my shelter. Years ago it had been robbed of all its windows and doors. It was a scrambled mess of old pieces of plywood and bits of lumber. I once again sat in the doorway but this time I swung my feet around onto the floor, then managed with the help of my cane and the door frame to make it up onto my feet again. I picked up several larger pieces of wet plywood and threw them out the door. Lowering myself back onto the ground I started dragging the mouldy plywood over to the other road — the one I had just walked down.

I propped them up against some brush to make a blockade wide enough to force any traffic coming up the river road to veer towards the shack, or at least stop and clear away my crude barricade. I hoped this would at least force them to hesitate long enough to let me get their attention. I had done all I could. I had to get back to shelter and get off my feet.

I had only just got in out of the rain when I saw headlights coming towards me. Which road would they take? Praying that

I was guessing right, and as fast as I could, I headed back out towards the barricade I had just finished.

Thank God! They saw me.

Three young men were in the cab. But for one awful moment, even though they had slowed down, I thought they were not going to stop. Perhaps they thought they'd seen a ghost coming towards them. I frantically waved my arms and yelled at them.

I asked the driver, who later said they were stunned to see me, if they had something to eat. I explained I was a diabetic and needed food immediately. He handed me a banana and a sandwich. Food never looked or tasted so good or was so desperately needed. I gulped down half the banana, told them I had been on the mountain all night, was wet to the bone and in bad shape and needed to get home as soon as possible.

"I've a couple of hundred dollar bills I'll gladly give you if you will take me home right away. My truck is stuck up near the top of the mountain above Fourth Lake."

"We don't want your money, thank you," Jason Dancy said. We'll see if we can help get your truck started. First, we'll unload our stuff at the dam. We'll be back here in fifteen minutes to take you up. Will you be okay?"

Sitting in the doorway, I finished the banana and devoured the sandwich. They arrived back as promised. Their big Ford had a high step and I was so stiff and cold I had to be pulled up into the warm cab. I sat between them. I was in heaven with the turned-up heat blasting out at me.

"What the hell are you doing up here?" Dancy asked. "There's nobody within miles. Everything's shut down for the winter. This is our very last trip in here until spring!"

I could only say, "This is the nearest thing to heaven I have ever felt."

"You're damn lucky," he repeated as we took off. "As I said, this is our last trip here." They were still loaded with some gravel and cement to give their big truck traction going up the steep hill. The heat flowed around us and my steaming wet clothes were fogging up the windshield as we ground on up the rough mountain road.

"You hiked down here in the dark?" one asked, amazed. "This road? At your age?"

They could tell I was not normal and kept asking me if I was sure we were on the right road. No one should travel this road, they were thinking. Near the top of the mountain, the

The following spring of 1993, wearing the same clothes and warm and comfortable, Joe sat again in the door of the shack that had given him shelter. The memories came flooding back.

divide between the east and west watershed of Vancouver Island, I told them to take the last turnoff to the left. To their obvious relief, within minutes we were stopped beside the stalled truck. I handed my key to the driver.

He put the key in the ignition. He found as I had that although the key fitted it would not turn. He got out, walked to the front of the truck and hit the hood with both hands, opened it and looked underneath. He had lots of mechanical experience but nothing looked wrong.

He went to the other side, opened the door and looked under the passenger's seat. Nothing there. He came back to the driver's side, brushed his hand on the floor under the seat and came up with my full set of keys on a ring. I wish I could remember the look on his face as he handed them to me saying,

"Try these."

Yes, I wish I had a photo of the look on my face. All I can say is that I felt amazed, incredulous and very stupid. How could I have stashed a duplicate set of keys — and forgotten I had. All this, the horror of it, for nothing.

I climbed up into the seat. I put the key in the ignition, gave it one turn, and the engine roared into life. I looked at him, "How did you know there would be another set of keys there?"

"I didn't," he replied, smiling. He knew what I now suddenly realized. When I parked, an eternity before, I had put my keys on the seat, or thought I had, but they had slipped off and onto the floor. The other key, the "dud" one was for another vehicle, my van. I truly was a victim of my own stupidity, or shall I call it carelessness? It doesn't matter, it very nearly cost me my life, and I wasn't ready to go yet.

He closed my door and said they would watch as I turned around and then follow me down. At the road into Fourth Lake I honked my horn and waved as they turned off to go back to work.

Driving past the shack slowly — I didn't trust speed just yet — I went around my barricade and felt I never wanted to even see the place again.

I thought only of a bowl of steaming porridge and my heated water bed. I would even get to enjoy my brand new carpet after all.

At the gate I stopped only long enough to tell the gate man, "This is the truck, and I'm the driver that didn't make it out last night. I'm just plain lucky to be alive."

He did not reply.

"What do you think I was doing alone in the cold rain and snow up there all night, playing tiddlywinks?"

I drove for home fast, afraid of falling asleep. I don't remember much about the 18-mile drive or how long it took. When I saw my log home appear over the slope at the end of the driveway I could hardly believe it was for real. As I walked through the door I scuffed my soggy feet on the new soft carpet.

I was home.

All I wanted was to sleep, but first I had to eat. That was vital, as any diabetic knows. I reached for the saucepan and turned on the stove. I know I was not right, not really functioning, but the inner strength that had kept me going all that dismal night still carried me. Any job I started I'd finish. So I went through my daily routine of cooking up a pot of rolled oats.

The long view Joe sees each morning as he eats his porridge, the
breakfast he knew he must eat when he made it home after an
ordeal he never thought he would survive.

I sat at the kitchen table with my steaming bowl of porridge
and looked out the window at the familiar scene. In the long
grass, I could see two does walking over towards the bush, each
with her fawn close by her flanks.

Could I be in heaven?

It was eight o'clock and the sky to the east was now clear.
I could see Mount Baker across the Strait of Georgia — a sight
I was extremely lucky to see again. In a way I didn't deserve
it. But in another way I did. I have been lucky in life, I have
worked hard for that life and I always have been a survivor.

Now more in control and fed, before climbing into bed and
instant oblivion, I wrote a short note to Joan:

J: Don't wake me. Walked seventeen miles last nite. One good thing about it — In the rain it shure wasn't the least bit Crowded. Will cancell nee operation. **J.**

Barely aware of what he was doing, Joe wrote this note for Joan Davis, who would arrive soon. Still clothed, he hit his waterbed and sank down, down into oblivion.

Crowded? At least I had been able to keep my sense of humour.

I woke in the early afternoon and, although I felt tired and shaky, I was remarkably well. There was no sign of a cold or cough. Could it be the flu shot I'd had earlier in the week?

And yes, I cancelled my knee operation.

The tiredness continued for days, even weeks, but I did not develop anything serious. My luck had not run out yet.

When I walked into the kitchen and told Joan what had happened, the Irish in her came out, and she said, "Sure you're too stubborn to die yet, Joe."

Joe takes his ease under the overhang of his log home, still wondering how, at the age of 84, he could have survived.

EPILOGUE

TRAIL'S END. I've had a good life, lived in a freer, less cluttered land. Alas, how times have changed, and how quickly. Live each day to the fullest and never, never waste a minute. The only thing we are all short of is time.

Yes, there are things I did that I should not have done. There are things I did which I did not have to do, but I did them for the good of my country, my community, my family and my friends. Sometimes I won and sometimes I lost. But that's the spice of life. Risk nothing, gain nothing. I've always rolled the dice.

There was an American writer and poet named T. Morris Longstreth who died long ago, but I'd like to leave you with this poem he wrote titled "The Old Fisherman":

> *Daily he comes there to the shrunken pool,*
> *   Made secret by its wind-guard of old pine,*
> *To smoke his pipe and loiter by the cool*
> *   Secret water, like Time's truant, with his line.*
> *Even a child would know no fish are left,*
> *   For streams like men fall on evil days,*
> *Yet still he lingers where his joy ran swift*
> *   As a trout leaping — Now the dusty rays*
> *Of afternoon lie golden on the land*
> *   And the tall dark creeps from the wood,*
> *And there he stoops, the old rod in his hand,*
> *   For one last try before he goes, for good.*
> *The line floats out — though not to water flung*
> *But far upon the days when he was young.*

My days are dwindling, but I'm not done yet. I see the sun going down, but sunsets are beautiful. Adios!

INDEX